For Annie

Contents

The Mountbatten Centre for International Studies

The Mountbatten Centre for International Studies (MCIS), located in the Department of Politics at the University of Southampton, conducts many cooperative and individual research programmes and activities. Current areas of research include nuclear non-proliferation, human rights, international environmental issues, naval peacekeeping, European and Asian security, civil-military relations and police studies.

MCIS activities include residential seminars by its Defence Studies Unit as well as a programme of seminars and public lectures. The Centre is interdisciplinary, relying for its resource base on many departments within the University, including History, Law, Education, and Aeronautics and Astronautics.

Links have been established with the Centre d'Histoire Militaire of the University of Montpellier, the Foundation Pour les Etudes de Défense Nationale, Paris, and the Faculté des Affaires Internationales, Université du Havre. The Centre also participates in the work of the team on Political Culture in Eastern Europe at the Ecole des Hautes Etudes en Sciences Sociales, Paris. Members of the Centre have participated in the work of the European Science Foundation and the International Congress of Historical Sciences.

Publications of the Centre include the Southampton Studies in International Policy monograph and book series, the latter in association with Macmillan, and a monograph and newsletter series produced by the programme on nuclear non-proliferation. MCIS was established in 1990 in succession to the Centre for International Policy Studies (founded in 1983). The Mountbatten Centre bears the name of the Earl Mountbatten of Burma (1900–79), whose papers are housed at the University of Southampton.

Acknowledgements

I am grateful to many people who have offered their support and encouragement. My special thanks go to Mark Hoffman and Paikiasothy Saravanamuttu for their generosity and time as I struggled to understand the complexity of international relations. I am also grateful to several people who, often without knowing it, have made a considerable contribution to the ideas found in this book. Among these are Julian Saurin and Peter Wilson whose intellectual integrity and friendship I value greatly. During my time at Aberystwyth my conversations with Ken Booth, Richard Wyn Jones, Jon Ferron-Jones and may others added considerably to by thoughts. Special thanks go to Howard Williams for his willingness to listen patiently to ideas that were often incomplete and misguided.

My thanks also go to a group of people who have given their support since I arrived at Southampton University. Among these are Jenny Steele, Tim Jewell, John Simpson, Darryl Howlett and Adrian Hyde-Price. Finally, my special thanks go to Caroline Thomas for both her friendship and intellectual understanding.

Introduction

Truth is the child of time, not authority. Our ignorance is infinite. Let us shorten it by one cubic centimetre. Why be obsessed with intellectual gymnastics — when now, at last, we can be a little less stupid.[1]

In his play The Life of Galileo, Bertolt Brecht explores the growth of ideas within an innately conservative society. During the second century A.D. Ptolemy, elaborating on ideas first put forward by Aristotle, developed a complete cosmological model of the universe that placed the moon, sun and the planets in orbit around the earth. Although this model was challenged by the Polish priest Nicholas Copernicus as early as 1514, the Catholic Church remained faithful to the Ptolemaic model throughout the sixteenth century for theological reasons to do with the centrality of humankind in God's creation. However, in 1609 Galileo utilised the newly invented telescope to provide evidence in support of Copernican ideas. For daring to promote these ideas Galileo was persecuted by the Church, made to discontinue his work and forced to renounce any notion that challenged the existing religious and social order.[2] The words given to Galileo by Brecht quoted above are a plea to conservatives to put aside their own interests in favour of the growth of knowledge and the wider interests of humankind. The persecution suffered by Galileo in his attempt to challenge accepted scientific thinking also finds a resonance in social and political ideas. Indeed, Brecht himself uses the trials of Galileo as an allegory for the persecution of Marxists. The underlying theme of this book is a similar assertion: that even after fifty years of struggle, the discourse on human rights has yet to achieve the necessary victory over previous thinking that places the interests of the state and the state system above the promotion of human dignity.

THE 'IDEA' OF HUMAN RIGHTS

While the post-1945 world cannot claim the idea of human rights as its own, interest in the field during this era can be distinguished from that of previous periods in two areas. First, those engaged in postwar international reconstruction recognised that violations of human rights could be the cause of war itself and not merely a consequence, i.e. the distinction between peace and human rights was acknowledged as artificial.[3] Therefore, in planning for a new, post-Second World War international order, human rights would have to assume a central position. Second, although the idea of rights as an attribute of humankind possessed a long history dating back to the time of Hume, rights had been usually seen as attached to specific classes of people.[4] To prefix rights with 'human', and to suggest that at least some rights existed that could be attributed to humankind as a species was a departure from previous thinking. Moreover, through accepting rights as universally applicable the idea of human rights became an international issue by definition. While other concerns of international relations might continue to be thought of as limited by the interests of those directly involved, violations of universal human rights became the legitimate concern of all people everywhere.

Today it is common to find commentators claiming human rights as the 'idea of our time'.[5] Since the time of the General Assembly resolution that accepted the Universal Declaration of Human Rights, human rights have found their way into national constitutions, inspired an extensive body of international law, underpinned peace treaties and inspired the creation of a burgeoning number of nongovernmental organisations devoted to righting injustices throughout the world. The idea of human rights has also offered a justification for civil war, terrorist and separatist movements, and for military intervention in the name of humanitarianism. It is an idea used to challenge existing economic structures and political institutions, to rally public opinion to a cause and to provoke a sense of guilt or shame in those countries where violations are systematic. It has been claimed as a 'trump card' to arouse the approbation of international society in order to cement alliances with friends and as a 'stick' with which to beat ideological enemies.

However, despite the universalisation of the 'idea' of human rights, and all the political and legal activity that this has brought, there are few reassuring signs that human rights are any better protected than in the past. Increased awareness of human rights as a legitimate international concern, and the enormous resources expended in the UN on the issue, have hardly touched the historically accepted relationship between the state and its citizens. The unresolved tensions between the attributes of statehood and the demands of human rights — often expressed as dichotomies such as the national interest and cosmopolitanism, domestic jurisdiction and intervention, realism and idealism, or 'realpolitik' and morality — remain unresolved. On the one hand states have placed human rights on the international political agenda by linking rights to peace and creating machinery for the promotion of rights, while on the other states have often retreated behind the institution of statehood to prevent effective remedies for violations.

Furthermore, for all the heightened interest, political rhetoric and burgeoning literature, there remains considerable disagreement and confusion over the place, status and nature of universal human rights in international relations. In some ways enthusiasm for the idea of human rights is dependent upon confusion and indeterminacy, for human rights provide a convenient banner on which to pin political and ideological values without the need for expressing preferences or going into detail over the content of the idea. Claiming to uphold human rights, like claiming to support the idea of democracy, can offer legitimacy without explicit responsibility. As A J M Milne has written, 'like all influential ideas, the idea of human rights is in danger of degenerating into a slogan'.[6] This is nowhere more obvious than in questions concerning agreement on lists of rights, correlative duties, and international methods for the protection of human rights. Such questions are of considerable significance for the theory of international relations since they represent a potential challenge to long held and cherished beliefs about the nature of the discipline.[7]

THE STUDY OF HUMAN RIGHTS

An examination of the literature suggests that matters relating to international human rights can be divided between three distinct debates: the philosophical, the legal and the political. The philosophical debate is concerned with the meaning, source, justification and force of values upon which rights claims can be made. More specifically for international relations, this debate attempts to detect normative changes in behaviour that have seen the issue of human rights increase in significance such that human rights must now be included in policy and public opinion calculation. Since it is often claimed that human rights have now achieved a measure of international political legitimacy, which is expressed in both political and economic terms, we might reasonably expect to find normative changes. The nature of these changes remains unclear at this time but could be located within either the existing international system or in a process of change from the old order to some new conception based upon human need for identity and self-expression.[8]

The legal debate focuses on disagreements over the nature of international law as law, the internal coherence of existing human rights instruments, and methods of enforcement. Broadly, this debate focuses on detecting qualitative changes in organisational means intended to promote newly legitimated concerns. Importantly, the legal debate focuses on the United Nations, the major instruments of international law on human rights generated by the UN, and on the development of implementational procedures for the protection of human rights. The legal debate therefore provides the most visible aspect of the development of human rights. However, visibility and weight of paper are no proof of efficacy. All too often in the literature there is an implicit assumption that a clear relationship exists between human rights, international law and international politics. This provides the false impression that provided we can find the correct form of words to get an international convention ratified, a specific problem has been satisfactorily solved. Without taking proper regard of the political context of human rights the profusion of international law produced since the Universal Declaration can often give a more optimistic picture than is justified.

The political debate questions the scope of human rights in the tension between universal and international principles, and seeks to understand the character of domestic jurisdiction, sovereignty and the role of non-intervention in a changing world. It therefore questions the extent to which qualitative changes can be discerned in the nature of international society. As we shall see, while some authors attempt to accommodate human rights broadly within traditional Realist thinking on international relations, others argue that all attempts to explain the contradictions between the universal nature of human rights and the state system are futile. This argument runs that as human rights become progressively regarded as regulating the behaviour of states, Realist assumptions about the state and the international system lose credibility. In response to the demand for human rights, both state and nonstate actors are responding to human needs for organisational control, identity and a sense of participation rather than to the self-interest of states.[9] Seen in this way, the advent of human rights represents a glimpse into a new and emerging world of international relations, or more correctly global politics, which has not yet been fully realised but is expressed in the work of World Society analysts like John Burton.[10] Consequently, as followers of Thomas Kuhn would argue, we are witnessing a period where the traditional language and concepts of international relations have become outmoded, but where new thinking for explaining contemporary social and political processes has not yet reached maturity.[11]

It is rare to find any clear distinction between these three debates such that authors often move unselfconsciously from one to the other. Accordingly, legal questions may be given a moral philosophical answer, which in turn is deflected by some political objection. As J S Watson has observed, the potential circularity of this process leads to conclusions in the form of

an exhortation to optimism or hope, almost invariably expressed in the passive voice in order to increase its apparent authority. What such remarks indicate is of course that the true basis for the writer's argument is not to be found within the confines of international law, but rather in his or her perceptions of human nature.[12]

Attempting to address some of the questions outlined above is problematic because until recent years human rights literature received so little attention from students of international politics. The greater portion of research emanates from departments of law and legal practitioners and often displays an amazing lack of insight into the political environment in which the law is formulated and operates. Furthermore, even when attempts are made by students of international relations to understand political aspects of human rights there is often a tendency to defer to the instruments of international law. As one author has noted, having encountered the literature on human rights for the first time, a visitor from outer-space might easily report to its home planet that the protection of human rights was the great achievement of us earthlings.[13] Such political research that does exist typically focuses on specific case studies, often in an attempt to discover how existing international law might be applied. However, more often such research pays more attention to recording violations rather than attempting to understand the political conditions necessary to reduce them.

Making the assumption that a secure relationship has already been established between human rights, international politics and international law has led some authors to describe the advent of the idea of human rights as 'revolutionary', in the sense that it differs radically from traditionally held views of interstate law and politics. An example of this is Louis Henkin's assertion that adding human rights to the list of legitimate international concerns has buried the old dogma that the individual is not a subject of international law, and that a government's behaviour towards its citizens is solely a matter of domestic concern.[14]

While there may be some cause to assume that the idea of human rights now demands attention when in the past it did not, the political facts of torture, arbitrary arrest, genocide, structural economic deprivation and racial discrimination make grand claims of success premature. For those interested in understanding the place of human rights in international politics, the rhetoric of human rights often obscures our vision when attempting to determine how far the idea of human rights represents a normative change in the expectations of actors at the international level. The assumption of much of the literature is that the world is indeed undergoing a normative transformation away from a society of states towards a broader social framework for ordering the relations among the world's peoples. Although such an assumption may be valid, it cannot rest upon the existence of international law alone. Indeed, the examination of international law —

understood as the law between states — may be an inappropriate means for examining human rights in an emergent world society. Equally important in assessing normative change must be the energy, vigour and conviction of international actors as they condemn, condone and defend violations.

THE INTERNATIONAL HUMAN RIGHTS REGIME

Underlying the disagreement between pessimists and optimists over the status of human rights in the current international political sphere is a confusion over the distinction between goals and values. According to the Oxford Dictionary, goals are the 'object of ambition or effort'.[15] By contrast, values are 'one's principles or standards; one's judgement of what is valuable or important to life'.[16] This suggests that goals should be associated with characteristics like aspirations, desires, enthusiasms and endeavours, while values are concerned with merit, virtue and social worth. Therefore, when referring to values, moral and normative attributes are a necessary defining feature, but this is not so when speaking of goals. The literature on human rights, and indeed the human rights debate in general, suffers from confusion concerning this distinction. As suggested in the previous section, the legal approach looks optimistically at goals set by the international law on human rights, often ignoring cultural, political and ideological conflicts over values that represent barriers to achieving these goals. This is not to claim that all authors from a legal background think and write about goals, or all philosophers about values, with the political scientists hovering somewhere between the two. However, in noting that human rights authors are commonly prone to reaching conclusions of immoderate hope, drawing attention to the distinction does ensure a measure of caution. In the field of human rights, a field of study that is often at an interface between the traditional principles of international relations and the more radical principles of world society thinking, the distinction between goals and values places both optimists and pessimists in perspective.

This book attempts to examine the tensions and conflicts between the accepted understanding of inter-state relations and the evolution of universal human rights as a legitimate issue that increasingly commands the attention of international and transnational actors. It is therefore an attempt to understand the political debate on international human rights and the reasons why the wide acceptance of the 'idea' of human rights has not been matched by successful actions to protect the rights of people everywhere. While the legal and philosophical debates cannot be entirely ignored, no attempt to conduct a detailed analysis of legal method or philosophical issues concerning the nature of rights will be made. This is because the politics of human rights is more concerned with disputes over differing legal and philosophical approaches to rights, rather than attempts to define rights legally or philosophically. When legal and philosophical issues are discussed they are placed within a political context.

The distinctive character claimed for international regime theory rests on the importance of normative relationships and is particularly appropriate for a study on human rights. However, as we shall see, the regime approach lends itself to both pessimism and optimism over the future of human rights. This is because of a diversity of opinion on the nature of international regime theory itself. In some approaches the existence of a regime is coterminous with the existence of empirically observable machinery designed to implement agreement on negotiated principles and norms. At another level regimes can be inferred from the behaviour of international and transnational actors: in other words, few or no formal arrangements need exist to claim the existence of a regime.[17] At yet another level some authors are content to use regime analysis as a framework for structuring their ideas or research findings and attach little or no significance to normative issues. However, adopting one or other of these approaches exclusively misses an important opportunity offered by regime analysis. This is the possibility of gaining an insight into the complex relationship between value oriented, normative and interpretative aspects of international life on the one hand and formal, political, goal oriented and empirical aspects on the other.

More specifically, a regime approach to examining the growth of the idea of human rights since 1945 offers several advantages. First, and to stress the point already made above, matters relating to human rights can be divided into three debates — philosophical, legal and political — each with its own language and epistemology. Much of the literature attempts to confine itself to one or other of these debates, although this often proves an impossible task. The regime approach allows the possibility of bringing the connections among the three debates into sharper focus. This is particularly important in a field like human rights where the relationship between normative expectations, legal method and political compliance remains unclear.

Second, while rights may be located within a moral debate, rights claims remain in the political debate.[18] If the moral debate tells us what 'ought' to be in an ideal world, then the political debate offers an insight into what 'is' and suggests how we can move further towards achieving the ideal. For example, although it is possible to identify distinctive philosophical approaches within negotiations over the promotion and protection of human rights, political, ideological and foreign policy considerations circumscribe the ideas that finally find expression as international law or declarations of intent. Attempting to view human rights as an international regime allows us to find some underlying reasons why there is frequently a disparity between the 'ought' and the 'is', and to place the philosophical debate within a political context.

Third, although human rights are now accepted as a legitimate international concern their implementation remains firmly the responsibility of individual states. The links between foreign policy, international relations and, importantly, domestic politics are therefore an essential consideration. The current status of human rights can be characterised as the distinction between accepting the moral imperative of universal human rights but denying universal solutions. Put another way, the growth of ideas identified with the wider communitarian values derived from transnationalism, interdependence and processes of globalisation have found expression in human rights, but these values remain suppressed because the state retains the central role in implementing those rights.[19] This is particularly important when considering hegemonic states like the United States of America, whose role in determining the scope of human rights was, and remains considerable. Indeed, this book argues that interests within the USA played an important role in placing human rights on the international political agenda, and an equally important role in ensuring that only the weakest procedures for protecting human rights were adopted. The processes that have seen human rights become a significant part of international politics can therefore be understood only by considering both the vertical and horizontal images of the state.[20]

Fourth, according to Joseph Nye 'end point utopias' frequently lead to pessimism because of the gulf between some vision of the future and current political and social conditions that present barriers to achieving desired ends. Consequently when human rights scholars look at the relatively meagre achievements of international law and international organisations created to protect human rights, they can come to the pessimistic and despairing conclusion that no further progress is likely to be seen in the future. However, Nye suggests that the alternative approach of 'process utopia' allows us to hypothesise 'benign or pacific trends, though the end point of the trend is uncertain'. Thus, the pessimism engendered by pursuing a particular but unattainable end point is replaced by optimism through the possibility of moving towards some desirable utopian future world, though this utopian world remains too distant to be achieved.[21] Importantly, process utopia moves away from concern with empirically observable machinery towards examining social attitudes and the development of new social institutions. Regime theory lends itself to analysis of these processes.

Fifth, regime theory accepts the importance of hegemonic power in processes of regime formation. During the decades in which the human rights regime was emerging Cold War conflicts impinged on all international issues where ideological differences could be illustrated, imagined, created or invented. Human rights offered both sides considerable opportunities for engaging in the ideological struggle conducted at the United Nations. In particular, the struggle to win the hearts and minds of less developed states often focused on claims to self-determination, the right to dispose of natural resources and the demand for a more equitable international economic system. Finding such demands unacceptable and irresistible, the United States withdrew its early support for a human rights regime, leaving the regime without hegemonic leadership.

It should be stressed that the focus of this book is the activities of the Councils, Commissions and Committees of the United Nations that have sought to develop the major instruments for the universal protection of human rights. Since the advent of the Universal Declaration of Human Rights, several regional conventions have come into force.[22] Furthermore, human rights have become an important part of several nonbinding agreements, the most important being the Final Act of the Helsinki Conference on Security and Cooperation in Europe.[23] While the existence of these conventions and agreements adds emphasis to the claim that human rights have now achieved an important status in international relations, the human rights debate at the United Nations remains central to any attempt at understanding the place human rights holds within contemporary international politics. Regional arrangements remain important, but they represent an understanding of human rights that reflects a particular culture or region.[24] They cannot therefore be seen as universal in the same way that the United Nations' attempt at constructing a human rights regime might be.

OUTLINE OF THE BOOK

Chapter 1 places the field of international human rights in an international regime context. It begins by looking briefly at the existing literature on international regimes and continues with an analysis of regime components understood as different types of rules. It then moves to a discussion of the uses and abuses of international law in the academic literature. Through this analysis it is argued that the development of the idea of human rights as an international regime can be understood in both a weak and a strong sense. In the weak sense, while the regime boasts an ever increasing amount of international law and receives considerable attention and resources from international organisations, attempts to achieve a significant reduction of gross violations of human rights through formal means have proved largely ineffectual. Understanding the regime in the weak sense often leads to pessimism and the view that no further progress in the field of human rights is expected.[25] However, in the stronger sense the institutionalisation of the idea of human rights has seen it become part of the day-to-day dialogue of international relations to such an extent that foreign ministers, statespeople and diplomats cannot ignore the consequeneces of their actions upon human rights.[26] Finally, the role of hegemonic power in regime formation in general and the human rights regime in particular is examined. Hegemonic power has long been recognised as central to regime formation. However, little attention has been given to the argument presented here; that a hegemon has the capacity to prevent the formation of a regime.

Chapters 2 and 3 look at the debates and disagreements over the principles and norms that were intended to provide the foundation for the postwar human rights regime. Following the rhetoric of universal human rights during the war years, and the consequent increased interest by national and international publics, international leaders became increasingly concerned to respond by including a provision for the protection of human rights in the new postwar order. However, the fundamental contradictions and tensions between sovereignty and universally recognised human rights could not be resolved easily. The UN's reluctance to try to resolve these tensions meant that the foundations of the formal regime were never fully defined. Similarly, disagreements arose during the discussion about universally acceptable norms for human rights. Importantly, as the character of the Cold War unfolded human rights, in common with all other international issues, provided a further platform on which to conduct the ideological struggle. Again, these disagreements led to less than universal acceptance of the content of rights claims and further confused the objectives of the regime.

Chapter 4 looks at the role of the United States of America as the hegemonic leader of the world, following the end of the Second World War. It argues that during the early years of the United Nations a growing majority of socialist and less developed states began to reject the Unites States historically narrow view of economic, political and social relationships. The Commission on Human Rights, together with the Economic and Social Council, provided a convenient stage for challenging the dominant view of the United States. As the formal development of the human rights regime progressed, domestic actors within the United States became increasingly alarmed by the need to make concessions in response to this challenge. These domestic actors took decisive action to ensure that the United States would not become a full member of the human rights regime; leaving the regime without hegemonic leadership and ensuring that the regime would remain impotent.

Chapter 5 looks at the attempts made to develop the rules of the human rights regime as international law. Following the failure of influential members of the United Nations to realise the need for fundamental changes in the rules of the international system to include human rights, the lengthy debate on international law became increasingly politicised. This is seen most vividly as the process of decolonisation gained momentum and an increasing number of countries saw their interests diverge from traditionally held western views of rights.

Chapter 6 looks at the progress made in devising decision-making procedures for implementing human rights on a universal basis. It is argued that the machinery for implementing international human rights remains weak, because of the failure to resolve fundamental difficulties when attempting to establish sound principles and norms on which to build the regime. Furthermore, it is argued that although state rhetoric on human rights remains high, this interest is not reflected in the foreign policies pursued by states.

Finally, chapter 7 will offer some speculation about the future of international human rights in a post-Cold War world.

NOTES

1. Bertolt Brecht, *The Life of Galileo*, translated by Howard Brenton, (Eyre Methuen, London, 1980), p. 30.
2. For a good, brief history of the development of ideas on the cosmos from Ptolemy to Copernicus and then to Newton see Stephen Hawking, *A Brief History of Time*, (Bantum Press, London, 1988), ch. 1.
3. For example, the well known 'four freedoms' speech by President Roosevelt to Congress in 1941; Prime Minister Attlee's speech at the First General Assembly of the United Nations on 10th January, 1946; and the speech by V K Wellington Koo (China) on 15th January at the same Assembly.
4. Kenneth Minogue, 'The history of the idea of human rights', in W Laqueur and B Rubin (eds), *The Human Rights Reader*, (Meridian Books, NY, 1977), p. 3-17.
5. Louis Henkin is fond of stressing this point. See his introduction to Louis Henkin (ed), *The International Bill of Rights*, (University of Chicago Press, Chicago, 1967), p. 1.
6. A J M Milne, 'The idea of human rights: a critical inquiry', in R E Dorwich (ed), *Human Rights: Problems, Perspectives and Texts*, (Saxon House, London, 1979), p. 24.
7. It is interesting to note that while the study of democracy is inevitably a component of undergraduate degrees, human rights has not achieved a place in departments of politics and international relations either in Britain or the USA. If human rights is offered as a course at all it is usually in departments of law.

8. For examples of these two approaches see Terry Nardin, *Law, Morality, and the Relations of States*, (Princeton University Press, Princeton, NJ, 1983); and Lynn H Miller, *Global Order: Values and Power in International Politics*, (Westview, London, 1985).

9. Richard L O'Meara, 'Regimes and their implications for international theory', *Millennium*, 13:3, 1984, pp. 245-64.

10. John Burton, *World Society*, (Cambridge University Press, Cambridge, 1972).

11. Thomas Kuhn, *The Structure of Scientific Revolutions*, (Chicago University Press, Chicage, 1970).

12. J S Watson, 'Legal theory, efficacy and validity in the development of human rights norms in international law', *University of Illinois Law Forum*, vol. 3, 1979, p. 367.

13. Oscar Schachter, 'The obligation to implement the Covenant in domestic law', in Louis Henkin, *The International Bill of Rights: The Covenant on Civil and Political Rights*, (Columbia University Press, Columbia, 1970).

14. Louis Henkin, 'The United Nations and human rights', *International Organization*, 19:3, 1965, p. 506.

15. *Concise Oxford Dictionary*, (1990), p. 505.

16. ibid., pp. 1356-7

17. Tony Evans and Peter Wilson, 'International regimes and the English school of international relations: A comparison', *Millennium*, 21:3, 1992, pp. 329-351.

18. Friedrich Kratochwil, *Rules, Norms and Decisions*, (Cambridge University Press, Cambridge, 1989), esp. ch. 6.

19. ibid., ch. 4, particularly p. 115.

20. Richard K Ashley, 'Untying the sovereign state: a double reading of the anarchy problematique', *Millennium*, 17:2, 1988, pp. 227-62. Oran Young also makes the point that a domestic debate exists parallel to all international debates. See his 'The politics of international regime formation: managing natural resources and the environment', *International Organization*, 43:3, 1989, pp. 349-75.

21. Joseph Nye, 'The long-term future of nuclear deterrence', in Roman Kolkowicz (ed), *The Logic of Nuclear Deterrence*, (Allen and Unwin, London, 1987), pp. 233-50.

22. These include the European Convention on Human Rights, the American Convention on Human Rights and the Banjul Charter which envisages an African Commission of Human and People's Rights.

23. For text, see Ian Brownlie (ed), *Basic Documents on Human Rights*, (Clarendon Press, Oxford, 1981), pp. 320-77.

24. John Vincent, *Human Rights and International Relations*, (Cambridge University Press, Cambridge, 1986), p. 95-6.

25. For example, this is the view of Jack Donnelly, 'International human rights: a regime analysis', *International Organization*, 40:3, 1986, pp. 599-642.

26. This more optimistic view is tentatively suggested by John G Ruggie, 'Human rights and the future of international community', *Daedalus*, 112:4, 1983, pp. 93-110.

1 Universal Human Rights and International Regimes

Examining the literature that comes under the general rubric of 'human rights talk',[1] the reader is likely to suffer rapid fluctuations of mood between hope and despair. This is because of a fundamental incompatibility between accepting the principles of state sovereignty while simultaneously advocating the universal protection of human rights. The literature can be divided into two broad approaches, which I shall call the cosmopolitan and the statist. The first of these assumes that the world is currently in a state of transition from that characterised by a society of states to that more appropriately described as a world society. The culmination of this transition will see the existing principles of state sovereignty and nonintervention replaced by new principles generated by the continued expansion of complex interdependence, transnationalism, globalisation and the cosmopolitan ideal of 'one world'. Early evidence of such a transformation, it is claimed, is seen in both popular movements that spawn influential nongovernmental organisations, and in the growth of supranational organisations that develop a hierarchical character above the state.[2] Such an approach looks forward to fundamental changes in the international normative order, expressed in the language of 'idealism', and draws upon moral and philosophical literature concerned with defining, assessing and evaluating the scope of human rights as a basis of analysis and subsequent action. It is thus an 'open' discourse in that its focus is the legitimation of values, principles and norms in a social environment where disagreement and contestability are the inevitable result of social dynamism.[3]

The second approach, the statist discourse, assumes the continuation of a society of states and the principle of nonintervention in the domestic affairs of sovereign actors. It is part of a long tradition of Realist thinking which places the relationship between the state and its citizens beyond the reach of other international actors. Universal moral claims, like human rights, are therefore inappropriate issues to include in foreign policy.[4] Where states have agreed specific standards for human rights, these are defined by reference to positive international law, thus avoiding moral questions inherent in appeals to a divine authority, natural law or self-evidence in support of rights claims. This approach offers a 'closed' discourse, which is limited to the modest goals set by the society of states. Its central focus is the rules and decision-making procedures provided by international law, and the roles played by international organisations in determining legitimate or illegitimate behaviour.[5]

Both discourses offer insights into particular problems concerning the protection and promotion of human rights at the global level. Although at times their divergent approaches seem mutually blind, neither is entirely unaware of the other's existence. Indeed, it is rare today to find literature that attempts to retain the full consequences of the statist discourse by asserting that the relationship between a government and its citizens remains the exclusive concern of separate states. However, sovereignty and non-intervention remain central in most international political analysis, suggesting that the cosmopolitan discourse has achieved at best only limited impact on traditional thinking. While the idea of human rights has achieved a measure of international legitimacy, as exemplified by the enormous investment of resources by both governmental and nongovernmental organisations since 1945, the international community has thus far made very little progress in turning profession into practice through finding satisfactory solutions to gross violations. This remains the central paradox of human rights.

For some authors, turning to the new vogue of international regimes offers the opportunity of understanding the relationship between the limited goals that states have set and the values articulated increasingly by a wider cosmopolitan community. An international regime approach promises to give an insight into the contradiction between the growth of human rights as the 'normal stuff of international politics'[6] and the evident failure of the international community to respond to known, widespread and persistent cases of officially sanctioned murder, political imprisonment, torture and racial and religious discrimination. Put another way, understanding human rights as a regime should offer an insight into why, from time to time, butchers such as Pol Pot and Idi Amin shock the conscience of humankind while failing to stimulate any action from members of the international community.

The still expanding catalogues of case studies suggests that the introduction of regime theory has indeed touched a nerve, exciting an interest in many authors who have found previous approaches to international cooperation wanting. Indeed, the term 'international regime' has entered general usage and can now be found in the work of many authors not explicitly engaged in operationalising the concept. For example, in his attack on the over reliance on legal instruments as evidence of improvements in international human rights, Watson argues that the 'practice of states does not show that there is an international regime of human rights'.[7] Similarly, in his analysis of international justice Terry Nardin refers to the 'international human rights regime' and suggests that improvements to human rights will be achieved only through strengthening international rules and practices.[8] More recently John Vincent has asked 'what regimes have been established in regard to human rights',[9] and suggests that institutional arrangements for the promotion and protection of human rights 'constitute international human rights regimes'.[10]

Apart from these somewhat unspecific allusions to the possibility of an international human rights regime, at least four essays have attempted to cast human rights in such terms.[11] However, in common with much of the literature that uses the concept, these essays demonstrate considerable differences in their understanding of international regimes. For example, while Ruggie wants to use the concept to gain an insight into how the idea of human rights 'alters the day-to-day conduct of international relations',[12] Bergesen uses it as a framework for describing the development of international law on civil and political rights over the last five decades.

While case studies proliferate, a 'theory' of international regimes remains to be articulated in any generally accepted form. Few empirical studies go beyond a brief reference to the work of those writers who have attempted to develop the concept.[13] However, it is clear from an examination of these contributions that fundamental underlying assumptions, definitions and theoretical perspectives remain divergent, with the consequence that much empirical work remains unclear.

CONCEPTUAL MODELS

The development of regime theory can be understood as a response to three problems within the discipline of international relations. The first of these was a growing concern for pragmatic solutions to new and genuinely global problems like environmental degradation and the depletion of energy resources, which were encouraged throughout the 1970s by imagery such as 'spaceship earth'. According to Ruggie, 'we are being told that on our "only one earth" we are, for the first time, living a single history'.[14] The second problem was the failure of complex interdependence to undermine realism as the dominant paradigm in international relations theory. The final problem was a continuing and growing dissatisfaction with current general theory. These three areas are not unconnected, because the failure of complex interdependence, or rather its absorption as a supplement to Realism, still left the phenomenon of greater levels of cooperation to be explained. By using such phrases as 'sets of mutual expectations, rules and regulations' and 'collective arrangements among states',[15] early proponents of international regimes articulated this difficulty but said little about how expectations, rules and collective arrangements are caused or stimulated in an environment thought of as anarchic. For these early essayists the use of regime analysis expressed a need to understand the empirical fact of a growing number and type of cooperative international organisations — an observation that fitted uneasily into accepted Realist thinking.

Since 1982 most authors have taken as their starting point Stephen Krasner's definition for an international regime as:

> sets of implicit or explicit principles, norms, rules, and decision-making procedures around which actors' expectations converge in a given area of international relations.[16]

Thus defined, regimes provide standards for behaviour, which limit action through the acceptance of norms and rules designed to help shape expectations. While the four central components of a regime are not discrete or exclusive, Krasner attempts to describe their intended use in greater detail:

> Principles are beliefs of fact, causation and rectitude. Norms are standards of behaviour in terms of rights and obligations. Rules are specific prescriptions or proscriptions for action. Decision-making procedures are prevailing practices for making and implementing collective choices.[17]

Importantly for international human rights, it is the inclusion of principles and norms that distinguishes regime analysis from previous approaches to international organisation. According to Finlayson and Zacher, norms together with principles 'provide[s] the foundations of a regime'.[18] Krasner argues that they 'constitute the general obligations and rights that are a guide to states' behaviour in designing decision-making procedures.' Furthermore, these components are intended to suggest relationships that are 'considered something more than temporary arrangements that change with every shift of power'.[19] Including principles and norms, it is claimed, distinguishes regime activity from that associated with traditional thinking on international relations, which assumes behaviour is motivated solely by egoistic self-interest. Including principles defined as rectitude assumes a moral dimension to which international actors must respond by modifying their preferred behaviour. Duties as well as rights assume an influence over action.

The Krasner definition of an international regime has achieved such wide acceptance that few empirical studies find the need to do more than repeat it. This may not be important if the regime definition is utilised as a methodological framework; it does after all provide a handy checklist for describing particular features of existing organisational structures. Whether the mere identification of these features is sufficient to claim the existence of a regime as a social institution remains unclear however. At the level of explanation, on the other hand, the definition needs clarification, particularly when using normative language that places regimes within the domain of societal values. Four questions need an answer at this level of analysis. These questions offer a focus for the remainder of this chapter.

The first, and perhaps most important, concerns the nature of the society in which regimes emerge. The discipline of international relations is undergoing increasing turbulence such that fundamental assumptions no longer claim a consensus.[20] This has exposed considerable disagreement on the social context of global politics and therefore the social context of international regimes. Are we to assume a society of independent sovereign states with a moral code, set of values and normative order separate and distinct from that normally associated with domestic society? Or does the emergence of regimes offer a further indication of important changes towards a cosmopolitan or world society that expresses an emerging set of normative expectations no longer appropriately expressed through the state?[21]

The second question concerns the role of power in regime formation. This is one area that has received considerable attention from regime analysts. Most agree that while the presence of a hegemon is a necessary requirement for regime formation, once established a regime may become self-sustaining. However, little consideration has been given to the potential for a hegemon to resist or deny the formation of a regime, even in the face of widespread demand. Given the global interest in the idea of human rights, we might ask what role the post-World War II hegemon played in establishing a human rights regime. More particularly, given the ideological importance that the USA attached to human rights, we might ask why the regime remains so weak.

The third question follows from the first. It concerns epistemological issues about the nature of institutions, how they can be identified and their significance in altering the behaviour of international actors.[22] This concerns the important distinction between social institutions and organisations, which will be considered in greater detail later. It is sufficient here to note that many regime studies deduce the existence of institutions from the constitutions and practices of international organisations and the requirements of international law. This allows analysis to assess the success or failure of a regime by comparing actual behaviour to prior, formal rules. While such an approach does not in itself deny the existence of social institutions, it provides little insight into questions concerning how regimes affect the behaviour of members or how they are formed in the first instance.

Some minimum level of international organisation may be a necessary requirement of all international regimes, but it can never be sufficient.

The fourth question concerns the nature of rules and again follows from the first. Since all four components of a regime can be understood as types of rules, there remains a difficulty in determining the normative content of regimes, particularly when principles and norms are seen as so central. In some meanings given to the term principle, for example the principles of physics, the intention is to describe the physical world. In this usage the physical world does not, except metaphysically speaking, obey these principles, nor can it be altered through human intervention. Principle in this meaning offers the student of international relations the possibility of understanding the world as structural relationships perceived as unchanging. In another meaning, related to the moral world, principles can be seen as prescriptive in that they point to moral precepts that demand our compliance but, through human intervention and the exercise of choice, offer the possibility of deviant or irregular behaviour.[23] Moral principles are intended to integrate behaviour and allow individuals to make sense of social life through a knowledge of their own and others' expectations. Understood in this way principles can be amended, reformed or replaced as the needs and expectations of society demand new values through which to make sense of a dynamic social world.[24]

The norm component of a regime presents similar possibilities. At one level norms can be viewed as dynamic social phenomena, in a continuous process of flux, which result from complex relationships between national, transnational and state actors who constitute a global community.[25] At another level norms can be found in the formal protocols, conventions and treaties that constitute international law. In traditional Realist thinking on international regimes these are the rules and norms that are reluctantly accepted by states in recognition of a failure to persuade others to embrace their own preferred values.[26] This does not necessarily deny the existence of the first level, but it is a narrow view and can be considered as an attempt to legitimise and reify a particular normative order at a particular level of international life.

Given that norms and principles can be understood in different ways, the conceptualisation of the normative content of regimes becomes problematic. Accepting the descriptive view of principles and the formal view of norms assumes a normative order with few similarities to that generally held to be present in domestic society. Alternatively, the prescriptive view of principles and the view of norms as the outcome of dynamic social processes suggests a basis for international regimes in a growing awareness of a community of humankind. This is to do with questions about 'duties beyond borders'[27] and the obligations individuals and groups have both to their own state and the wider international community.

INTERNATIONAL REGIMES AND RULES

It is of course quite possible to view all four central components of a regime as particular types of the generic term rules. In both the statist and the cosmopolitan discourses rules can convey the idea of regimes as part of a moral normative order. But what form does this order take? This question arises because of a supposed dichotomy between sovereignty and anarchy, where sovereignty is defined as a culturally specific, ideal view of a moral community with shared values and purposes, while anarchy represents the rejection of this ideal. It is, in part, the well-known distinction between domestic and international politics, which requires individuals to accept what Richard Ashley has called the 'heroic practice' of limiting the moral domain to the territorial boundaries of the State.[28]

Within the cosmopolitan discourse on human rights this dichotomy, if not totally rejected, is brought into question. Given current political and economic conditions, so the argument runs, the state alone cannot hope to perform all the tasks associated with the continued expansion of the world economy. This is because of increasing complexity, specialisation and the emergence of a range of global ecological problems characteristic of the expansion process. Non-state actors therefore become an essential element in sustaining and managing the world economy.

> Should the mobility of non-state actors be too constrained, they would no longer be able to take advantage of economies of global scale. Should transnational communications be too restricted, social and economic progress would suffer. World markets would collapse, economic contraction would set in, and in all locales, environmental deterioration, social dislocation, and political instability would result.[29]

Thus there is an increasing realisation that both the material and moral well-being of people everywhere is dependent on social, political and economic relationships that transcend traditional state boundaries, and this weakens any normative distinctions between international and domestic society.

The statist discourse on the other hand, assumes that a clear qualitative distinction can be drawn between the moral life found within the state and that common to international behaviour. It is a situation that arises because an informed sense of right and wrong requires education:

and this is particularly so in the field of interpersonal relations. Whereas it may be argued that interpersonal morality emerges from the educational experience of living together in a society, no such sustained moral competence can be assumed when it comes to international morality. The moral problems thrown up by the existence of multiple, autonomous, political communities are not experienced directly by ordinary citizens, and it is not necessarily the case that criteria for moral judgments can be extrapolated from criteria employed in ordinary day-to-day life.[30]

Therefore, if any level of moral behaviour can be said to exist at the international level, it is qualitatively distinct from that associated with domestic society.

One way of conceptualising the nature of rules might be to begin with the well-known distinction between rules of 'purposive association' and those of 'practical association' suggested by Terry Nardin. Nardin begins by rejecting the international moral scepticism of structuralists, arguing instead that human consciousness, invention and intention allows the possibility of maintaining international order through such things as diplomacy and international law. However, acknowledging the sovereignty–anarchy problematique, Nardin argues that while normative association can be said to exist at the international level it is neither of the same kind nor qualities as that found in domestic societies. The existence of domestic society presupposes the existence of a moral community possessed of a set of common values, norms and rules. The domestic normative order therefore derives from some notion of common purposes or what Nardin calls 'purposive association', which is based upon the moral integrity of the individual within a culturally specific social environment oriented around some commonly held vision of the 'good life'. However, because of cultural diversity and the existence of states,

> it would be a mistake to regard all international relations as defined and governed by the pursuit of shared purpose ... there is another mode of relationships that is more fundamental because it exists among those pursuing divergent as well as shared purposes. Durable relations among adversaries presuppose a framework of common practices and rules capable of providing some unifying bond where shared purposes are lacking.[31]

These are the non-purposive rules of 'practical association', the most important expression of which is found in the authoritative practices and principles of international law.

Rules of practical association at the international level include such things as nonintervention, the rule *pacta sunt servanda*, rules on the legitimate use of force and diplomatic immunity. Such rules, according to Nardin, require no commitment to shared purposes or values, but they provide a formal unity, an association of states, based upon restraint and accommodation.

> It is the sort of unity enjoyed by those who, having failed to get others to adopt their own ideas and institutions, have little choice but to tolerate the existence of differences they are unable to eradicate.[32]

Understanding the normative content of the rules of practical association therefore entails an analysis of the application of these rules rather than an examination of their content or relevance to some moral purpose. To speak of justice when referring to practical association, is to be concerned with the equal application of rules rather than the consequence or outcome of their application. To utilise a term that has fallen into disuse in recent times, the 'law of nations' becomes the law governing relations between nations as opposed to an alternative meaning that assumes a common purpose of humankind or laws common to all nations.[33]

The characterisation of international society as a non-purposive, practical association helps clarify the two discourses on international regimes, and particularly the human rights regime. The cosmopolitan discourse sees the emergence of regimes as a significant indication of a growth in international purposive association. It suggests an expansion of the moral boundaries set by individuals and culturally specific groups to one more appropriately characterised as a world or universal society. Importantly, it allows normative enquiry to consider justice in moral rather than in legal, formal terms. This allows international cooperation, and particularly cooperation on overtly moral issues like human rights, to be understood as part of an expanding world society with commonly held aspirations, values and goals. Such an approach represents a direct threat to traditional thinking. It poses questions about the continued moral legitimacy of the state, about the moral standing of individuals as both citizens and human beings and, importantly, epistemological questions about the premise we might adopt in beginning to analyse the field of international politics itself.

The statist discourse, on the other hand, views regimes within the framework of rules of practical association. Since this conception stresses those rules considered necessary for coexistence and the maintenance of the international system, rather than human aspirations and values, cooperative arrangements like regimes are seen as practical structures designed to secure order and increase predictability. Although nothing in the idea of practical association precludes the possibility that the moral concerns of purposive association cannot emerge within a society of states, there remains a powerful, if tacit implication that practical rules must take priority over purposive rules. That is, the preservation of the existing society of states is taken as an end in itself. Progress in human rights, for example, can be expected only if 'human rights are given a foundation in the common rules of conduct governing the society of states'.[34] It follows that revolutionary changes must be made in the existing practices of international society before any progress can be made in reducing human rights violations. Important among these would be a relaxation of the principle of domestic jurisdiction, including a redefinition of the scope of intervention, and the acceptance of new restrictions on the traditionally held understanding of state sovereignty.[35]

The classification offered by Nardin emphasises the idea that the preservation of the society of states should itself be seen as the single most important value in international life. Order should take precedence over justice, where justice concerns the rights of individual human beings as part of a global community rather than the rights of states as expressed through international law. The priority afforded to non-purposive practical association becomes an important factor in confining moral and normative concerns within the boundaries of the state. This is to claim that the state itself assumes a moral legitimacy that has a potential to satisfy fully the moral needs of the individual. Placed in this context, international regimes might be seen as structures designed to provide the necessary means of satisfying purely domestic demands, with no thought given to the consequences for others outside the state. In this interpretation regimes are not, as the cosmopolitan discourse would have it, an expression of the growing awareness of emergent world society — a society that presents a challenge to existing rules of practical association — but evidence of the operation of those rules themselves. The normative content of regimes should therefore be seen as part of the existing international order and not as derived from the moral claims of individuals in a world society. The point to note here is that through confining the moral claims of individuals to the state, the state itself is presumed to possess moral legitimacy.[36]

This section has attempted to clarify further the two discourses on the nature of international regimes. It has focused upon the distinction between purposive and practical rules of association as suggested by Nardin. This analysis shows that those who understand international regimes within the statist discourse view them as embedded in the practical rules of coexistence that define international society. Such an approach necessarily places international regimes within the normative order of a society of states. This means that the limits of a regime as a social institution can be found in international law and the international organisations that are concerned primarily with preserving that particular social identity. This entails denying any moral claims that derive from the purposive association associated with the cosmopolitan discourse. Seen from this perspective, international purposive association, if it can be said to exist at all, is severely limited in its scope.

To sustain this view requires the acceptance of several important premises. First, it assumes that the state provides the sole means for the expression of human values. This means that at the international level normative analysis is confined to the society of states. Second, it understands the state as an active participant on the international stage as opposed to a reactive entity responding to the demands of national and international publics. Third, it overlooks the possibility of international law and international organisations producing negative outcomes for many people. This is to argue that international law and international organisations are designed to limit expressions of values present in the wider international community in the name of preserving the higher value of international society.

INTERNATIONAL LAW AND HUMAN RIGHTS

Confusion over purposive and practical association has caused those who think and write about the international law on human rights, and the organisations designed for its implementation, to be called notoriously 'wishful thinkers'.[37] This is because of the predilection of academics for empiricism, formalism and written evidence. A contrary methodology would be to attempt the more difficult task of understanding less visible changes in normative expectations and values. Authors who attempt to examine a particular case of violation or deprivation of human rights commonly resort to extensive analysis of covenants, declarations, constitutions, and General Assembly resolutions rather than an examination of actual behaviour in its political and social context. To adopt the latter approach is of course arduous and often fraught with difficulties in collecting reliable information. The interpretative approach is also full of pitfalls and open to criticisms well known to the social and political sciences. Furthermore, most governments are obsessed with secrecy, particularly in areas of domestic life where openness may result in vilification by other members of international society. Of course, many transnational organizations, like Amnesty International for example, attempt to overcome this problem, but there remains a tendency among many authors to treat these sources as 'political' and, therefore, with suspicion. This academic self-censorship leaves little else but an examination of legal material. But, as Michael Barkun has pointed out:

> [a] narrow concern for the assertions of documents or for the power of legally constituted organs of government mistakes appearances for

reality, confuses visibility with significance and substitutes (however inadvertently) sophisticated description for explanation.[38]

Moreover, using formalism as a methodology mistakenly focuses attention on disagreements and arguments concerned with such things as the internal logic of the 'law', its coherence, extent and meaning, excluding more troublesome problems to do with efficacy, application and obligation.[39] Furthermore, formalism accepts without question that the 'law' in its present form plays a consistently positive role in reducing violations without regard for the context in which it is being applied.[40]

Following these arguments, those engaged in analysing the human rights regime have confused the existence of international law with the political and social norms of the regime. As discussed previously, the existence of international legal norms does not necessarily indicate a widely accepted normative order in the sense of one derived from complex social relationships. Although regime analysis seems to offer an attractive approach to human rights specialists because 'the centrality of norms is mirrored in their field', existing attempts at casting human rights as a regime have achieved little more than might be expected through employing traditional concepts and language.[41] This is because the essays under discussion here make the assumption that legal norms and the norms of universal human rights are both located in the instruments of international law — an assumption that leads to formalism derived from the expectations of the statist discourse. For example, Onuf and Peterson argue that regime analysis allows an examination of political aspects of human rights, particularly in the move from norm 'creation' to effective international law. On one hand they acknowledge that the regime underpins the relationship between the individual beneath the state and the institutions above the state, while on the other they assert that this remains acceptable only while states remain confident that norms, rules and procedures remain generalised, unenforceable and poorly defined.[42] At the outset of his essay, Donnelly asserts that regimes 'involve regularities that arise only when actors *conform* their conduct to norms and procedures they accept as legitimate',[43] but he then proceeds to devote the greater proportion of his essay to an examination of law and formally agreed measures of implementation. Ruggie is perhaps the least sanguine. He considers that as a rhetorical idea human rights have found their way into normal diplomatic and political debate, but he argues that the failure to reach a consensus on norms has hindered progress in establishing routinely adhered to rules and procedures.

In common with most research, these studies make an implied assumption that international law is the most efficacious method of tackling human rights violations. It is rare to find any justification for this assumption or to be given guidance on how we are supposed to understand the relationship between the existing body of international law on human rights and a reduction in the number of violations. This is a particularly important criticism if many violations of human rights owe as much to current economic and political structures as they do to the 'evil' side of human nature. Johan Galtung, for example, has argued that the legal approach assumes that those who violate human rights can be identified, made to answer for their crimes and suffer whatever punishment society decides is appropriate. Such an understanding of the processes and nature of law overlooks the fact that '[s]tructures cannot be juridical persons with intentions and capabilities', although structures may be the cause of repression, exploitation or starvation.[44] This leaves many unasked questions that have significant bearing on our understanding of the regime's development. For example, what positive role is assumed for international law? Does the international law approach offer only positive outcomes or might we find negative aspects also? What is the relationship between international law and the political environment in which it emerges and in which it must be implemented? Does the attention given to international law and formalism deflect attention from pursuing political and economic methods of reducing violations that may prove more efficacious? Are the existing international political structures such that international law will inevitably remain inadequate, no matter how well intentioned or constructed?

For those who write and think about human rights in the context of international law, several areas deserve special attention. These are the debate over the use of a domestic law analogy in relation to international law; the still detectable spectre of the natural law assumption when writing about the international law; the tendency to confuse legal norms with political norms and to collapse them into one another so that they are used synonymously; the assumption that international law offers no negative consequences for the area of international life in which it purports to intervene; and finally, the often overlooked cultural diversity in approaches to law.

At the heart of the propensity to formalism is an assumed analogy between domestic and international law. This is not the place to pick up the old debate between those who view international law in some hierarchical relationship with other systems of law and those who see international law, in the words of H L A Hart, as something 'clean different'.[45] The important question for international regime analysis, and for international theory in general, is whether a body of rules governing international action exists in the absence of central authoritative institutions, not whether these rules can be properly defined as law in the domestic sense.[46] If part of the utility of regime analysis is that it allows us to integrate formalism with normative expectations, our interest in normative rules should concentrate on the conditions for the existence of rules rather than on nebulous arguments about whether rules may be appropriately called law at the international level.

This being said, the confusion caused by those who imply some hierarchical relationship between domestic and international law is important. In a notable critique of the international law approach that dominates the study of human rights, J S Watson draws a distinction between the coercive nature of domestic law as opposed to the reciprocal nature of international law.[47] He argues that domestic law is coercive in the sense that its operation relies upon enforcement procedures that ensure compliance despite the immediate social and political environment in which it is applied. International law, on the other hand, relies upon reciprocity and can be identified only through constantly checking its validity against the actual practices and behaviour of states. The idea of enforcement, such as that reflected in domestic law, does not exist at the international level. Instead, compliance with international law relies upon some version of 'do unto others as you would have them do unto you' under similar circumstances. Sanctions for non-compliance, such as they exist, are not administered by a disinterested third party, as assumed in domestic law, but by those whose political and social interests may have been violated.[48] In the case of human rights the need for reciprocity is more difficult to establish than in other areas covered by international law since, in most cases, how another state treats its citizens bears little on the interests of others.[49] Watson writes:

> if the subject matter of a norm does not affect another state to a sufficient extent to make it willing, or likely, to respond to the violations, then there is no motivation for compliance beyond pure self-limitation on the part of the violator or potential violator. Such self-limitation needs no legal system at all.[50]

In short, a failure to understand the distinction between coercion and reciprocity allows many human rights authors to make assumptions about the potency of international law, which do not stand up to scrutiny.

As a consequence of the domestic law analogy writers on human rights regularly confuse international law with what might be termed supranational or transnational law. Underlying this confusion is a 'breathtakingly naive over generalization',[51] an unspoken but discernible call for the abolition of the nation-state and its replacement with some form of central world government. This error marks much academic work on human rights as little more than an article of faith because it ignores the current structures of international politics and instead affords international law an authority that it could only possess in a more cosmopolitan world. Even the most respected of human rights scholars are subject to this delusion. For example, Hersch Lauterpacht writes:

> a matter may be according to international law as it stands at present within the exclusive domestic jurisdiction of the state, while at the same time, because of its international implications and the growing interdependence of States, it may be essentially an international matter as distinguished from a matter of domestic jurisdiction. In particular, it is not essentially a matter of domestic jurisdiction if it has become the subject of international obligation undertaken by the State.[52]

Emphasising this point, Watson reports a remark by the distinguished legal scholar Rosalyn Higgins. During a conference on human rights and international law, she was asked to distinguish between states' practice and states' attitudes towards sources of international law. Watson reports that she replied, 'in essence the attitude of a government leads to the practice and there is not a great distinction between the two'.[53] While this may be a laudable utopian goal for international law and international lawyers, students of politics may treat it with some scepticism if not cynicism, and look upon it as a wholly unsatisfactory basis for the study of universal human rights. As Watson argues:

> [with] depressing regularity the reader of human rights literature in the international law field will find in the concluding paragraphs of typical articles an exhortation to optimism or hope, almost always expressed in the passive voice to increase its apparent authority. What such remarks indicate is of course that the true basis of the writer's argument is not to be found within the confines of international law but rather in his or her perceptions of human nature.[54]

A further complexity that springs from the passion for focusing on legal analysis in writing about human rights is to confuse and conflate natural law with international law.[55] The cosmopolitan nature of natural law offers an attractive philosophy for those interested in universal human rights because natural rights offers a coherent claim to authority over the state. However, following the work of twentieth century legal scholars, who have succeeded in discrediting the natural law assumption through showing that it is a façade for ideological purpose, subjective and incapable of discovery,[56] human rights scholars have been forced to turn to international law when attempting to give substance to the positive law of nation-states. Since the authority of natural law assumptions is no longer accepted, human rights has become a 'boundless sphere' deprived of any possibility of 'closure', and therefore open to the inclusion of many rights claims that under natural law are excluded.[57] Thus the status afforded to the international law of human rights is sustained by accepting two premises that remain contestable. First, that international law and natural law are synonymous, and second, the assumption that international and domestic law are in a hierarchical relationship with international law at the top.[58] This confusion ensures that international law receives what little credibility remains in the natural law assumption and supports the superiority claim of international law.

To press the point further, there is a difficulty in looking towards formal instruments if the assumption is that the international law on human rights reflects a well established, generally accepted set of norms derived from a sense of global society, because it remains open to question whether such a sense of global community does yet exist. This is reflected in the continuing political debate concerning the nature of rights; a debate dominated mostly by western thinking. This thinking understands law as articulating the dominant social order, which in the West assumes the primacy of the individual whose sense of both legal rights and, importantly, obligation offers the basis for maintaining social order. However, as many Third World statespeople and academics tirelessly point out, most of the world's peoples do not come from this tradition. Many societies in Africa and Asia, for example, assign the individual a role-playing function subordinated to the custom and authority of the group or community.[59] International Bills of Rights, which generally express an order taken for granted in the West, will therefore continue to offer less than a complete picture of the real state of human rights as they stand today.[60] The idea of rights for most non-western states concerns establishing justice for their community as a whole. This looks not to individual rights within a state but the rights of peoples and communities to participate in a global economic, social and political system on a basis of equality and fairness. The role of international law is therefore to articulate the norms of some future world order, which remains an order of states, rather than to formalise the well-established western idea of the rights of the individual. As such, the propensity to analyse human rights through the instruments of existing international law ignores important insights into the socio-political content of human rights that bear upon the norms and rules of the human rights regime.

Connected with this is the problem of cultural diversity. Although much has been written on the problem of cultural diversity, particularly in the attempt to establish a foundation for claims of universality, the existence of different traditions of law, and therefore competing interpretations of international law, seems to have escaped criticism.[61] This is of greater importance in fields like international human rights law, where implementation remains firmly in the hands of the state and domestic legal systems. Under such conditions the scope for conflicts caused by different understandings, conceptions, interpretations and readings of the law is legion. For example, the Latin American legal tradition attaches considerable importance to sustaining and enforcing existing formal legal norms, even when social practice has long since failed to demonstrate compliance. Although in these countries the formal norm is not understood as providing solutions to real world problems, 'the verbal solution is important in its own right, with all the social cultural connotations that it carries.'[62] Contrast this with the more flexible Anglo-Saxon tradition. In this tradition the failure of social compliance is treated as an opportunity to reform existing legal norms, 'to make the normative order work better as a prediction of social reality'.[63] While many who write on the international law of human rights assume that the principles of law are themselves universal, this assumption does not hold, because law means different things to different traditions of law. The importance of this point becomes more obvious in the following chapters that deal with conflicts over drafting processes for the International Bill of Human Rights.

Finally, it is important to be aware of some potentially negative aspects of international law and the international law approach to human rights. The first in this regard is to recognize that complexity often leads regime members to seek the 'lowest common denominator' that satisfies all participants and allows them to give public support to emergent international law in areas of moral concern.[64] Having once engaged in the debate on human rights, having given the idea of human rights political force and legitimacy by placing it as a central plank of the UN Charter, and having promoted the cause of human rights as a central value in the emerging postwar order, the founding members of the UN had invested considerable political currency in establishing a human rights regime. Any state seen to be openly obstructive, uncooperative or refusing to participate in processes that would translate that investment into international law laid itself open to charges of illegitimacy. However, many statespeople engaged in translating the idea of human rights into the language of international law equivocated for several reasons. First, the political and economic implications of establishing human rights as an additional, legitimate item on the international political agenda remained unclear. Second, uncertainty remained over the exact nature of the challenge human rights represented to existing principles of international relations, including the definition of sovereignty. Last, there was an acute awareness that establishing norms expressed as international law not only limited others' freedom to act but might also limit one's own freedom.

Such equivocation is common in regime formation when making the move from generalized expressions of concern to particular, detailed and binding legal rules. As the obligations attached to international law force regime members into making hard choices, they must assess the costs of altering their domestic and foreign policies to accommodate new agreements. At this crucial stage of regime formation, where costs and benefits typically remain uncertain, regime members are often reluctant to move beyond non-binding declarations of intent to more formal, detailed treaties or conventions.[65] If this is true as a general point for all regime formation, it is perhaps of greater significance in the area of human rights. Associating a state's name with a particular nonbinding declaration may be preferable to entering a binding agreement with uncertain future costs.

All of the above uncertainties are reflected throughout the history of the human rights regime and, indeed, in the duality of human rights talk itself. On the one hand human rights talk offers an abstract, metaphysical discourse concerned with absolutes, while on the other it is concerned with limiting the scope of these absolutes through international law, which is open to interpretation.[66] This echoes the opposition between natural law claims and those of positive law referred to earlier. It is further reflected in human rights law, which typically follows a two-step structure: a truth statement followed by a limitation clause. The truth statement embraces the concept of universal values. It allows governments to claim an adherence to moral values and virtues common to a wider society. It provides the conditions of moral legitimacy, including the claim that the state is the defender of human rights. Conversely, the limitation clause sets out the conditions whereby universal claims are legitimately proscribed or ignored in the name of public order, security or the national interest. It is an escape clause that allows the state to reassert its own authority over the truth statement.

For example, the fundamental right to life inevitably includes an escape clause, which once enshrined in binding covenants, permits capital punishment under due process of law. Defining universal human rights as a limitation to the truth claim, as international law does, legitimises the authority of the state over the moral claims of the individual. As Teson expresses it:

> [an] enlightened moral and political global reality is ill served by the statist model of international law. The model promotes states and not individuals, governments not persons, order not rights, compliance not justice. It insists that rulers be permitted to exercise whatever amount of coercion is necessary to politically control their subjects.[67]

Thus the normative order becomes that order which conforms to the demands of positive international law rather than that of universal moral claims. Moral questions therefore, need not enter the international political agenda.

This has the negative effect of allowing states to claim legitimacy of action provided their behaviour remains within the limits described by international law. Instead of attempting to understand their actions within the contemporary moral and political context, states can compare all acts against international law and claim legitimacy without regard for justice. In this way the international law of human rights is seen as an obstacle to further moral understanding because it offers governments the opportunity to match and compare all acts against legally binding obligations.[68] This offers an illusion of orderliness that deflects attention from wide-ranging, fundamental disagreements when thinking about human rights. Furthermore, it deflects attention from the purpose of human rights, which is to create the conditions of justice.[69] Since it is generally accepted that international law, including that body of law dealing with human rights, represents a basis for transactions between states, as opposed to a contrary view implicit in human rights that it represents a cosmopolitan idea of a universal morality claimed on behalf of all members of humankind, human rights talk confined to the level of formalism excludes the idea of justice. This is the distinction between law as 'order' and law as 'justice' intended to secure the rights of the individual.[70] Indeed, as discussed earlier, for many scholars, achieving the conditions of 'practical association' in a world of states must take priority over securing the rights of the individual.

In summary, according to one scholar, publications on human rights that pin their hopes on international law for solutions are rather like a man who has lost his wallet in the street and, having mislaid it, looks for it under the street light, not because he dropped it there, but simply because there is greater light.[71] However, such criticisms remain the exception. Although many are aware that a gap exists between legal formulae and the reality of a world where human rights are denied or ignored, they continue to be disappointed and pessimistic, and respond by doubling their efforts to produce even more international legal instruments. If the criticisms offered here are well founded however, these efforts will be equally futile and lead to equally pessimistic conclusions.

What seems clear from the above analysis is that the presentation of the international law of human rights as law in its formality and language, which intentionally or not attracts some prestige and authority, does not attract the full rigour or consequences of the law.[72] To focus on formalism and the legal approach as a way of gaining an insight into the globalisation of the idea of human rights presents a distorted picture: optimistic at one time in that a vast body of law now exists, but pessimistic at another because of its fragility and its failure to command compliance. What this suggests is that greater attention should be paid to the political environment in which the idea of human rights has emerged.[73]

The arguments presented here shows that the legal-formal approach to analysis offers great dangers for those interested in using the regime concept, particularly when attempting to draw together legal, social and political norms in the field of human rights. This is not to argue that the existence of a large and growing body of international law is insignificant. The political energy consumed in making this law, together with the fact that it is cited in national constitutions, treaties, settlements of conflict and in the speeches of statespeople, should be evidence enough that human rights now represent a significant addition to the international political agenda. But it is, and has always been, political. Focusing so singularly on international law elevates the legal approach beyond its potential, offers a distorted view of progress on human rights and overlooks the inconvenient fact that international law, in the accepted classical sense, is politically motivated because it represents a body of rules made by states to regulate behaviour between states.

If human rights talk is in large part about facets of human nature that concern such things as love, care, justice, obligation and the other characteristics thought of as peculiar to human society, it cannot be captured by reducing it to the concepts and language of the law alone. To do so is to confuse philosophical and political debates on human rights with the technique of the law. Kaplan and Katzenbach's observation of over thirty years ago seems to have had little influence on contemporary writing on human rights:

> The difficulty with most writing about international law is that it does not differentiate between myth and technique, and does not provide the student with any basis for judging the policy considerations that constrain the decisions of the legal system. There is a sense of frustration in the discussion of the sources of law that brings the student no closer to understanding the process. In fact, we are talking here merely of technique, the mechanics of the process, and this provides no clue for answering questions of what the legal norm is in any given situation.[74]

Some of this confusion results from the move away from natural rights to rights as positive legal rights referred to earlier. Such a move has allowed the scholar of human rights to focus on the techniques and mechanics of the law but offers few insights into important questions concerned with obligation and compliance.[75]

INTERNATIONAL REGIMES AND INTERNATIONAL INSTITUTIONS

The distinction between institutions and organisations adds further confusion to the uncertainty over the source and nature of human rights norms discussed above. This distinction is important for epistemological reasons that determine how authors write and think about regimes.

Institutions can be thought of as expressions of prized social values found in shared moral convictions about some aspect of the 'good life'. They assign actors recognisable roles that describe rules or conventions which govern relations between role occupants. To describe an institution requires an examination of the patterns of social relationships that are the customs or habits found in social life. The existence of an institution therefore 'sets up a network or pattern of behavioural relationships that lends order or predictability to human affairs'.[76] Organisations, on the other hand, are physical entities possessing offices, personnel, equipment and budgets. They are bureaucratic entities designed to achieve specific, well-defined goals or objective needs. In attempting to understand regimes or any other form of international cooperation commentators:

> make a mistake when they say that international society features few effective institutions; what they mean to assert is that it has few effective international organisations.[77]

It follows that if international regimes are understood as institutions, as most regime authors attempt to assert, then they cannot be found in the practices and bureaucratic arrangements of international organisations alone. Rather, they are to be found in the attitudes, convictions, expectations and social needs of actors expressing themselves in ways understood as moral, apposite and appropriate to their social environment.[78] Therefore, regimes as institutions are 'conceptual creations not concrete entities'.[79] However, an examination of the literature reveals that the distinction between institutions and organisations is seldom recognised.

Understood as social institutions, international regimes possess a dynamic nature in that they result from a social environment of continuous interaction both with other institutions and the natural world.[80] It is therefore inappropriate to assess a regime by simply comparing behaviour in relation to compliance with a set of prior, formal rules; for this tells us nothing about the social environment in which current actions take place. For example, to gain an insight into prevailing attitudes towards nuclear nonproliferation it is not sufficient simply to measure the rate and degree of proliferation, but we must also attempt to understand how the contemporary international community assesses and responds to proliferation.[81] Similarly, assessing the efficacy of existing measures for the promotion and protection of human rights through comparing the requirements of international law, regional conventions and UN committees with the legislative activity of states, does not in itself tell us anything about the status of human rights as a legitimate international moral and political issue.

This is not to argue that such machinery is of no significance when attempting to understand a particular regime. However, it is to assert that confining enquiry to formalism, whether this involves the study of constitutions to see what organisations are supposed to do, or a study of what they actually do, tells us little about how regimes shape behaviour. Formalism may provide an insight into agreements reached in a particular historic period but, since expectations change over time through repeated attempts to accommodate new environments, including the existence of regimes themselves, formalism will tell us nothing about regime dynamics or about how regime norms actually affect behaviour.[82] Of greater interest is an attempt to understand how actors' behaviour within regimes is interpreted by fellow regime members. This is because:

> the rationales and justifications for behaviour which are proffered, together with pleas for understanding or admissions of guilt, as well as the responsiveness to such reasoning on the part of the states, are all absolutely crucial component parts of any explanations involving the efficacy of norms. Indeed, such communicative dynamics may well tell us more about how robust a regime is than overt behaviour.[83]

The differentiation of organisations from institutions is important when looking at human rights regimes because it exemplifies the distinction between goals and values in international relations in general and human rights in particular. Several authors have recognised this distinction previously. Kenneth Minogue, for example, suggests such a distinction when he argues that goals and values have long inhabited the 'uneasy borderland between peoples' demands on the one hand (goals) and their moral convictions on the other (values)'.[84] This suggests that political and social activity cannot be understood exclusively as objective goals and material means whose ends are the satisfaction of needs. Rather, such activity is also an end in itself because it satisfies important human needs for participation, place and social identity. According to Robert Jackson, this offers a 'schizo-phrenic' existence to actors in a social environment where goal oriented organisations, designed to fulfil particular ends, fail to meet the requirements of newly evolving, dynamic social institutions.[85] In modern times the growth of complex interdependence and transnationalism leads international, transnational and domestic actors to seek new forms of organisation that regularise new relationships and institutionalise emerging norms.[86]

At the level of international relations the dynamism of social institutions — made more complex with the rise of transnationalism — can be thought of as a challenge to the current system of states, and particularly to those who are best served by its preservation. The outcome of placing the source of human rights norms within international instruments, which are determined by a state-centric organisation like the United Nations, is that cosmopolitan normative claims are expressed in statist terms. Global leaders, perhaps with half an eye on avoiding the erosion of their own domestic authority by acknowledging universal values, turn instead to defining human rights by reference to international law as a measure of 'good' or 'bad' behaviour, and in so doing avoid moral questions.[87] While such a view supports Maurice Cranston's assertion that the only legitimate human rights claims are those that can be delivered through the law[88] — and for Cranston this excludes all economic and social claims — it overlooks the possibility that international law is often drafted and ratified for political purposes that do not necessarily represent the values held by statespeople, national communities, diplomats or governments engaged in the drafting process. However, as Alison Dundas Renteln has observed, these same groups are called upon to implement the law in their own countries, even when the values that the law expresses may be contrary to culturally held values.[89]

Since ideas, intentions and values are the outcome of dynamic, complex social interactions, there remains a tension between the authoritative goals of international law and international institutions.[90] If human rights have anything to do with the 'good life' — which concerns political organisation and human welfare — confining analysis of the regime solely to international law and treaties, including the organisations brought into existence through such agreements, excludes important normative dimensions of the human rights debate. Understanding human rights as legal, formal arrangements allows states to consign them to foreign policy, which is concerned with the behaviour of other states rather than the rights of people everywhere.[91] Few who have an interest in human rights would support such a view because human rights represent a commitment to life itself.[92] In a world where transnationalism is acknowledged as a factor in conditioning our beliefs and perceptions, and where there is a growing awareness that all human beings share a common history, values are transmitted to international society through domestic political processes, international economic structures and transnational organisations like Amnesty International who have gained access to international channels of communication. Therefore, to view the human rights regime in statist terms alone ignores important social and political structures that ultimately determine its success and strength. This does not, of course, suggest that a totally universalistic approach that ignores the state should be adopted. But it does suggest that in any attempt to discover how these relationships help determine the emergence and form of the regime an effort should be made to account for all these structures and to include the linkages between all significant actors. If the utility of regime analysis is that it allows us to integrate analysis of goal-specific organisations with normative aspects of international behaviour then the emphasis on formalism is misplaced.

Finally, as James Mayall has pointed out, the state is an intellectual construct or notional entity, an idea rather than a territory or a political fact.[93] If the state is a notional entity then it cannot be seen as a necessary or inevitable form of political or moral life. Furthermore, if the state is a notional entity then international society, as a society of states, must itself be a notional entity. This raises the question of how to understand notional entities as holding or expressing values and expectations? While values and institutions are integral to defining social relationships between individuals, the same cannot be claimed for notional entities. If this were possible then it would be necessary to sustain the claim that notional entities beget further notional entities without the need for human intervention. This difficulty again explains the preoccupation of the statists with formalism and deducing the existence of regimes by reference to organisations. It allows regimes within international society to be deduced through the application of formal rules and organisational procedures rather than from evidence of their acceptance. As James Keeley has argued, while this approach does not in itself preclude the existence of a more inclusive universal society, it avoids questions concerning obligation, legitimacy, benevolence and other concerns that are generally associated with the presence of society.[94] Moreover, there is a presumed assumption that the activities of these organisations produce outcomes that are 'good' for all members of society. This ignores the demands of those whose values are left unfulfilled or even impaired by particular regimes. Furthermore, such an approach has little to say about those areas of international life where no regime emerges but where a growing consensus displays the evolution of new values, for example, in concern over environmental degradation.

HEGEMONY AND THE HUMAN RIGHTS REGIME

The most widely employed explanation of regime formation and dynamics is the theory of 'hegemonic stability'.[95] This theory argues that the establishment and maintenance of enduring international organisations and institutions depends upon the existence of a single dominant state. In forming and maintaining a regime, such a state must possess both the capability and, importantly, the will to structure regime rules and enforce them. Following the theory suggests that the importance, efficacy and saliency of international institutions ride upon the rise and decline of the hegemon's interests and capabilities. In short, the rise and decline of a particular hegemon is parallelled by the rise and decline of particular regimes in which it has an interest. This is the Realists' view of hegemony. It relies on the notion of a dominant state utilizing its power in ordering the actions of weaker states, by imposing cooperative, rule governed institutions.

As Robert Keohane has pointed out, this crude version of hegemonic stability, although useful as a starting point for the analysis of international cooperation, fails to stand up to historic scrutiny. Keohane argues that from the end of the World War II until the mid-1960s, the USA did indeed seem to exert its authority on world order through its leading role in creating international cooperative organisations. However, Keohane asserts that the longevity of existing international organisations, coupled with a sustained interest in developing new cooperative arrangements, cannot be so easily understood as US power as coercion. As an alternative he argues that:

> rather than being a component of a scientific generalization — that power is a necessary or sufficient condition for cooperation — the concept of hegemony, defined in the terms of willingness as well as ability to lead, helps us to think about the incentives facing the potential hegemon....Thinking about the calculations of secondary powers raises the question of deference. Theories of hegemony should seek not only to analyse dominant powers' decisions to engage in rule-making and rule-enforcement, but also explore why secondary states defer to the leadership of the hegemon.[96]

Keohane argues that 'valuable clues' to the answers for these questions can be found in Marxian analysis, and particularly in the ideas of the Italian Marxist Antonio Gramsci. To the Realist conception of hegemony as dominance, Gramsci adds the notion of hegemony maintained as much through consensus as through coercion.[97] He argues that a dominant social group manifests itself in two ways: as 'coercive force' and through the legitimation of 'intellectual and moral' leadership.[98] While analysis of economic capabilities remains a necessary task in understanding hegemony, reducing hegemony to economics alone misses important insights concerned with moral, social and ideological conditions. This implies that secondary states undergo processes of socialization that promote the 'common acceptance of a consensual order that binds the ruler and the ruled and

legitimizes power',[99] enabling the hegemon to enhance rules based on might
with those based on right.

Noting the Gramscian notion of ideological hegemony, and that the world
capitalist system remains the overwhelmingly dominant mode of production,
Keohane argues that weaker states perceive their interests as fundamentally
integrated within that system. Secondary states are therefore willing to defer
to the hegemon who, in return, performs the necessary tasks associated with
supervising cooperative relationships between politically independent states.
International regimes, in this understanding of hegemony, facilitate both
material and ideological transactions. Regimes legitimise the articulation of
rules and norms as described by the dominant state with the acquiescence of
lesser states. Put succinctly by Robert Cox, another author who has drawn
upon the ideas of Gramsci:

> world hegemony is describable as a social structure, an economic
> structure and a political structure: and it cannot be simply one of these
> things but must be all three. World hegemony, therefore, is expressed in
> universal norms, institutions and mechanisms which lay down general
> rules of behaviour for states and those forms of civil society that act across
> national boundaries — rules which support the dominant mode of
> production.[100]

Taking up Gramsci's concept of ideological hegemony, Keohane offers a
way of understanding regimes that are not concerned primarily with
economic and material exchange. However, several points should be stressed
before considering hegemony and human rights. First, and to reiterate,
Keohane's analysis attempts to associate hegemony, complex interdependence and international regimes as a way of explaining enduring
international economic relationships. In the field of human rights we are
more interested in exploring the existence of 'moral interdependence',[101]
which may make many of Keohane's assumptions less sure. Second,
Gramscian analysis takes class as its basic unit of analysis and is concerned
with the relationship between state and civil society. Keohane, on the other
hand, is interested in asymmetrical, inter-state power relationships where
power is disaggregated across a wide number of issue-areas. Therefore,
Keohane's attempt to utilize the Gramscian concept of hegemony, which is
largely concerned with the domestic life of the state, may be less appropriate
than at first sight. Third, Keohane makes a tacit assumption that regime
formation is inherently 'good' and fails to recognize any possible 'bad' or
negative consequences of their operation for a significant number of other
actors. This is of particular importance for human rights and is a recurring
theme throughout this book. Fourth, like most scholars who have shown an

interest in regime analysis, Keohane confines his analysis to those institutions and associated organizations that are currently operative. He has little to say about the failure of some regimes to develop beyond the weakest form or those that do not emerge at all. Important here is the power of the hegemon to deny the formation of a regime that promises to benefit secondary states at the expense of the hegemon, or runs the risk of undermining hegemonic authority.

This being said, we might ask whether the United States did boast the prerequisites (capabilities and will) to develop a human rights regime after 1945. Those rights promoted by the United States derive from liberal ideology and include freedom of individual action, noninterference by the state in economic and social matters and the principle of laissez-faire.[102] This meant that human rights became defined as those rights that required government abstention from acts that impaired the freedom of the individual.[103] As far as is possible within the confines of a necessary minimum order, liberal ideology offers the individual the widest possible freedom to innovate and to invest time, capital and resources in the processes of economic production and exchange. Applying the laissez-faire principle to human rights thus points to acts of omission rather than those of commission. Crucially, acts of omission confine human rights to civil and political rights, which some have argued demand little or no additional state resources to maintain.[104]

Of course, the implementation of civil and political rights does require such things as legislation, courts and a police force, and this is why the word 'additional' must be emphasised. If however, as Richard Falk has argued, 'hegemonic logic'[105] determines that human rights, like any other tool of foreign policy, furthers the interests of the hegemon, then applying the laissez-faire principle to human rights is exposed as part of a postwar programme of reparation or punishment to be pressed upon the defeated by the victors, rather than as a serious attempt at formulating a regime for the universal protection of human rights.[106] This suggests that if a human rights regime is possible it should include only those civil and political rights largely enjoyed by the allies. Any rights claims that demanded changes to the hegemon's domestic or foreign policies, or presented a challenge to their existing interests, could not be accepted as legitimate. Several other authors support this view. Many rights promoted by the victorious states during the war years and after, for example, the right to self-determination and racial equality, were never intended as universally applicable principles, particularly where their application appeared to challenge existing hegemonic superstructures.[107]

Following the attempt by the USA to establish the idea of human rights in the immediate postwar years, it became increasingly difficult to limit the debate to those areas that best suited America's interests. First, influential groups in the USA were concerned about a possible challenge to liberalism and the American way of life. Furthermore, in some southern states there was concern over a potential challenge (often seen as a 'threat') to their racist and discriminatory laws. Both groups found expression in the run up to the 1952 presidential election and the subsequent change of administration. As many have noted before, policies and regimes intended to promote the long-term global interests of a hegemon often undermine the confidence of domestic publics.[108] Second, the Soviet Union, together with other socialist states, offered leadership to less developed founding members of the UN who perceived their interests as best served through claiming economic rights and rejecting the primacy of civil and political rights. Third, less developed states were enthusiastic to give expression to their new found status as 'equal' sovereign members of the UN. They soon realized the advantages of building coalitions for supporting their own agenda at the expense of that of the USA. Fourth, human rights offered a fertile ideological battleground in the Cold War atmosphere that rapidly developed following the formation of the UN. Human rights presented a significant issue on which both sides could set out their ideological differences. Last, the less developed states were encouraged and supported by the socialist states to take the principles of self-determination and racial equality at face value. What less developed states expected from their membership of the United Nations was to be treated as equals and to have an equal voice in world affairs. The principles of self-determination and equality were also used to support the claims of those remaining under colonial rule in their fight for independence. The success of the decolonisation movement promised, at some time in the future, to further increase the majority against the USA in the General Assembly.

Taken together, these features of the early debates on human rights weakened both the will and the capacity of the USA to develop a strong regime. The USA was also unable to inspire deference in others. As it became clear that economic rights were not on the agenda, and support for self-determination was ambiguous, less developed states became less inclined to defer to the USA. Indeed, the less developed and socialist states soon began to promote a conception of human rights contrary to the expectations of the United States. As the less developed states natural majority in the Assembly emerged, the threat to outvote the United States and its allies increased. To avoid this risk, with its attendant perceived loss of status and increasing unrest among dominant domestic groups like bankers, industrialists and financiers,[109] the United States calculated that withdrawal from the debate was politically preferable.[110]

In conclusion it should be noted that most advocates of regime theory attempt to understand the actions of a hegemon in regime formation as positive and beneficial in achieving desired ends. In the field of human rights the United States became increasingly aware that it could not hope to limit the extent of the regime to its own interests. Instead, it set about diminishing the consequences of its initial, postwar enthusiasm for human rights. While existing studies of the human rights regime recognize that the regime is weak, and is likely to remain so for the foreseeable future, they fail to acknowledge the negative influence of the hegemon. Put simply, the weakness of the regime can be attributed to domestic and international forces upon the hegemon. These forces caused the hegemon to change its emphasis on human rights in an attempt to marginalise an issue that promised to gain an importance beyond its control and against its own interests.

CONCLUSION

Pointing to the distinction between the statist and the cosmopolitan discourses on human rights does not require us to choose between the two. The emergence of international organisations and administrative machinery cannot be wholly divorced from demands based on expressions of human values. Nor for that matter can the activities of organisations like the United Nations, which are engaged in seeking consensus and building regimes in almost all areas of international life, be seen as irrelevant. However, to confine analysis to the practices of international organisations or the demands of international law is likely, at best, to reveal only the most visible signs that a regime exists, or at worst, to offer false reassurances that a satisfactory regime already exists. Furthermore, the statist discourse seems incapable of providing satisfactory explanations of how institutions emerge, how they are amended or how they collapse.

To understand the growth of a regime requires a more inclusive approach that takes account of its social and political context. For human rights, attempts to construct a regime were conducted within the context of the Cold War and rapid decolonisation. Taken together, these political conditions meant that the USA could not resist the growing movement to cast human rights in a way that challenged its interests. What follows in the remaining chapters is an attempt to understand how human rights have emerged as one of the twentieth century's most powerful ideas and why that idea has failed to inspire a strong regime.

NOTES

1. John Vincent, *Human Rights and International Relations*, (Cambridge University Press, Cambridge, 1986), p. 54.
2. Richard Falk, *Human Rights and State Sovereignty*, (Holmes & Meier, London, 1981).
3. Roger Smith, 'Institutionalization as a measure of regime stability: insights for international regime analysis from the study of domestic politics', *Millennium*, 18:2, 1989, pp. 227–44. See also, Friedrich Kratochwil and John Ruggie, 'International organization: The state of the art or the art of the state', *International Organization*, 40:4, 1986, pp. 753–75.
4. George Kennan, 'Morality and foreign policy', *Foreign Affairs*, 64:2, 1985, pp. 205–18. For a contrary view see, Cyrus R Vance, 'The human rights imperative', *Foreign Policy*, 64, summer 1986, pp. 3–19.
5. For an analysis and critique of this type of traditional thinking see, Andrew Linklater, *Men and Citizens in the Theory of International Relations*, (Macmillan, London, 1981), particularly chapters 1 and 2.
6. Evan Luard, *The Globalization of Politics: The Changing Focus of Political Action in the Modern World*, (Macmillan, Basingstoke, 1990), p.101.
7. J S Watson, 'Legal theory, efficacy and validity in the development of human rights in international law', *University of Illinois Law Forum*, vol. 3, 1979, p. 611.
8. Terry Nardin, *Law, Morality, and the Relations of States*, (Princeton University Press, New Jersey, 1983), p. 275.
9. Vincent, op. cit., p. 92.
10. ibid., p. 99.
11. Helge Ole Bergesen, 'The power to embarrass: the UN human rights regime between realism and utopia', paper presented to the International Studies Association, Rio de Janeiro, August, 1982; John G Ruggie, 'Human rights and the future of international community', *Daedalus*, 112:4, 1983, pp. 93–110; N G Onuf and V Spike Peterson, 'Human rights from an international regime perspective', *Journal of International Affairs*, 32:2, 1984, pp. 329–43; and, Jack Donnelly, 'International human rights: a regime analysis', *International Organization*, 40:3, 1986, pp. 599–642.
12. ibid., p. 100
13. Prominent among these writers are Robert Keohane, John Ruggie, Oran Young and others who regularly contribute to *International Organisation*.
14. John G Ruggie, 'International responses to technology: concepts and trends', *International Organization*, 29:3, 1975, p. 557.
15. Ernst Haas, 'On systems and international regimes', *World Politics*, 27:2, 1975, pp 147–74 and Ruggie, op. cit. Although Ruggie's article was published some months before that of Haas, Ruggie acknowledges that Haas was the first to coin the phrase 'international regime'.
16. Stephen Krasner, 'Structural causes and regime consequences: regimes as intervening variables', *International Organization*, 36:2, 1982, p. 186.
17. ibid., p. 196.
18. J A Finlayson & M Zacher, 'The GATT and the regulation of trade barriers: regime dynamics and function', in S Krasner (ed), *International Regimes*, (Cornell University Press, London, 1983), pp. 237–314.
19. Krasner, op. cit., p. 186.

20. See, for example, Mark Hoffman, 'Critical theory and the inter-paradigm debate', *Millennium*, 16:2, 1987, pp. 231–49.
21. For an essay that asserts the relevance of regime theory within a world society perspective see Richard L O'Meara, 'Regimes and their implications for international theory', *Millennium*, 13:3, 1984, pp. 245–64.
22. Kratochwil and Ruggie, op. cit.
23. Michael Barkun, *Law Without Sanctions*, (Yale University Press, New Haven and London, 1968), ch. 4.
24. For a discussion of the possible meanings and usages of the term 'principles' see, Felix Openheim, *Political Concepts: A Reconstruction*, (Blackwell, Oxford, 1981) and, *Moral Principles in Political Philosophy*, (Random House, New York, 1976).
25. For further discussion on the nature of norms see, Friedrich Kratochwil, *Rules, Norms and Decisions*, (Cambridge University Press, Cambridge, 1989); Adda Bozeman, *The Future of Law in a Multicultural World*, (Princeton University Press, New Jersey, 1971); and Georg Henrik von Wright, *Norm and Action*, (Routledge and Kegan Paul, London, 1963).
26. Richard K Ashley, 'Untying the sovereign state: a double reading of the anarchy problematique', *Millennium*, 17:2, 1988, pp. 227–62.
27. These questions have become a central issue in recent IR theory. See, for example, C Brown, *International Relations Theory: A New Normative Approach*, (Harvester Wheatsheaf, London, 1992).
28. Ashley, op. cit.
29. ibid., p. 247.
30. Chris Brown, 'Not my department? Normative theory and international relations', *Paradigms: The Kent Journal of International Relations*, 1:2, 1987, p. 108.
31. Nardin, op. cit., p. 5.
32. ibid. p. 57.
33. Vladimir Idelson, 'The law of nations and the individual', *The Grotius Society: Transactions for the Year 1944*, (Wiley & Sons, London, 1962), pp. 50–73.
34. Nardin, op. cit., p. 275.
35. Other similar approaches have been attempted also. See, for example, Hedley Bull's analysis of rules in *The Anarchical Society*, (Macmillan, Basingstoke, 1988), pp. 68–70. For another analysis of rules see, J Rawls, 'Two concepts of rules', *Philosophical Review*, 64:1, 1955, pp. 3–32.
36. For a full analysis and critique of Nardin see Mark Hoffman, 'States, cosmopolitanism and normative international relations', *Paradigms*, 2:1, 1988, pp. 6–25; and Chris Brown, 'Not my department?', op. cit.
37. Vincent, op. cit., p. 45.
38. Barkun, op. cit., p. 102.
39. Oran Young has consistently argued that focusing exclusively on formalism and the processes of bargaining and negotiation that lead to international law misses important elements in regime analysis. This is because the limits of the agenda have more usually been set and agreed before these processes are entered into. Formal bargaining, according to Young, is therefore more concerned with legal, technical, presentational and linguistic problems. See, for example, his 'The politics of international regime formation: Managing natural resources and the environment', *International Organization*, 43:3, 1989, pp. 349–75.

40. Many examples of this legal approach can be found. See, F Capotorli, 'Human rights: The hard road towards universality', in R S MacDonald & D M Johnson (eds), *The Structure and Process of International Law*, (Nijhoff, Dordrecht, 1983); K Vasak, 'Introduction', in K Vasak (ed), *The International Dimensions of Human Rights*, (Greenwood Press, Westpoint, 1982). For an example of the despair of many writers see, H Gross-Espiell, 'The evolving concept of human rights — Western, Socialist and Third World views', in B G Ramcharan, *Human Rights: Thirty Years After the Universal Declaration*, (Nijhoff, London, 1979), pp. 42–65. For a discussion of some of the problems noted above see, Oscar Schachter, 'Towards a theory of obligation', *Virginia Journal of International Law*, 8:2, 1968, pp. 300–22.
41. Conway Henderson, 'Human rights and regimes: a bibliographical essay', *Human Rights Quarterly*, vol. 10, 1988, pp. 525–43.
42. Onuf and Peterson, op. cit., p. 339.
43. Donnelly, op. cit., p. 602. Emphasis in the original.
44. Johan Galtung, *Human Rights in Another Key*, (Polity Press, Cambridge, 1994), p. 32.
45. For an example of this type of discussion see, H L A Hart, *The Concept of Law*, (Clarendon Press, Oxford, 1969), ch. 10.
46. Nardin, op. cit., ch. 6.
47. Watson, op. cit.
48. Watson acknowledges the existence of international courts. However, he argues that human rights claims are essentially political. It is therefore inappropriate to submit human rights claims to legal adjudication because courts must act as independent third parties, not as arbiters of differing political claims.
49. Watson uses this argument to demonstrate why some areas of human rights, for example the treatment of aliens and the movement of refugees, are afforded greater interest in international politics. In both cases the physical movement of peoples holds potential costs for recipient states.
50. ibid., p. 619.
51. ibid., p. 638.
52. Hersch Lauterpacht, *International Law and Human Rights*, (Archon Books, London, 1968), p. 176.
53. Watson, op. cit., p. 632.
54. ibid., p. 627.
55. H L A Hart, 'Are there any natural rights', in A Quinton (ed), *Political Philosophy*, (Oxford University Press, Oxford, 1977).
56. Watson cites J Kelsen, *What is Justice*, (University of Columbia Press, Berkeley, 1957).
57. R G Brisenco, 'The Negative Aspects of International Law: A Study of Law and Ideology', (Unpublished PhD thesis, LSE, 1987)
58. For a recent discussion of these problems from a Kantian perspective see Fernando R Teson, 'The Kantian theory of international law', *Columbia Law Review*, 92:1, 1992, pp. 53–102.
59. See, for example, Abdullahi Ahmed An-Na'im, *Towards an Islamic Reformation: Civil Liberties, Human Rights, and International Law*, (Syracuse University Press, Syracuse, 1990); Muhammad Zafrulla Khan, *Islam and Human Rights*, (The London Mosque, London, 1976); R Thaper, 'The Hindu and Buddhist tradition', *International Social Science Journal*, 18:1, 1966, pp. 31–40; and, V N Kudryartov, 'Human rights and the Soviet Constitution', in

Philosophical Foundations of Human Rights, (UNESCO, New York, 1986). The most widely known example of ascribed roles for individuals in some societies is the special role given to women.

60. Martin Wight, *System of States*, (Leicester University Press, Leicester, 1977), ch. 6. Wight reminds us that the representative of the USSR (Mr Vyshinsky) in the early days of the United Nations, often warned the USA and its supporters that it represented only the minority of the peoples of the world but that the minority in the Assembly represented the majority.

61. Bozeman, op. cit., and Barkun, op. cit. do take this question on.

62. Galtung, op. cit., p. 44

63. ibid., p. 42.

64. M A Kaplan and N B Katzenbach, *The Politics and Foundations of International Law*, (John Wiley, London, 1961). Also, Antonio Cassese, 'Progressive transnational promotion of human rights', in B Ramcharan (ed), *Human Rights: Thirty Years After the Universal Declaration*, (Mijhoff, London, 1979).

65. Young, op. cit., 'The politics of international regime formation'.

66. Brisenco, op. cit., ch. 3.

67. Teson, op. cit., p. 101.

68. Bozeman, op. cit., pp. 183–4.

69. Vincent, op. cit., ch. 3.

70. M Barkun, *Law Without Sanction*, (Yale University Press, London, 1968), p. 155. Barkun argues that this distinction represents a major difficulty for international relations analysis on rights and causes considerable confusion in the literature.

71. W M Reisman, 'International incidents: A new study in the genre of international law', in W M Reisman and A R Willard (eds), *International Incidents: The Law That Counts In World Politics*, (Princeton University Press, Princeton, 1988), pp. 3–24.

72. P Allott, 'The international protection of human rights: A stocktaking', paper given to the 'British International Studies Association', Annual Conference, 1977.

73. Ruggie, op. cit., p. 98, argues that the continued dialogue on the nature of particular rights provides further evidence that rights as international law remain closely dependent on power and interests among states.

74. Kaplan and Katzenbach, op. cit., p. 264.

75. John Kleinig, 'Human rights, legal rights and social change', in E Kamenka and A Erh-Soon Tay (eds), *Human Rights*, (Edward Arnold, London, 1978), pp. 36–47. Kleinig likens the use of law as the methodology for the study of human rights to the introduction of a new plant or species to a country as a means of preventing disease in indigenous species. The introduced species may perform its desired task but in time it can become a pest itself.

76. Oran Young, *International Co-operation: Building Regimes for Natural Resources and the Environment*, (Cornell University Press, London, 1989), p. 32.

77. Oran Young, 'International regimes: towards a new theory of institutions', *World Politics*, 39:1, 1986, p. 108. For a more detailed expression of Young's concern to distinguish institutions from organisations see his *International Co-operation*, op. cit., ch. 2.

78. Puchala and Hopkins, op. cit.

79. Kratochwil and Ruggie, op. cit., p. 763.

80. ibid. Examples of this can be seen in several areas of contemporary international life. For example, the monetary regime which moved from the gold standard, to fixed exchange rates (Bretton Woods), to the floating exchange rates of the present time. See, Benjamin J Cohen, 'Balance of payments financing: Evolution of a regime', in S Krasner (ed), *International Regimes*, op. cit., pp. 315–36.

81. Smith, op. cit.

82. Philip Action, 'Regimes and hegemony', *Paradigms: The Kent Journal of International Relations*, 3:1, 1987, pp. 47–55.

83. Kratochwil and Ruggie, op. cit., p. 768. Kratochwil and Ruggie liken this process to 'interstitial law making', a term used by lawyers to indicate the process of the development of law through interpretation.

84. Kenneth Minogue, 'Natural rights, ideology and the game of life', in E Kamenka and A Erh-Soon Tay (eds), *Human Rights*, (Edward Arnold, London, 1978), p. 16. Words in brackets added.

85. Robert H Jackson, 'Quasi-states, dual regimes, and neo-classical theory: International jurisprudence and the Third World', *International Organization*, 41:4, 1987, p. 519–49.

86. Yale H Ferguson and Richard W Mansbach, 'Between celebration and despair: Constructive suggestions for future international theory', *International Studies Quarterly*, 35:4, 1991, pp. 363–386.

87. Ralph Pettman, *State and Class: A Sociology of International Affairs*, (Croom Helm, London, 1979), ch. 3. See also Harold K Jacobson, 'The global system and the realization of human dignity and justice', *International Studies Quarterly*, 26:2, 1982, pp. 315–32. Jacobson points out that the development of positive international law since 1945 is paralleled by the intellectual dominance of Realism.

88. Maurice Cranston, 'Human rights, real and supposed', in D D Raphael (ed), *Political Theory and the Rights of Man*, (Macmillan, London, 1967), pp. 43–53.

89. Alison Dundas Renteln, 'A cross-cultural approach to validating international human rights: The case of retribution ties to proportionality', in D L Cingranelli (ed), *Human Rights: Theory and Measurement*, (Macmillan, London, 1988).

90. Charles R Beitz, *Political Theory and International Relations*, (Princeton University Press, New Jersey, 1979). See also, R G Brisenco, *The Negative Aspects of Human Rights: A Study of Law and Ideology*, (unpublished PhD thesis, LSE, 1987). Brisenco argues that international law is concerned with legitimating state action not with expressing moral concerns.

91. Richard Falk, *Human Rights and State Sovereignty*, (Holmes and Meier, London, 1981).

92. Vincent, op. cit., p. 125.

93. James Mayall, 'International society and intervention', in Michael Donelan (ed), *The Reason of States*, (Allen & Unwin, London, 1978), pp. 122–42.

94. James F Keeley, 'Towards a Foucauldian analysis of international regimes', *International Organization*, 44:1, 1990, pp. 83–105.

95. Stephen Haggard and Beth A Simmons, 'Theories of international regimes', *International Organization*, 41:3, 1987, pp. 419–517. For the definitive article on hegemony and international regimes see Robert O Keohane, 'The theory of hegemonic stability and changes in international economic regimes,

1967–77', in Ole Holsti et al., *Change in the International System*, (Westview Press, Boulder, 1980), pp. 131–62.

96. Keohane, *After Hegemony*, op. cit., p. 39.
97. Joseph Femia, *Gramsci's Political Thoughts: Hegemony, Consciousness and the Revolutionary Process*, (Clarendon Press, Oxford, 1987).
98. Antonio Gramsci, *Selections from Prison Notebooks*, Q Hoare and G Howell (eds & trans), (Lawrence and Wishart, London, 1971), pp. 57–8.
99. G John Ikenberry and Charles A Kupchan, 'Socialisation and hegemonic power', *International Organization*, 44:3, 1990, p. 287.
100. Robert Cox, 'Gramsci, hegemony and international relations: an essay in method', *Millennium*, 12:2, 1983, pp. 171–2.
101. Donnelly, op. cit., p. 618.
102. M K Addo, 'The implications for some aspects of contemporary international economic law on international human rights law' (Unpublished PhD thesis, University of Essex, 1987) and J Saurin, 'Hegemony, the state and civil society' (Unpublished PhD thesis Southampton University, 1990). Both argue from a Gramscian perspective of hegemony that the economic system derived from 'laissez-faire' capitalism is presented as 'natural' while human rights are understood as determined by human factors. Crucially, these two factors are not seen as causally related.
103. Tetrault, op. cit. See also Addo, ibid.
104. See, for example, the well known arguments of Maurice Cranston, 'Are there human rights?', *Daedalus*, 112:4, 1983, pp. 1–18.
105. Richard Falk, 'Theoretical foundations of human rights', in R P Newburg (ed), *The Politics of Human Rights*, (New York University Press, NY, 1980), pp. 65–109.
106. Ruggie, op. cit. See also Louis Henkin, 'The United Nations and human rights', *International Organization*, 19:3, 1965, pp. 504–17.
107. P G Laurens, *Power and Prejudice: the Politics and Diplomacy of Racial Discrimination*, (Westview, Boulder, 1988). Laurens points out that Churchill made it clear that the rights included in the Atlantic Charter would not be extended to all the peoples of the British Empire. He also argues that promoting racial equality was a necessary feature for drawing all racial groups into the fight against fascism.
108. Alan W Cafruny, *Ruling the Waves: The Political Economy of International Shipping*, (University of California Press, Berkeley, 1987), pp. 33–4.
109. Noam Chomsky, *Human Rights and American Foreign Policy*, (Spokesman Books, Nottingham, 1978).
110. M Glen Johnson, 'Human rights in divergent conceptual settings: How do ideas influence policy choices?', in D L Cingranelli (ed), *Human Rights: Theory and Measurement*, (Macmillan, London, 1988).

2   Human Rights and Post-War Reconstruction

This chapter focuses on the post-Second World War concern to place human rights on the international political agenda. In particular, it will look at the tensions between a human rights regime built upon the traditional principles of the international system and those principles associated with the idea of establishing universally accepted norms. Although these tensions had long been acknowledged, apart from a brief period between 1941 and the early months of the United Nations the principles of the international system prevailed. Wartime rhetoric suggesting that the postwar order give greater priority to the place of the individual under international law remained unfulfilled. Consequently, it is argued that the human rights regime is built upon principles that often leave victims of violations in a struggle with authoritarian governments legitimised and supported by international society.[1]

To reiterate some central points made in chapter 1, principles have two meanings when applied to international regimes, and particularly to a human rights regime. In the first, principles refer to the fundamental or primary sources of international action. This is the long established doctrine of Westphalia based upon a set of international principles that include sovereignty, nonintervention and domestic jurisdiction. Such an approach implicitly rejects the notion that regime analysis should include a deeper understanding that pays attention to values and 'raises our vision above the horizons set by governments and their (often limited and shortsighted) perceptions of national interest'.[2] It implicitly assumes that regimes can be regarded as simply a further addition to the existing tools of analysis that allows us to see what we already 'know' in a different light.[3] What we already 'know', in this perspective, is that international principles concerning the preservation of the international system take precedence over all other considerations. Thus the principle of internationalism allows no other actor to assume higher authority than the state. In as far as human rights has achieved a prominence on the international political agenda it has done so with the consent of states.

Internationalism has its roots in the approach adopted by statespeople, academics and international lawyers following the end of the Second World War. In the atmosphere of international anomie that then prevailed, the formation of the United Nations represented a reassuring reaffirmation of a return to a Realist world of self-interested, egoistic states.[4] The spokespeople of all the countries involved at the birth of the UN accepted with few reservations that the new global order would be based on the sovereign equality of state members.[5] Consequently the UN Charter formally articulated the principles of internationalism, including the important principles of nonintervention and self-determination that allow the separation of internal from external affairs. Legitimate international affairs were therefore confined exclusively to state-to-state relationships. If the founding members of the United Nations did accept that human rights represented a new, legitimate issue to be represented in the post-World War order — and in 1945 most international leaders did in fact accept this rhetorically — it was based upon the principles of internationalism. Importantly, internationalism tolerates political processes to establish generally accepted standards but denies methods of implementation if this implies domestic interference.

The principles of international society are in opposition to the principles of universal human rights. As a universal principle, human rights offer a fundamental challenge to existing assumptions about the place of the individual in international politics. They raise questions concerning the changing role of international law, the traditionally conceived relationship between government and the individual and the emergence of a global order, away from a society of states, towards a world society. Universalism is therefore a challenge to the assumption that the language and concepts of interstate politics satisfactorily explain current international political and social conditions. The challenge of universalism is fostered by the increasing complexity of economic life, including technological advances in transport and communications, which generates greater numbers of transnational actors whose interests go beyond old ideas of the national interest. Such changes have stimulated what Zacher has called 'common heritage regimes'[6] that attempt to solve problems associated with issues like pollution, the protection of the global commons and the management of scarce global resources. The human rights regime is part of this movement. It is part of the crisis of modernity that makes us increasingly aware that humankind shares a common history.

Viewed as part of a normative debate, the principles of the human rights regime can be understood as universal and defined as the rights everyone has by virtue of their membership of the human race. According to this principle, the subjects of human rights are members of the community of humankind and rights cannot therefore be seen as solely attached to particular societies or states.[7] Seen in this way, human rights cannot be guaranteed through international organisations like the UN, which places the principle of internationalism above all other considerations. Although John Vincent has argued that the principle of internationalism is not necessarily incompatible with universalism,[8] since no authority can be higher than the state the implementation of human rights is realistic only in as far as states consent. It is the principle of internationalism, which allows the state to remain in control of the application or non-application of international law, that many writers on human rights conveniently overlook.[9]

In the atmosphere of hope and euphoria that infused the creation and early organisation of the United Nations, many came to believe in the inevitability of restructuring the principles of international relations after the immorality of Naziism. Central to this was a growing belief that the new world order should include provision for protecting and promoting human rights. However, the feeling of unity, of being engaged in the 'great adventure' as one author has put it,[10] grew largely from the residue of a solidarity found in the defeat of the common enemy of fascism. Once victory was achieved, this feeling of solidarity waned. Idealistic talk of a new order based upon the rights of the individual dwindled and was replaced by old antagonisms that soon resurfaced. By the time the Commission on Human Rights began its task of preparing an International Bill of Rights, the high hopes of this idealism had already degenerated and human rights became a further weapon of the Cold War, utilised by both sides as a measure of their ideological verity. Rather than grasping the nettle of a new postwar order, the international community quickly reverted to 'normal' international relations in the form of known and understood principles, formalised and institutionalised through the UN. In this environment, human rights ceased to be an issue that demanded reflection, contemplation and a thorough examination of existing assumptions about the strategic goals of international politics. Rather than becoming an issue that demanded active attention to planning, and collective action that cut across national borders, human rights came to represent a set of problems to which each state reacted as independent, self-interested members of the international society.[11] As one participant engaged in the early effort to place human rights high on the international political agenda has observed:

> I soon discovered....that many of the nationals of certain powers — and I'm not referring to only one side of the Cold War — looked upon themselves, as their governments looked upon them, primarily as watchdogs of the national interest.[12]

However, the idea of human rights survived and grew in the immediate postwar period partly because of the domination of western states in the UN, but also because both East and West identified the field of human rights as fertile ground on which to conduct their ideological battles. That the development of the regime has made such little progress since it was first included on the international agenda can also be attributed to these same causes.

This chapter will concentrate on the tensions that emerged between the postwar demand to include universal human rights in the new order and the conflicting demand of states to maintain the traditional character of international society. It will proceed by looking at the origins of human rights thinking during the war years, and particularly at the reasons why the United States, as the emerging hegemonic leader of the future order, found in human rights an ideal vehicle for supporting its economic and foreign policy. This focus will be maintained in the following two sections. These will look at the preparatory work that was carried out prior to the formation of the United Nations Organisation whose purpose was to promote world peace and human rights. A further section will examine the outcome of the tensions between universalism and internationalism regarding domestic jurisdiction and the protection of human rights in the UN Charter.

WAR AND THE DEMAND FOR HUMAN RIGHTS

Wartime leaders in the fight against fascism saw the idea of human rights as a symbol that would inspire the necessary ethos needed to sustain public support for a prolonged struggle. Calling for the universal application of human rights inspired a sense of solidarity. People were not asked to fight for some patriotic cause alone but for the survival of human freedom itself. For the administration of President Roosevelt in particular, appeals to human rights offered a partial solution to several pressing problems. One of these was public resistance to America's entry into the war.

Before entering the war, and to some extent throughout the war years, significant sections of the American public saw the fight against Naziism as an exclusively European problem. To win over public opinion Roosevelt sought to justify the United States' involvement by appeal to American values that many believed to be the rationale for the very existence of America itself — human rights, human freedom and the 'American way of life'. Furthermore, the Roosevelt Administration saw the idea of human rights as an issue which held considerable potential in the effort to avoid foreseen postwar problems. These problems related to the increasing importance that the Administration felt it must give to postwar international economic and political planning. As the United States was the only major economy to grow during the war years, the Roosevelt Administration became anxious that unless new markets could be found postwar overproduction would lead to high unemployment and social unrest.[13] The rapid demobilisation of troops would further exacerbate this problem. For example, Under-Secretary of State Stettinius argued that the United States resist the call for the immediate return of troops on the cessation war. According to Stettinius, the United States' new postwar role in economic and political planning offered the opportunity to ensure high levels of employment for the American people. Stettinius sought to link America's traditional love of freedom with global economic engagement as a way of getting the United States out of the 'vicious circle of isolation, depression, and war'.[14] In similar vein the report of the American Conference on Problems of War and Peace urged the government to:

> direct the economic policies of American Republics towards the creation of conditions which encourage....the attainment everywhere of high levels of real income....in order that their people may be adequately fed, housed, and clothed, have access to services for health, education, and well-being, and enjoy the rewards of their labor in dignity and in freedom.[15]

It was therefore important that the United States did not return to its historic policy of isolation. Supporting human rights as a universal principle, as a symbol of solidarity related to ideas of freedom and laissez-faire, offered the potential to mitigate some of these difficulties by mobilising public support for an active United States' postwar international political and economic role.[16]

According to some authors, such thinking has its foundations in an American ideology characterised by the twin ideas of 'liberalism' and 'destiny'. These ideas have historically informed the United States' economic and foreign policies. For example, following the conception of hegemony developed by Antonio Gramsci, Augelli and Murphy argue that the ideas of 'liberalism' and 'destiny' have achieved such intellectual predominance in the USA that American foreign policy decision-makers have long regarded them as nothing short of 'common sense'.[17] They go on to argue that understanding the nature of this phenomenon helps explain two potentially contradictory aspects of much America foreign policy — isolationism and an almost evangelical need to spread the message of the 'American Dream'.[18] Isolationism has its historic roots in the motivations of early American settlers who, having suffered religious and social persecution in their native lands, sought to withdraw from the wider world both physically and culturally. Emigration to America was therefore instrumental in instilling a group of ideas to do with identity, 'with who Americans are' and 'with the view that many Americans have of their own exceptionalism and destiny'.[19] But the act of emigration also contains the seeds of liberalism.

The early settlers achieved their freedom not through eliciting the help of existing social structures or relying on the intervention of the state, but by exercising their own initiative and imagination, which they saw as the right of all people. Accordingly, Augelli and Murphy argue that rights became associated with political and economic liberalism to the extent that today many Americans are incredulous that others do not share their 'common sense' definition of freedom or their vision of a free market society.

Thus, if the ideas of such writers as Thomas Paine in the *Rights of Man* are the inspiration for the Constitution of the United States, and the rationale for the very existence of America is based upon the notion of free individuals fleeing the suppression of tyrannical governments, it is difficult to see how human rights can remain confined to the state. As Tracy Strong has so succinctly put it:

> To act as an American is to pursue a view of rights as universal and general; ... It is not enough simply to recognise general rights — one must also act on them. This indicates that the quality of being American is something that is constantly in question, especially so in relation to the question of human rights in other countries. Human rights, taken generally, are all that is necessary to be an American. If one is an American, it follows that one can remain indifferent to appeals that are premised upon claims of general rights only with difficulty; were one not to acknowledge, in some manner, that those demands were legitimate, then the definition of being an American could also be threatened. In some sense, being an American means that anyone has a potentially legitimate claim on you. Reciprocally, anyone is entitled, in some sense, to make demands on Americans and America, simply by being human.[20]

The traditional claim of moral sceptics in international relations is that states have no obligations to the citizens of other states; a claim which E H Carr noted had attained 'the status of professional orthodoxy in both academic and policy circles' in pre-war Europe. However, according to Carr, for the United States moral scepticism 'is a most implausible view, especially in a culture conscious of itself as an attempt to realise a certain moral ideal in its domestic political life'.[21] This is to argue that if one believes in the values of individualism and liberty, and in the liberal economic and social order that these values imply, it is not enough to confine them to the domestic environment alone. It does not necessarily follow from this that human rights should be at the centre of foreign policy, but it does suggest that foreign policy should include a sense of idealism and values. Capturing this in relation to American society, Stanley Hoffmann argues that human rights is:

a way of rooting foreign policy in the American public, which wants some idealism in its foreign policy. ... If one believes in the values of liberalism, it is not enough merely to try to have practised them at home; and if one wants to establish a livable world order, human rights must be taken into account, since governments have a disturbing way of connecting behaviour at home with behaviour abroad.[22]

Human rights therefore had the potential of appealing to an American consciousness that included many other potent ideological ideas like liberalism, minimum government, the market and tolerance. However, ideas of tolerance and indulgence did not extend to criticism of these ideas themselves, for this would have entailed a challenge to the very idea of America's destiny and the 'common sense' of the American way.[23] This contradiction became crucial once discussions began on giving substance to human rights, particularly in drawing up lists of rights.

Both liberalism and isolationism are readily detected in the United States' foreign policy from the earliest days of preparing for a postwar world. The United States followed a dual policy: a public policy that described an idealised world that focused on issues of high moral content like human rights, human dignity and human freedom; and a less visible policy that saw the United States, conscious of its position as the most powerful country to emerge from the conflict, as the hegemonic leader of a new world order.[24] This less publicly articulated policy was intended to take the opportunity of extending America's sphere of influence, including the United States' share of world markets, over a much wider area once victory had been won.[25] Roosevelt and his administration realised that these interests could not be accomplished if those who called for withdrawal from Europe — and a further period of isolationism such as that following First World War — struck a receptive chord with public opinion. Roosevelt saw that human rights offered an issue that served America's future economic needs while simultaneously allowing full expression of the values associated with being American. As John Vincent has pointed out, such an approach is not dissimilar to the liberal argument over trade most closely associated with Richard Cobden, i.e., that trade has a 'meliorist's influence on barbarous countries by keeping them in contact with the civilised'.[26] Through this contact the 'enlightened and elevating values and practices' of the United States would 'serve to undermine the unenlightened and stagnant values and practices' of a decimated Europe.[27]

Roosevelt's annual message to Congress of January 1941, which is frequently cited as evidence of a commitment to the cause of human rights, also gives an insight into the United States' hopes for economic prosperity.

In that speech Roosevelt looked forward to a new world order founded upon four essential freedoms; freedom of speech, freedom of religion, freedom from want and freedom from fear.

> That is no vision of some distant millennium. It is a definite basis for a kind of world attainable in our own time and generation. That kind of world is the very antithesis of the so-called new order of tyranny which the dictators seek to create with the crash of the bomb.
> — To that new order we oppose the greater conception — the moral order.[28]

However, in the same speech the links between moral aspirations and economic necessity were expressed more overtly, even if they appear as an afterthought.

> No realistic American can expect from a dictator's peace international generosity, or return to true independence, or world disarmament, or freedom of expression, or freedom of religion — or even good business.[29]

In similar vein, Secretary of State Cordell Hull published a statement in March of the same year arguing that material power was not sufficient to overcome the present tyranny and promote American values. He urged the American people to make an 'unprecedented effort', and to undertake 'heavy sacrifices', to preserve the American way of life, to fulfil the promise of an unshakeable faith in the everlasting worth of freedom, honour, truth, justice and intellectual and spiritual integrity.[30]

The links between ideology, economic prosperity and human rights also found their way into several important wartime documents. The Declaration of Principles of 14 August 1941, known as the Atlantic Charter,[31] was careful to emphasise the growing importance that the international community was attaching to the rights of individuals and peoples, rather than the rights of states as members of international society. States were mentioned only once so that, taken as a whole, signatory states promised to take the significant step of introducing the individual as a legitimate concern of the Law of Nations. Furthermore, signatory states promised to respect not only the rights of nations but also those of peoples and 'all the men in all the lands.'[32] In similar vein the first reference to cooperative measures for the preservation and promotion of human rights is found in the Declaration by the United Nations made at Washington and dated 1 January 1942.[33] The purposes of those engaged in the war were clearly stated as the defence of 'life, liberty, independence and religious freedom, and to preserve human rights and justice in their own lands as well as in others.'[34] Such phrases suggested that humanitarian intervention, tentatively acknowledged as legitimate during the war, would remain so once victory had been won.

However, while these statements emphasised the importance of human rights and individual freedom as an addition to the international political agenda, debates on postwar international organisation did not lose sight of the need to reaffirm the principles of the international system. This is seen, for example, in the meetings held in Moscow between 19 and 30 October 1943 to discuss peacetime planning. These meetings, attended by China,[35] the United Kingdom, the USA and the USSR, produced the Moscow Declaration on General Security. Paragraph 4 of this document recognises:

> the necessity of establishing at the earliest practicable date a general international organisation, based on the principle of sovereign equality of all peace loving states and open to membership by all such states, large or small, for the maintenance of international peace and security.'[36]

Thus, while the Atlantic Charter and the UN Declaration both emphasise the values of human rights, liberty, concern for the individual and the potential for legitimate humanitarian intervention, the Moscow Conference restates the principles of sovereignty and the centrality of the state. If those engaged in developing a new world order were serious in their intention to place human rights at the centre of international politics — and as we shall see later in this and the following chapter there are doubts about this assumption — the resolution of tensions and contradictions between the moral demands of people and the political demands of states could not be avoided.

HUMAN RIGHTS AND THE DUMBARTON OAKS CONVERSATIONS

As prospects for peace increased, national publics turned to world leaders for reassurance that new institutions and organisations would be established to ensure that human life would never again be threatened by the excesses of tyrannical governments. Once victory was assured, and publics became more aware of the horrors brought by Naziism — the holocaust, concentration camps, medical experimentation, torture, and the destructive power of modern warfare — world leaders sought to reassure their people that such atrocities would not be repeated in the future. The shock of Naziism made satisfying the moral outcry a priority. Urgency meant that potential contradictions and tensions between the principles of universalism and internationalism remained unexplored when the four great powers met at Dumbarton Oaks between August and October 1944.[37] The document that resulted from these discussions, known as the Dumbarton Oaks Conversations on World Organisation,[38] was circulated to all states that had contributed to the victory of the Allied Powers and became the basis for discussions on establishing a new organisation designed to effect a lasting peace.

The Conversations were split into two parts, the first between the USA, the USSR and the UK and the second between the USA, the UK and China.[39] There was early agreement that any new organisation would be based upon the sovereign equality of its member states. Indeed, an examination of the records of the Conversations demonstrates that the idea of a new world order was limited to legitimising new priorities and power centres defined in terms of the existing order rather than making radical changes to the order itself. The new order was new only in the sense that now the United States, rather than the old European countries, predominated in international affairs. The defining characteristics of the order remained unchallenged. For example, in his opening address at the Conversations Secretary of State Cordell Hull declared that any international organisation designed to ensure order in the postwar world must promote 'the principle of sovereign equality of all peace loving states, irrespective of size and strength, as partners in a system of order under law.' Ambassador Gromyko's concurring view was that 'postwar international order must be based upon the sovereign equality of all freedom loving nations, great and small.'[40] Significantly for the future of human rights, the four powers agreed that international disputes would be defined as conflicts of interest between states who alone would be subjects under international law. Furthermore, effective means for settling these disputes would remain the sole responsibility of states. That is to say, while acknowledging that human rights represented claims by individuals against all peoples everywhere, states alone would have the right to appeal to an International Court of Justice that would become the principle judicial organ of the new organisation.[41]

The state centric approach to international organisation adopted at Dumbarton Oaks was tempered by a continued affirmation that the rights of the individual would be given central importance in maintaining peace, security and economic development. Of particular interest to this study are the provisions set out in chapter IX of the Dumbarton Oaks Conversations, which outlined proposals for the protection of human rights. Chapter IX proposes an Economic and Social Council (ECOSOC), which under the authority of the General Assembly would 'facilitate international economic, social and other humanitarian problems and promote respect for human rights and fundamental freedoms.'[42] This would be achieved by utilising existing specialist agencies identified as already possessing expertise in their respective fields, for example, the International Labour Organisation.

Although the introduction of specialist agencies suggested some possibility that the guardianship of human rights would not be entirely left to states, the identification and status of these agencies remained unclear. For example, when ECOSOC consulted with specialist agencies, would they be used for their expertise in exposing human rights violations, or for active involvement in providing solutions? Would they retain their independence as political lobbying groups or would they sacrifice this role by becoming agents for implementing UN policy? What would be their formal relationship to ECOSOC? Were they to be called in as advisers at the discretion of ECOSOC if and when their services were needed? Or would they be placed in a more formal relationship with ECOSOC and given rights to investigate, judge and take corrective action where violations were proven? These questions were frequently debated during the Conversations but were deferred to some unspecified future date. While the great powers were clearly aware of the need to find a speedy response to appease the moral outrage of their publics, they were also acutely aware that the tensions between international and universal principles presented immense difficulties.

Similar ambiguities and questions focused on the proposed structure of ECOSOC itself. The Dumbarton Oaks Conversations proposed that ECOSOC would consist of 18 member states, that it be set a wide range of tasks and responsibilities, and that it be given powers to promote its aims. Important among these was the power to 'receive and consider reports from economic, social and other organisations' and the power to 'make recommendations on its own initiative with respect to international, economic, social and other humanitarian matters.'[43] To assist in the success of these matters the Council was instructed to set up a series of Commissions. Significantly, in a move that seems to challenge the strict principles of Westphalia, it was proposed that the membership of these Commissions be 'experts in their field', not the official representatives of states, a tacit recognition that social and humanitarian issues could not be successfully conceived as existing wholly within the domestic jurisdiction of the state.[44] This proposed concession to universalism became a central and continuing point of contention during the early days of the UN and particularly during the earlier meetings of the Commission on Human Rights. This issue will be discussed in the next chapter.

Three areas must be emphasised concerning the outcome of preparatory negotiations for a postwar world. Firstly, none of the four participants in the Dumbarton Oaks Conversations seriously countenanced a radical overhaul of the existing principles of the international system so that human rights could be better accommodated. The jurisdiction of the proposed international court included only settlement of disputes between self-interested states; i.e., states remained the subjects of international law. Secondly, there was general recognition by the four parties to the Conversations that nongovernmental organisations offered an important insight into public opinion. It was therefore thought expedient to find a role for these organisations in planning for the protection of human rights. However, perhaps more than any other issue this proposal sensitised states to the complex tensions between universal and international principles. While the representatives of states continued to express concern for the future of human rights, they were also concerned to ensure the integrity of the state and the international system. Thirdly, the pressure of time weighed heavily on many governments whose publics demanded swift action on human rights. The contradictions and tensions inherent in the promotion of the universal principle of human rights within the existing structures of international relations brought a tacit agreement between the most powerful states to continue with the rhetoric, fudge the difficulties and reach conclusions in only the broadest of non-binding terms.

THE UNITED NATIONS AND HUMAN RIGHTS

The rhetoric of human rights continued to offer a sense of unity and purpose following the cessation of war. Beneath this rhetoric, however, international leaders were already beginning to realise the complexities of placing human rights at the centre of international relations. To some, these complexities were perceived as threats to a familiar international political system that gave them their authority.[45] This can be seen throughout the debate over human rights at the United Nations Conference on International Organisation (UNCIO) held at San Francisco between 25th April and 26th June 1945. Although many observers took some satisfaction from the fact that several sections of the Dumbarton Oaks Conversations dealing with human rights were greatly enhanced in the UN Charter, others remained pessimistic and warned that increased prominence should not be mistaken for progress.[46] As will be made clear later, although the sponsoring countries remained faithful to their rhetoric by expanding the human rights content proposed at Dumbarton Oaks, overall the effect of these changes was to shift the balance away from the promise of protection of human rights towards the traditional values of international society which stress the impermeability of the state.[47]

Notwithstanding this, the speeches of world leaders, particularly at the first General Assembly, which followed UNCIO in January 1946, continued to stress their devotion to the cause of human rights. Prime Minister Attlee, for example, reaffirmed the UK's faith in fundamental human rights:

We see the freedom of the individual within the state as an essential complement to the freedom of the state in the world community of nations. We stress too that social justice and the best possible standards of life are all essential factors in promoting and maintaining the peace of the world.[48]

Similarly, in his opening address to the Assembly, the Chinese representative Dr V K Wellington Koo said:

> We are gratified that of the five Commissions recommended to be established by the Economic and Social Council, the one on Human Rights is placed at the top of the list. ... This is a matter in which the peoples of the world are deeply interested. ...
>
> If the world is to enjoy lasting peace, the dignity of man must be respected as the first principle of the new order: and the implementation of this principle will not only strengthen the basis of our civilisation but remove suspicion between nations and thus contribute to the cause of peace.[49]

However, as early as the first meeting of the Commission on Human Rights this idealistic high moral tone was already showing signs of erosion as states became nervous of the unknown consequences of making radical changes to traditional principles of international behaviour.[50]

As already mentioned, the Charter gives greater prominence to human rights than the Dumbarton Oaks Conversations. This reflects the influence of two lobbies that showed great determination in promoting the cause of human rights. The first of these was the group of 42 organisations that the United States Department of State had invited to San Francisco as consultants,[51] including representatives of church, business, labour, and civic organisations.[52] In a private meeting with the leader of the United States delegation (Mr Stettinius), this group urged the adoption of a strong human rights policy.[53] Decisive among the arguments presented was that such a policy would have the virtue of winning favour with both American and western publics whatever the outcome. This supported the USA's claim to be the moral leader of the western world and the moral track of the Administration's dual policy.

According to Walter Kotsching, who was present at the meeting, the arguments presented by the consultants left Mr Stettinius 'deeply impressed by the discussion'.[54] When Stettinius met later with the American delegation he was determined that the USA would adopt a policy of support for maintaining the centrality of human rights in the Charter. Kotsching reports:

> I accompanied Mr Stettinius at the end of that meeting (with the consultants) to a meeting of the American delegation. We went straight there. And all the way up in the elevator, then down the long corridor on

the fifth floor, down to the room where the American delegation was meeting, he didn't say a word. He was obviously moved. ... But he did speak strongly and convincingly at the delegation meeting. It was the afternoon that the Commission on Human Rights was born.[55]

The minutes of the United States' delegation meeting reveal that many of its members reiterated their scepticism about giving human rights too central a place in the postwar order.[56] For example, some delegates showed disquiet over the potential incompatibilities inherent in the promotion and protection of human rights on a universal scale within an organisation of sovereign states. Similarly, several delegates suggested that to take a strong view before knowing exactly which rights were included in the list of internationally recognised human rights would be imprudent. Related to this was the concern that any agreement made by the United States' delegation might run foul of influential domestic lobbies and thus be overturned by the Senate.[57] However, after hearing Stettinius's report of his meeting with the consultants, and recognising the need to win over American public opinion in favour of the United States engaging fully in the new international organisation, the delegation was persuaded not to let these worries stand in its way.[58]

The second significant lobby was that presented by a group of small, mainly South American states. Of these Panama, Chile and Cuba pressed for the Charter to go much further than it finally did. Panama, in particular, urged the incorporation of an International Bill of Rights into the Charter that would guarantee specific rights and impose specific obligations on members. The Mexican proposal went even further and attempted to introduce amendments that would have set up human rights organisations charged with ensuring the protection of human rights. These efforts were not successful, partly because of the caution shown by participating states, but also because of the activities of the invited NGO consultants who argued that to reach conclusions over lists of rights prematurely risked excluding important rights that mature reflection would otherwise include.

However, although acknowledging that both lobbies made a major contribution to maintaining the prominence of human rights in the Charter, their activities also brought some negative effects.[59] Some commentators have argued that the effort to persuade the sponsoring countries to adopt a strong human rights stance served also to alert powerful interests to the challenge of including universal principles in international affairs. The outcome of this, according to Hersch Lauterpacht, was that lobbying activities were directly instrumental in ensuring that the original intention to 'protect' human rights suggested in the Dumbarton Oaks Conversations, including the implication that states would have a duty to intervene in the domestic affairs of violators, was changed to the less exacting duty to 'promote' human rights.[60]

The efforts of these two lobbies did contribute towards more detailed proposals in the Charter than the Dumbarton Oaks Conversations promised, but this should not be taken as an indication of increased efficacy. Throughout the Charter the idea of human rights is intended to give purpose and meaning to the future of postwar international cooperation. The preamble reaffirms 'faith in fundamental human rights, [and] in the dignity and worth of the human person'.[61] Article 1 (Purposes and Principles), paragraph 3 pledges 'respect for human rights and fundamental freedoms for all without distinction as to race, sex, language, or religion'. Article 13 (b), which sets out the functions and powers of the General Assembly, calls for the Assembly to 'assist in the realisation of human rights and fundamental freedoms for all'.

There are three specific mentions of human rights in the articles dealing with ECOSOC and its Commissions. Article 55(c) instructs ECOSOC to promote 'universal respect for, and observance of, human rights and fundamental freedoms for all without distinction as to race, sex, language or religion'. The powers and functions of ECOSOC allow it to 'make recommendations for the purpose of promoting respect for, and observance of, human rights and fundamental freedoms for all'. Many authors attach particular importance to Article 68. This Article allows ECOSOC to set up commissions in economic and social fields 'as may be required for its functions'. However, it instructs the Council to set up a Commission on Human Rights — the only Commission named explicitly in the Charter. The final mention of human rights is found in Article 76, which deals with the Trusteeship system. Objective (c) of this article reiterates the purposes of the UN, which are 'to encourage respect for human rights and fundamental freedoms for all without discrimination as to race, sex language, or religion'. These provisions, Stettinius noted, were not mere general expressions in a preamble but were woven throughout the document. Moreover, he stressed that they were closely tied to the all important provisions on economic and social development.

However, the principle of internationalism upon which the UN was founded predominated, even while the Charter vigorously advocated the universalism of human rights.

> The provisions proposed in the Charter will not, of course, ensure by themselves the realisation of human rights and fundamental freedoms for all people. The provisions are not made enforceable by any international machinery. The responsibility rests with the member governments to carry them out. ... Whether the opportunity is used effectively or not will

depend, as it must, upon the governments of the member nations and upon the people who elect them to office.[62]

The two chapters that define the principles under which ECOSOC was established show some notable differences from those of Dumbarton Oaks. Firstly, the unclear role given to specialist agencies in the Dumbarton Oaks Conversations noted earlier is resolved by giving intergovernmental and non-governmental organisations separate roles. Article 57 allows specialised agencies, defined as those established by intergovernmental agreement, to be brought into relationship with the UN, but Article 71 restricts non-governmental organisations to merely a nonvoting consultative role.[63] Secondly, Article 62(1) makes provision for ECOSOC to commission 'studies and reports with respect to international economic, social, cultural, educational, health and related matters'. However, although Article 62(2) specifically refers to human rights, it makes no mention of these tools, suggesting only that ECOSOC 'make recommendations for the purpose of promoting respect for, and observance of, human rights and fundamental freedoms.' Thirdly, although several South American states attempted to include the promise to 'promote' and 'protect' human rights in these sections, the great powers were successful in avoiding any possible suggestion that humanitarian intervention was now legitimate by including only the lesser pledge to 'promote' human rights.[64] Lastly, for the first time there is some hint of the content of human rights. Article 55(a) includes 'Higher standards of living, full employment, and conditions of economic and social progress and development', while Article 55(b) and (c) call for 'solutions to social, health and economic problems and cooperation in education' in the observance of human rights.

The final form and content of the Charter reflects an awareness by the great powers that human rights should not be allowed to predominate when other more fundamental principles — sovereignty, nonintervention and domestic jurisdiction — might be threatened. This emerged in two questions discussed at separate meetings among the four sponsoring powers at UNICD and also in the meetings of the US delegation.[65] The first was the debate over naming specific rights in the Charter, particularly the Soviet proposal to include the right to work. Had the United States delegation accepted this amendment it would have presented an enormous barrier to the Roosevelt Administration's attempt to gain Senate ratification of the Charter because of the challenge it represented to American liberal ideology. In recognition of the emerging struggle between the East and West during the postwar period, the United States' delegation chose to label this amendment a mischievous 'playing up to the small nations.'[66] Although the Soviets pressed for this amendment it was dropped, partly because all the sponsoring nations remained uncertain of the consequences of accepting certain rights, and partly because the United States argued that to include specific rights at this stage would imply the exclusion of other rights not specifically mentioned.[67]

The second area that found agreement between the sponsoring states in their separate consultations was the need to find a form of words that supported the idea of universal human rights while leaving the question of methods for implementation to a later date. This difficulty was exemplified by the promise to 'promote' rather than 'protect' human rights and the shift of the domestic jurisdiction paragraph to Article 2, which is discussed below. In effect, what the sponsoring states sought was to retain the emphasis on human rights demanded by public opinion while ensuring that the new principles of universal human rights did not interfere with a return to 'normal' international politics.

DOMESTIC JURISDICTION AND UNIVERSAL HUMAN RIGHTS

The question of domestic jurisdiction, and the right of the international community to intervene on humanitarian grounds, became the focal point of tensions between the conflicting principles of internationalism and universalism. The conflict of interest between human rights and the rights claimed by states was the subject of debate by many interested parties during the period between Dumbarton Oaks and the San Francisco Conference.[68] In submitting their revisions to the proposals, some governments suggested that after the horror of war certain issues that were previously considered as solely within the domestic jurisdiction of the state were now international questions, making it inappropriate to confine them to domestic solutions.[69] Many remained sceptical, expressing the view that while doubts existed about the meaning of domestic jurisdiction further developments in the international protection of human rights could not be assured. In short, unless this difficulty was resolved, the human rights proposals would not match the 'expectations of public opinion shocked by the atrocities of the war.'[70]

Concerned that the importance afforded to human rights in international affairs might lead to measures that would inevitably challenge the principle of sovereignty, the four sponsoring nations jointly proposed several important amendments at UNICO. The first of these was to amend Chapter VIII of the Dumbarton Oaks Conversations, dealing with the maintenance of international peace and security, by replacing the term 'solely' within the domestic jurisdiction of the state with 'essentially'.[71] The effect of this was to avoid the necessity of defining what was, or was not, within the domestic jurisdiction of the state, making it more difficult to distinguish between domestic and international behaviour and confusing the authority of the UN

Councils, particularly the Security Council. The second amendment, which appeared in the same paragraph as the first, was to add the word 'intervene'. Again, because the meaning given to this word was never satisfactorily defined, the effect (if not the intention) was to obscure the definition of legitimate intervention. This obfuscation was understood at the time and remains a considerable source of academic, legal and political disagreement to this day.[72]

The third and most important amendment to the Dumbarton Oaks Conversations was to move the domestic jurisdiction provisions from Chapter VIII to Chapter I of the Charter. In the Dumbarton Oaks Conversations the paragraph dealing with domestic jurisdiction was exclusively associated with pacific settlement of disputes, referring only to matters defined in section (A) of Chapter VIII dealing with the powers of the Security Council. By relocating this paragraph within Article 2 on the principles of the new organisation the emphasis was shifted to cover all its organs, including ECOSOC. When applied to human rights this proposal would have two implications. Firstly, the new organisation would have no authority to engage in matters claimed to fall within the meaning of paragraph 7 of Chapter I, including even the most blatant, gross violations of human rights. Since violations most often concern the relationship between the state and the individual in a domestic environment this seriously weakened the meaning and spirit of the Charter. It is further evidence of the conflict of principles inherent in planning for a postwar world. Paragraph 7 of Article 2 appears to deny the legitimacy of international action over what the Charter recognises throughout as a potential cause of international conflict and instability. Secondly, this difficulty was further compounded by the failure to define domestic jurisdiction or to determine which actors had the authority to decide those issues that fell within the realm of the term. If states were allowed to decide independently what was within their domestic jurisdiction then the new organisation would have little authority in pursuing one of its central aims — the promotion and protection of human rights. If, on the other hand, the new organisation, or an International Court on its behalf, possessed powers to determine what was or was not within a state's jurisdiction, then this threatened to produce an unacceptable level of interference in the domestic affairs of the state.

Proposing these amendments at the final session of the committee that dealt with domestic jurisdiction, John Foster Dulles (USA) was adamant that none of the sponsoring powers had envisaged that ECOSOC — which represented only eighteen of the member states — would have the right to decide universal standards for domestic order or the right under international law to impose that order on the entire membership of the UN.[73] He argued that the UN was an organisation of state members whose governments cooperated in solving common problems through international relations, not an organisation deeply involved in the domestic affairs of its members. This position reflected the concern of all the major powers that the UN should give the utmost priority to respect for sovereignty and should on no account attempt to dictate to members a specific type of social and economic order.

CONCLUSION

In as much as human rights embodied the rationale for creating the United Nations, the Charter represents a compromise between universal and international principles. During the war human rights were exploited politically to provide purpose and solidarity for those fighting against a fascist ideology that celebrated the superiority of the strong and justified the violation of the weak. Following the outbreak of peace, international publics looked forward to the realisation of the rhetoric of human rights by placing rights at the centre of a new world order. Largely for historic and economic reasons, the United States took the lead during the creation of the United Nations, ensuring that human rights continued to attract considerable attention in planning for the postwar order. As a result, for the first decade of its existence the General Assembly reflected the views and values of its pro-western majority.[74]

However, many of those engaged in postwar planning both in America and elsewhere, saw considerable flaws in including moral issues on the international political agenda. They argued, for example, that moral principles were too vague or too open to differing cultural interpretations for any widely acceptable international law to be agreed, that states would never surrender sovereignty for a universal cause, and that foreign policy costs would be too high for any consistent human rights policy to be adopted.[75]

The Charter was an attempt to satisfy both sides of the argument. The public demand that governments include human rights as an important postwar issue that would contribute to a lasting peace was appeased, at least for the moment, by including extensive sections on social and humanitarian issues in the Charter. The Charter gained legitimacy and the support of the peoples of the world because it appeared to emphasise the new importance of humanitarian issues. Similarly, and in contradiction to many commitments found in the Charter on human rights, those who rejected the idea of a moral international world order were pacified by guarantees for the principles of sovereignty, nonintervention and domestic jurisdiction. The Charter did not, of course, resolve the tensions between these two demands as many of those involved at the time were aware, but the urgent need to respond to public demand, and to articulate the principles of the new order, left little option other than to ignore or fudge important contradictions.[76] If the Charter cannot be said to have guaranteed human rights by extending the reach of international relations, it did ensure that, in the perceptions of international publics, human rights had at last achieved an international legitimacy that states ignored at their peril.

The Charter was not intended to offer detailed plans on how to achieve the purposes it set out. This task was the responsibility of the councils, committees and commissions that the Charter itself created. It is therefore unreasonable to expect the Charter to resolve all of the philosophical and practical questions presented in setting up machinery for the protection of human rights. However, the tensions between the principles of universalism and internationalism remained in need of urgent resolution before further progress was possible. This should have been one of the first responsibilities undertaken by the Commission on Human Rights but, as we shall see in the following chapter, the constraints of time, the realisation that many complexities and disagreements existed for which compromise could not easily be found, and the onset of the Cold War all saw to it that this primary task remained unfulfilled.

NOTES

1. Making a similar point, Robert Jackson argues that although decolonization bestowed the trappings of international society on many countries — sovereignty, non-intervention, reciprocity and judicial independence — they were neither capable of effective internal government nor economically viable. Thus Jackson argues that the principles of international society have provided 'negative sovereignty' in that these populations cannot hope to achieve the freedom and liberty associated with self-determination within international society, nor can they hope for a response to their appeals for help. See his, *Quasi-States: Sovereignty, International Relations and the Third World*, (Cambridge University Press, Cambridge, 1990).
2. Susan Strange, 'Cave! hic dragones: a critique of regime analysis', in Stephen Krasner (ed), *International Regimes*, (Cornell University Press, London, 1983) p. 354.
3. Jack Donnelly, 'International human rights: A regime analysis', *International Organization*, 40:3, 1986, p. 640.
4. Lynn Miller has argued that even today the UN General Assembly is 'Westphalian in its purest form'. See, *Global Order: Values and Power in International Relations*, (Westview, London, 1985), p. 51.
5. For an excellent analysis of postwar inconsistence between rhetoric and action on sovereign equality see Frank Furedi, *The New Ideology of Imperialism*, (Pluto Press, London, 1994)
6. Mark W Zacher, 'Towards a theory of international regimes', *Journal of International Studies*, 44:1, 1990, p. 148.

7. John Vincent, *Human Rights and International Relations*, (Cambridge University Press, Cambridge, 1986), p. 9.
8. Vincent, op. cit.
9. Jost Delbrueck, 'International protection of human rights and state sovereignty', *Indiana Law Journal*, 57:4, 1982, pp. 567–78.
10. John Humphrey, *Human Rights and the United Nations: The Great Adventure*, (Transnational Publishers, Dobbs Ferry, 1984).
11. See, Moses Moskovitz, *International Concern with Human Rights*, (Oceana Publications, Dobbs Ferry, NY, 1974), ch. 3.
12. Humphrey, op. cit., p. 7. Professor John Humphrey was the Director of the Commission for Human Rights from 1946 until his retirement in 1966.
13. For example, while manufacturing output in the UK declined slightly during the war years, output in the USA nearly doubled.
    Manufacturing output — index 100, 1937.

	USA	UK
1938	79	94
1946	150	90

Statistical Yearbook for 1948, (United Nations, New York, 1949).
14. Statement by Secretary of State Stettinius, *Department of State Bulletin*, vol. 12, no. 301, June 3rd, 1945, pp. 1007–13.
15. Marion Parks, 'American Conference on Problems of War and Peace', *Department of State Bulletin*, vol. 12, No. 304, April 1945, p. 732.
16. Wilfred Loth, *The Division of the World — 1941–45*, (Routledge, London, 1988), esp. ch. 1.
17. Enrico Augelli and Craig Murphy, *America's Quest and the Third World*, (Pinter Publishers, London, 1988), esp. chs. 2 & 3.
18. The contradiction between the desire for isolation and the need to participate in international society can be found in some measure in all societies. It was described by Kant as the phenomenon of 'social-unsociability', which includes the need for social exchange in co-operation with others but also the need to distinguish ourselves from others through isolation. See, Howard Williams, *International Relations in Political Theory*, (Open University Press, Buckingham, 1992), ch. 8.
19. Augelli and Murphy, op. cit., p. 37.
20. Tracy B Strong, 'Taking the rank with what is ours: American political thought, foreign policy, and the question of rights', in P R Newburg (ed), *The Politics of Human Rights*, (New York University Press, London, 1980), p. 51.
21. E H Carr, *The Twenty Years' Crisis*, (Macmillan and Co. Ltd., London, 1962), p. 15.
22. Stanley Hoffmann, 'The hell of good intentions', *Foreign Policy*, vol.29, winter 1977, p. 5.
23. Augelli and Murphy argue that the idea of tolerance did not operate within the new religious communities that gave identity to the early settlers. Indeed, they argue that strict observance of the rules was demanded, the ultimate sanction for disobedience being exclusion. See also Stephen D Krasner, 'Sovereignty, Regimes, and Human Rights', in Volker Rittberger (ed), *Regime Theory and International Relations*, (Clarendon Press, Oxford, 1993), pp. 139–67.
24. Loth, op. cit.
25. Noam Chomsky, *Human Rights and American Foreign Policy*, (Spokesman Books, Nottingham, 1978).

26. John Vincent, 'Human rights and foreign policy', *Australian Outlook*, 22:3, 1982, p. 2.
27. Peter Wilson, 'Human rights: Ideal or ideology', unpublished paper prepared for the Annual Isle of Thorns Conference, University of Sussex, January, 1988.
28. Franklin D Roosevelt, Annual Message to Congress, 6th January 1941. Published in S Shepard Jones and Denys P Myers, (eds), *Documents on America Foreign Policy*, vol. 1, (World Peace Foundation, Boston, 1941), p. 26.
29. ibid. p. 28.
30. See, *Department of State Bulletin*, vol. IV, p. 335.
31. Reprinted in, Royal Institute of International Affairs, *United Nations Documents — 1941-45*, (OUP, 1946), pp. 9-10.
32. ibid.
33. Reprinted in, ibid, p. 11.
34. ibid.
35. China was brought in at the last minute at the insistence of President Roosevelt through Cordell Hull and against the wishes of both the UK and the USSR. See, memorandum of conversation between Hull and Molotov, 21st December 1942, *Foreign Relations of the United States — 1942*, vol. 1, (Dept of State Publication No. 7585, 1963), p. 602.
36. Declaration of the Four Nations on General Security, reprinted in, *UN Documents*, op. cit., p. 13
37. These meetings, which were at Under Secretary and Senior Ambassador level, were held between 21st August and 7th October, 1945. The four delegations were led by Edward R Stettinius, US Under Secretary of State, Sir Alexander Cadogan, British Permanent Under Secretary to the Foreign Office, Andrei Gromyko, Soviet Ambassador in Washington, and Dr V K Wellington Koo, Chinese Ambassador to the Court of St James.
38. Dumbarton Oaks Conversations, reprinted in *UN Documents*, op. cit., pp. 92-104.
39. This was because the status of China remained uncertain, mainly through difficulties over the Chinese relationship with the Soviets on their border with Sinkiang Province.
40. *Keesing's Contemporary Archives 1944-5*, p. 6868.
41. Dumbarton Oaks Conversations, Ch. VII, op. cit.
42. ibid., Ch. IX(A)1.
43. ibid., Ch. IX(C)b and (C)d.
44. ibid., Ch. IX(D).
45. Ralph Pettman, *The State and Class: A Sociology of International Affairs*, (Croom Helm, London, 1979).
46. Contrast Phillip C Jessop, 'A good start', with N Peffer, 'A too remote goal' both in *Commentary*, January, 1946.
47. The sponsoring nations at UNICO were the USA, the UK, the USSR and China. France was also invited to become one of the sponsoring nations but declined on the grounds that it did not participate in the Dumbarton Oaks Conversations. See extract from the US government invitation to attend UNCIO, 5th March 1945, reprinted in L M Goodrich and M J Carroll (eds), *Documents of American Foreign Policy*, vol. VII, (World Peace Foundation, Princeton University Press, 1947).
48. The Earl of Lytton, *The First Assembly: The Birth of the United Nations Organization*, (Hutchinson, London, 1946), pp. 26-27.

49. ibid., pp. 36–40.
50. The first meeting of the Commission was held between 27 January and 10 February 1947.
51. Roger Stenson Clerk, *A United Nations Commissioner for Human Rights*, (Nijhoff, The Hague, 1972) and Humphrey, *The Great Adventure*, op. cit.
52. For a list of NGOs invited to attend the conference see, *Department of State Bulletin*, vol. 12, No. 304, April 1945, pp. 724–5.
53. James T Shotwell, one of the leading members of the consultative group, put forward a four point plan to the US delegation for amending chapter IX of Dumbarton Oaks. These included proposals to bring NGOs into a close consultative relationship with ECOSOC and the establishment of commissions for education and human rights. See, Chiang-Pei Leng, *Non-governmental Organizations at the United Nations*, (Praeger, New York, 1981), Ch. 2.
54. Minutes of the 26th meeting of the US delegation, San Francisco, May 2nd 1945, *Foreign Relations of the United States — 1945*, vol. 1, (Dept of State publication No. 8294), p. 532.
55. Quoted in, Howard Tolley, *The United Nations Commission on Human Rights*, (Westview, London, 1987), p. 6. It is perhaps some indication of America's new confidence in engaging in international affairs that Kotsching assumes that the decision of the American delegation determined whether or not human rights would be a central plank of postwar international organization.
56. The issue of human rights had been discussed fully by the delegation at a previous meeting. See, 12th meeting of the US delegation, 18th April 1945, Washington, *Foreign Relations of the United States — 1945*, op. cit., pp. 338–24.
57. This was a constant worry of the US delegation. See, Memorandum of Conversation between, Mrs Roosevelt, Senator Austin, Mr Ross, Mr. Winslow and Mr Hendricks, 3rd July, 1947. Roosevelt Library, Hyde Park, New York, Box No. 4587.
58. Chester S Williams also confirms the importance of the NGO lobby; 'One thing is certain, the American Delegation was profoundly influenced by the work of the representatives of all the organizations and especially the consultants.' See copy of speech made by Chester S Williams, Assistant Chief of the Department of State Division of Public Affairs, 21st June 1945. Box 4578, papers of Eleanor Roosevelt, Roosevelt Library, Hyde Park, New York, USA.
59. John P Humphrey, 'The UN Charter and the Universal Declaration of Human Rights' in, Evan Luard (ed) *The International Protection of Human Rights*, (Thomas Hudson, London, 1967).
60. H Lauterpacht, *International Law and Human Rights*, (Archon Books, London, 1968), p. 145.
61. It is ironic to note that this wording evolved from a suggestion by the Union of South Africa, which was used as a working basis for discussion. See, *Yearbook of the United Nations for 1946–7*, (UN publication No. 1947.1.18), p. 17.
62. Statement by Secretary of State Stettinius, San Francisco, 15th May 1945. Reprinted in L M Goodrich and M J Carrol (eds) *Documents of American Foreign Policy*, (World Peace Foundation, Princeton University Press, 1947), pp. 431–34.
63. The status of NGOs remains uncertain even today. For example, the 31st session of the General Assembly of 1975 saw a major attack on NGO activity,

an attempt to discipline NGOs and restrict their access to the UN. See, Chiang Pei-Leng, op. cit. The 1993 Human Rights Conference in Vienna also demonstrated that NGOs are treated with caution by states.

64. A Glen Mower, *The United States, the United Nations, and Human Rights*, (Greenwood Press, Westport, 1979), p. 7.
65. The sponsoring nations held private meetings throughout UNICO in an effort to find common areas of agreement and thus increase the speed of business at the formal meetings.
66. 26th meeting of the US delegation, San Francisco, 2nd May 1945. *Foreign Relations of the United States — 1945*, op. cit., p. 546.
67. To support its assertion that specific rights should be left out of the Charter the USA threatened to press for the right to own property if the USSR persisted in pressing for the right to work.
68. Discussions took place within the various governments which had received the proposals and also in wider fora like the Inter-American Conference on Problems of War and Peace, Mexico City, 21st February — 9th March 1945; the British Commonwealth Conference, London, April 4th — 13th 1945; and the Committee of Jurists, Washington, 9th — 20th April 1945.
69. See, for example, comments by Norway, *Documents of the United Nations Conference on International Organization* (UNCIO), vol. 3, p. 360.
70. John P Humphrey, 'The international law of human rights in the middle twentieth century' in M Bos, (ed) *The Present State of International Law*, (Kluwer, Netherlands, 1973), p. 83.
71. Dumbarton Oaks, Ch. VIII(A)7. The comparable paragraph became Article 2(7) in the Charter.
72. See, M S Rajan, *United Nations and Domestic Jurisdiction*, (Asia Publications, London, 1958) and R J Vincent, *Nonintervention and International Order*, (Princeton University Press, NJ, 1974).
73. Rajan, op. cit., pp. 42–43.
74. Evan Luard, *A History of the United Nations: The Years of Western Domination, 1945–55*, vol. 1, (Macmillan Press, London, 1982).
75. For a modern exposition of these arguments by someone influential in American foreign policy circles at the time see, George Kennan, 'Morality and foreign policy', *Foreign Affairs*, 64:2, 1985, pp. 205–18.
76. In a remark that sums up the unease with which many viewed the inclusion of human rights in the Charter, United States delegate Senator Vandenberg is reported to have said: 'Life was so much easier when I was an isolationist'. Interview with Covey T Oliver, Canadian Human Rights Foundation Annual Summer School, University of Prince Edward Island, Canada, 19th July 1990.

3 An International Bill of Human Rights

The Second World War provided the catalyst that led to calls for a new normative order, morally binding on all states and going beyond narrowly defined self-interest. Those planning for this new order came to accept that human suffering could be both a reaction to, and a cause of, political, social and economic chaos.[1] Human rights therefore became a central concern during the discussions to establish new institutions with the task of ensuring that the brutality of fascism would never emerge again. In effect this meant cooperation in all areas of political, social and economic life, including the development of new organisations to support and promote new postwar values. But new organisations could be constructed and supported only through the energy, resources, economic power and expertise of states that emerged from the war relatively unscathed. Since the United States was the only major power to be in this position it assumed the dominant role in determining the character of the new order. Consequently, the United States was well placed to promote those elements that supported its new hegemonic role while excluding those that appeared to offer a threat. From the early 1960s, particularly in the wake of rapid decolonisation, the legal, economic, political and cultural practices and principles established at the UN received increasing criticism from less developed countries. However, during the earlier period, dating from the end of the war until the mid-1950s, American and western values predominated.[2] The norms of the human rights regime were negotiated during this earlier period.

The tensions between the moral idealism represented by universal human rights and the pragmatic realism of self-interested states were not sufficient to stop the adoption of the Universal Declaration of Human Rights.[3] Indeed, in some measure the birth of the regime, and its subsequent development to the present day, owes much to the contradictions inherent in the existence of these two imperatives.[4] Pointing to the emergence of the Cold War, some authors have argued that the Third Session of the General Assembly (1948) presented the last opportunity for states to agree on the basic statement of human rights norms that the Declaration represents.[5] The Covenants, one on civil and political rights and the other on economic, social and cultural rights, were intended to provide legally binding rules for the regime, but took a further two decades before agreement could be reached. The final component of the regime — decision-making procedures in the form of measures of implementation — has never achieved general agreement in any but the weakest of forms. What is seen in the processes leading to the Declaration is the predominance of western values. Even today, these values circumscribe the agenda for the discourse on human rights. Furthermore, they determine both the language of the discourse and its limits.

Under the terms of the Charter, a Preparatory Commission was set up immediately following the United Nations Conference on International Organisation (UNCIO), to make provisional arrangements for the first session of the General Assembly and the other principal organs of the UN.[6] In preparing a provisional agenda for the first meeting of the Economic and Social Council (ECOSOC), the Preparatory Commission recommended the formation of five permanent Commissions, including a Commission on Human Rights. Following acceptance of these proposals at the first session of the General Assembly, ECOSOC set up a Nuclear Commission on Human Rights consisting of 'nine members appointed in their individual capacity'.[7] Furthermore, ECOSOC requested that this Nuclear Commission make recommendations on two further issues; first, the extent of its own powers and second, its competence to act in defence of human rights. Crucially, and of far reaching importance for the future of the human rights regime, ECOSOC defined the central task of the Nuclear Commission as drafting, without delay, a Bill of Rights establishing universal norms.

What follows here should not be seen as a drafting history of the Universal Declaration, an analysis of its moral force or a discussion of its legal implications, but an examination of the political processes that conditioned its final form. Before looking at the politics of drafting the Declaration three points should be stressed that provided the context for all UN debates on the human rights regime. Firstly, human rights offered a focus for exercising the divergent expectations of the communist east European states, the western capitalist democracies and the less developed states. This increased the awareness of all states to the conflicting expectations of these three groups and caused further delays in developing the regime. Secondly, as the debate unfolded it provided a greater insight into the challenge international human rights presented to sovereignty and traditional principles of international society. The early enthusiasm for human rights was therefore soon replaced with caution as the debate brought greater clarity. Thirdly, from the beginning the Cold War began to touch upon every area of international life, turning the UN into a theatre in which to play out well rehearsed ideological and political roles. Since the Cold War was concerned with the predominance of a particular set of values, and the work of the Commission was concerned with establishing universal values, the Commission soon became a focus for ideological struggle. The Declaration emerged in its final form because of tensions that existed in the UN's dual role: on the one hand fulfilling public expectations of higher international moral standards, while on the other guaranteeing the principle of sovereignty on which the United Nations was founded.[8]

Finally, many of the speeches and debates referred to here were conducted on the understanding that the International Bill of Rights would be legally binding. The decision to adopt a nonbinding Declaration in advance of a binding agreement was reached rather late in the period. It should therefore be kept in mind that speakers assumed they were addressing issues of international law and not solely the Declaration.

THE EXPECTATIONS OF A NEW INTERNATIONAL NORMATIVE ORDER

Before looking in more detail at events that helped shape the International Bill of Rights, including the Universal Declaration of Human Rights, it is necessary to examine the expectations of governments and their representatives during the early years of the United Nations. Three general approaches can be identified: that adopted by the east European socialist states led by the Soviet Union; that of the western democracies led by the United States; and that of the underdeveloped states.

Four features of the east European socialist states' expectations distinguish them from the West's approach. The first of these features concerns the socialist states' view of history, which understood the world as being in a state of transition from capitalism to socialism. From this it followed that any attempt to construct a durable human rights regime needed to focus on developing a range of rights that reflected the norms of some future socialist world. Among these were the right to social security and the right to work. Promoting this approach in the Commission, the communist states lost no opportunity in highlighting their 'progressive' approach and denigrating that of the West, which they claimed clung conservatively to outmoded values and attitudes. In the view of the socialist states the Declaration should express the values that represented a 'new and bright future for the individual in the vast field of social rights'[9]. Typical of this view was the assertion by Mr Heffmeister (Czechoslovakia) that the West's approach had parallels with the French Declaration of the Rights of Man and the Citizen. He argued that both the French Declaration and the Universal Declaration represented a reactionary attempt to legitimate outdated, middle-class, bourgeois values and to establish a new *status quo* with its authority dependant upon the suppression of the workers.[10] On another occasion Mr Mannilsky (Ukraine) described the final draft of the Declaration as the product of minds ignorant of the force of history, 'directed to the past not the future'.[11] Accordingly, the socialist states argued that human rights should not be seen as either 'natural' or 'inherent'. Rather, they should be determined by the forces of history that govern a peoples' level of economic and social development.[12]

The second distinguishing feature of the socialist states was their positivist view of international law.[13] According to the socialist states, international norms existed only in as far as they could be explicitly articulated in binding treaties. Furthermore, the legal norms agreed in treaties could not be generalised. That is to say, only those states that became a party to a particular treaty could be understood as bound by the norms it described. The Universal Declaration, which was intended to articulate general norms for the protection of human rights, had nothing to offer concerning the promotion of specific rights and, accordingly, could have no legal implications. To talk of general international legal norms therefore made no sense, because these could be established only in the extraordinary circumstances of universal ratification of specific treaties.[14] Throughout the debates in the Commission, ECOSOC and the Assembly, socialist states emphasised that a non-binding Declaration would be of little value. The socialist states argued that the UN Charter itself recognised human rights as a legitimate international issue, making the idea of a Declaration 'too abstract to be much practical use'.[15]

Thirdly, the socialist states remained inflexible on the issue of implementing human rights, which they argued should remain the sole responsibility of the state. They claimed that socialist constitutions already guaranteed rights for the citizens of socialist states. Therefore, the proper place for claiming rights was the domestic courts provided by the constitution. Further vague international generalisations, which the Declaration represented, made no contribution to this process because human rights remained a matter exclusively of national concern. Furthermore, the Charter articulated clearly the level at which human rights should be implemented. For example, while the Charter recognised human rights as a legitimate concern for the whole of the international community, it also recognised in Article 2(7) the sovereign right of all states. Throughout the debate on the Declaration socialist states vigorously promoted the state's exclusive right to implement human rights. At one time, for example, the Soviets attempted unsuccessfully to append the phrase 'This shall be enforced by the state' to every article.[16]

Finally, the socialist states saw no value in a Declaration that failed to condemn fascism and prohibit all fascist movements. In articles dealing with the freedom of expression, for example, the Soviet Union tried to introduce

amendments that denied fascist organisations access to the press.[17] At
another time during discussion on the same article, the Soviets introduced an
amendment that read: 'all societies, unions and the other organisations of a
fascist or anti-democratic nature, as well as their activities in any form, are
forbidden by law under pain of punishment'.[18] These measures were never
adopted because the majority argued that the Declaration was intended to
define general principles that could serve over time, and could not be
confined to those events that caused the Declaration to be written. In part,
the insistence of the socialist states to outlaw fascism in the Declaration had
its foundations in their determination to gain some form of restitution from
Nazi Germany. If Nazi war crimes provided the catalyst for elevating human
rights to a central position in the postwar new world order, then the
imposition of human rights on the evil, wicked and defeated represented a
kind of reparation that the socialist states felt justified in exacting.[19]

The western states also shared a common normative approach to human
rights. There are obviously dangers in thinking of western states as a
homogeneous group since distinctions between them are not difficult to find.
However, given the enormous political and economic power of the United
States at the time, and the role it played in establishing the UN, it is not an
unrealistic perspective to adopt. Moreover, the United States, the United
Kingdom and France represented a powerful grouping capable of finding and
articulating common interests. This group was also able to dictate the course,
shape and direction of the drafting process. In some respects the West's
position was not so dissimilar to that of the socialist states; but the Cold War
saw to it that conflicts were engineered, even on issues where agreement was
close. Human rights did not remain immune from the need of both East and
West to display diametrically opposed positions in every facet of political,
economic and social life.

Like the socialist states, western states were anxious to ensure the
protection of sovereignty, but given the high profile they afforded to the
universal protection of human rights this presented a problem. President
Roosevelt's twin track policy noted earlier — promoting high moral ideals
to win international public favour, while following policies of unspoken
realism to promote the economic interests of the United States — demanded
that the United States take action towards developing human rights within
the new world order but stop short of accepting any arrangements for their
international implementation.[20] To claim that human rights were exclusively
the concern of the state, as the socialist states did, would have been
unacceptable and have seriously weakened the moral tone that President
Roosevelt had set out to project. On the other hand, the racial laws in several
southern states of America presented potentially serious domestic problems

for a federal system of government bent on promoting the idea of universal human rights.[21]

Furthermore, for the United States in particular, the mere suggestion of economic and social rights threatened to outrage certain conservative sections of North American society. From the beginning of the debate over drafting a Bill of Rights, United States officials were aware of the difficulties involved in gaining Senate approval for anything that remotely challenged existing social and economic practices. James Hendrick, for example, wrote to Eleanor Roosevelt warning that 'certain elements among the southern contingent and the reactionaries from other parts of the country' would certainly resist any treaty that might serve either as a basis for federal civil rights legislation or for establishing economic and social rights enforceable under international law.[22] To avoid this difficulty, and to achieve both sides of the twin track policy, the United States sought some means of reiterating and reinforcing its rhetorical commitment to human rights, while deferring legally binding measures that threatened sovereignty and domestic constitutions.[23] This decision will be discussed in greater detail later.

In contrast to the communist states, the West was at pains to promote and include only political and civil rights in any internationally agreed list of rights, and to restrict as far as possible all references to economic and social measures that suggested 'state socialism'. The idea of social security was anathema to many western states, particularly the United States, so that the inclusion of any rights based upon socialist ideas ran the risk of domestic rejection. Civil and political rights derive, of course, from eighteenth century ideas of liberty that underpin most western democracies and define the individual's right to remain free of state interference.[24] Social, economic and cultural rights, including the right to social security, therefore presented a challenge to the state-individual relationship for many western states. In short, the problem for western states, and the United States in particular, was to promote their tradition of political values whilst diminishing the effect of articles concerned with economic, social and cultural rights.[25]

Although western states did not reject the idea that economic, social and cultural rights had a proper and appropriate place in any twentieth century declaration, they argued for these provisions to be defined in the broadest terms, for example, implying 'social justice' rather than the provision of 'social insurance'.[26] This was achieved in two ways. Firstly, western states opposed all references to state duties in relation to economic, social and cultural rights, thereby devaluing these claims as rights and consigning them to free market forces. Secondly, western states proposed that the Bill of Rights take a tripartite form: a nonbinding declaration to be made as quickly as possible, a legally binding covenant to be open to ratification at some future date, and methods of implementation, which could not be developed appropriately until the list of legally binding rights had been determined. Coupled with these concerns, and parallel to the communist states' anxieties over the dominance of western states at the UN, was the West's own paranoia over communism, as later manifested in the phenomenon McCarthyism.[27] Through Mrs Roosevelt, the Department of State ensured that any rights likely to cause reverberations at home were relegated to second place in the Declaration and that the Covenant made slow progress.[28]   On several occasions the US delegation was concerned over continued discussion on new obligations of a social and economic nature beyond the requirements of the Charter.[29] More particularly, these included a proposal that placed a duty on the state to provide social security, and a further proposal that denied the state the right to refuse employment to any individual on ideological grounds for reasons of security.   On these and many other proposals of a similar nature, the Department of State and the Attorney General's office made it clear that the United States would not be bound by any such rights and duties if they found their way into the Declaration.

If the socialist states' approach to human rights can be summarised as a point of 'departure' towards a new socialist world order, the West's perspective can perhaps be characterised as understanding human rights as a point of 'arrival'. For the West, after the horrors of the war, all nations should come to see the virtue of observing the liberal values of liberty, freedom and the Rights of Man [sic]. The International Bill of Rights was a visible sign of 'arrival', i.e., the acknowledgement that certain political and civil rights were an essential foundation for a just and peaceful world. By contrast, the socialist states saw the postwar reconstruction of international organisation as a point of 'departure' from which to develop and promote new values like economic and social justice and the rights of the citizen.[30] The overwhelming political and economic influence of the United States, however, meant that few concessions were made to socialist aims.[31]

If the West cannot be conceived as a homogeneous group, any attempts to understand less developed states as a single group with common characteristics are even more problematic. This was particularly so during the early years of the UN. The most influential states included in this group at the time were from South America, where culture, politics and legal practices could be understood as a rearticulation of European, mostly Spanish, values.   The normative expectations of less developed states differed in three important respects from socialist and western states. Firstly, they argued that the Charter itself had already made human rights a matter of international law, making all violations a legitimate concern for all members of the international community. Although the Charter accepted the principle of domestic jurisdiction, representatives of less developed states were the first to argue that this principle was not intended to apply in matters of human rights and that humanitarian intervention was therefore legitimate.[32] Secondly, from the earliest days of the UN underdeveloped states attempted to gain a legally binding status for human rights. This began with Panama's unsuccessful attempt to include a Bill of Rights in the Charter itself and continued throughout the Declaration debates. Thirdly, despite the essentially European cultural tradition of many representatives of less developed states, this group acknowledged economic, social and cultural rights as a radical addition to eighteenth century values and had no difficulty in including them in any list of rights.

These positions were far too stringent for either the United States or the USSR taken as a whole. From before the first meeting of the Commission, less developed states had attempted to move the debate away from drafting a declaration, with little or no legal standing, towards legally binding treaties that challenged traditional notions of domestic jurisdiction and provided the international community with the authority to intervene on matters of human rights. The tenacity of South American states in arguing for greater status to be given to human rights is demonstrated in their attempt to defer a vote on the Declaration, even at the last minute, because they thought it could still be improved.[33] There was little enthusiasm for this, mainly because many were coming to realise that further delays would almost certainly lead to the Declaration being lost completely with the coming of the Cold War.

Although the representatives of South American states often made subtle and penetrating comments, these states were too influenced by their cultural and political heritage for any independent approach to make much impact. This position changed as the process of decolonisation saw the creation of many new African and Asian states, turning this minority group into a majority.

No activity during the early years of the UN can be properly examined without placing it within the context of the Cold War. The development of a human rights regime is no exception to this. Indeed, human rights talk at the UN offered both sides in the Cold War conflict an opportunity to express their differences. Human rights gave an important focus to the struggle to win the hearts and minds of less developed states.

THE COLD WAR AND HUMAN RIGHTS NORMS

The idea of peace through cooperation as represented by the UN was attractive to both East and West, but the goals and aspirations they set out to achieve were quite contradictory. As discussed in the last chapter, following the war the United States saw the link between economic expansion and the elimination of want as a means of promoting a prolonged peace. The USA therefore set about developing a policy of 'one world', which included the USSR as a trading partner and recipient of United States aid. This assumed the restoration of the values of self-determination, equal access to raw materials and free-trade — liberal values that had served the cause of capitalism over many decades.[34]

In contrast, the Soviet Union, weakened and vulnerable after the fight against fascism, saw its priority as stabilising the nation and reasserting the authority of the communist party. The difficulties of achieving this goal brought further complexity because of the increased influence of military and industrial interests during the war years. Moreover, nationalist ferment in the Republics brought the possibility of domestic instability. Although United States aid offered an attractive option, the Soviet government saw intervention in any form, or into any area of domestic society, as a potential threat to the revolution and the authority of the communist party. With these uncertainties in mind, the United States notion of 'one world' was never a real option for the USSR. Furthermore, the USSR had experienced invasion from the west on three separate occasions during the previous thirty years so that security took precedence over economic necessity.

For these reasons the USSR saw the states on its western border as a legitimate sphere of influence. This presented the United States and the West with the choice between either recognising Soviet political and strategic interests in eastern Europe — a choice that in the perceptions of the West meant sacrificing the right of self-determination for which the war had been fought — or entering a period of uncertainty as the alliances of the war disintegrated.[35] Not all commentators denied that the Soviet Union had a legitimate interest in the 'buffer states'. For example, in an article sometimes attributed to E H Carr published in the Times during November 1944, the author argues that acknowledging the USSR's legitimate interests in eastern Europe need not be understood as a sign of belligerence:

> What role does Russia assign to herself in Europe? At such a moment as this questions will be universally asked in Europe and outside of it. Russia, like great Britain, has no aggressive or expansive designs in Europe. What she wants on her western front is security. What she asks from her western neighbours is a guarantee, the extent and form of which will be determined mainly by the experience of the past twenty-five years, that her security shall not be exposed to any threat from or across their territories. Admittedly she is not likely to regard with favour intervention by other Great Powers in these countries. But Britain has traditionally

resisted such intervention in the Low Countries or in the vicinity of the Suez Canal, and the United States in Central America — regions that these two powers have properly adjudged vital to their security. It would be incongruous to ask Russia to renounce a similar right of reassurance: and it would be foolish as well as hypocritical, to construe insistence on this right as a symptom of aggressive policy.[36]

The western world, however, was unable to accept that the USSR's interest in eastern Europe was so benign because, as the West saw it, it represented an infringement of the principle of self-determination. For the United States in particular the prospect of the Soviet Union establishing a separate sphere of influence left question marks over the possibility of developing a single world economy and opening new markets for American business. Furthermore, following a period of extensive cooperation in the decisive victory over fascism, western states were alarmed to find the old spectre of a socialist world revolution rising so quickly again.[37] Before the terms of reference of the Commission on Human Rights had been approved, Churchill had made his 'iron curtain' speech at Fulton, Missouri, and Truman was receiving top level advice on the dangers of Soviet expansionism. Of particular influence were the views of George Kennan, at the time posted to the United States' embassy in Moscow. In a communication to Secretary of State Dulles during the early part of February 1946, Kennan offered the view that a disjuncture existed between the Soviet government and the wishes of the Soviet people. Kennan argued that the people were eager to return to a friendly relationship with the West, to test their talents against their neighbours in an environment of peaceful competition, but that Soviet leaders remained resolute that the authority of the communist party should be protected from all external interference.[38] In Kennan's view, this discord between the people and the party offered an opportunity for the United States to cast itself as the champion of freedom and human rights, saving the Soviet people from their leaders, putting forward the United States as the leader of the free world and enabling it to stem any possible advance of socialism. Furthermore, Kennan warned that the Soviets would remain active in the United Nations only while the UN and its organs served the purpose of promoting socialist values.

The failure of the West to recognise the Soviet Union's claim that the states on its western border were within its legitimate sphere of interest, together with the Soviets' continued fear of western economic and cultural incursions and their fear of domestic unrest, held important consequences for human rights. Firstly, the rights of peoples living in the buffer states were violated by the Soviets who, having failed in their attempt to gain support for their legitimate interests, imposed pro-Soviet governments and sought to suppress any resistance to their continued influence. Secondly, the debate in the UN on the Bill of Rights presented an opportunity for both sides to extol their own ideological virtues, exemplify their differences and develop techniques that became a feature of Cold War politics for many years. Human rights, and the Declaration that expressed the norms of the new regime, offered the ideal opportunity for acting out Cold War imperatives that were more concerned with the process of the struggle itself rather than its ends.[39] Throughout the debate preceding the Declaration, charge and counter-charge became a characteristic feature, most noticeably over the conflict of emphasis on political or economic rights as both sides attempted to promote their own values.

One example should suffice to illustrate the potential for utilising the human rights debate in promoting Cold War aims. At the 102nd meeting of the Third Committee, Mr Pavlov, the Soviet representative, routinely accused the West of hypocrisy over its lack of support for economic and social rights, including an attack on British colonialism as an example of double standards. He argued that the West's lack of enthusiasm for human rights was a typically bourgeois response to the challenge represented by new, progressive, twentieth century rights claims — a challenge embraced willingly by all the socialist democracies.[40] The following day Christopher Mayhew (UK) delivered a scathing riposte. Brandishing a copy of the 'Soviet Corrective Labour Code' he detailed every available scrap of evidence about the treatment of forced labour, demanding to be told why there was silence and secrecy in the Soviet Union on these matters and accusing the USSR of a far worse human rights record than any western democracy.[41]

In itself this exchange is unremarkable, except perhaps for the fact that Mayhew's response was particularly highly charged, detailed and, in its style of delivery, came as a shock even to many western representatives. What makes this speech of greater interest, however, is that it was preconceived, meticulously planned and prepared some twelve months before delivery, giving an insight into the political atmosphere of the day and indicating the usefulness of the human rights debate in the Cold War struggle. During 1947 Mayhew had come to the conclusion that:

> Stalinist propaganda was having an influence, especially in the Third World, and needed to be answered; and if the answer was to be effective it must go beyond self-defence and carry the propaganda war into the enemy camp.[42]

With the full approval of Foreign Secretary Bevin and Prime Minister Attlee, extensive meetings had been held at the Foreign Office in early 1948 to discuss the Soviet Union's stance on the central issues then under debate at the UN. This culminated in the establishment of the Information Research Department, whose specific task was to collect and collate every possible detail about conditions in the communist countries. This intelligence, which was later circulated among British embassies, MPs, trade union leaders, journalists and broadcasters, allowed Mayhew to prepare his speech and wait his chance. Given such a political climate, it is often difficult to sift rhetoric from intention in the Commission. Instead of concerning themselves with universal aspects of human rights many representatives were encouraged by their governments to look upon themselves as Cold War warriors and guardians of the national interest. Progress was therefore slow and the real positions adopted on the issue often obscured.[43] Mayhew's reminiscences of the period confirm that human rights and the Commission were important political tools in the growing conflict with a Stalinist Soviet Union:

> Most of us thought the defeat of Stalinism was more important to the cause of human rights than the text of the Declaration.
> We were gaining a greater insight into conditions in the Soviet Union and, more importantly, into the ambitions of Stalin. What we knew then, and what horrified us so much, turned out to be only a pale image of the truth with the Gulags and all that implied. The only important thing was to defeat Stalinism and human rights offered a good opportunity in this.[44]

The commencement of the Cold War, and the conflicting expectations of important groups within the UN, provided the environment for the debate over the nature of the human rights regime. However, as we shall see in the following section, the normative debate, such as it was, failed to bring any maturity of thought to important questions that would have brought greater legitimacy to the human rights regime as it developed later.

THE NORMATIVE DEBATE IN THE COMMISSION ON HUMAN RIGHTS

Those who supported the idea of appointing experts acting in their own capacity as members of the Commission had argued that state members would be too constrained by the requirements of domestic and foreign policy. Furthermore, they argued that experts would take more time and greater care in deciding important philosophical issues considered to be crucial in achieving an international consensus for a Bill of Rights. These fears were realised from the first meetings of the Commission, for the meetings quickly took the character of a political forum, ideal for promoting the policies of particular countries but less suited to reasoned philosophical discourse.[45] In the prevailing atmosphere of urgency to reassure public opinion that the new world order included provisions on human rights, most states saw no advantage in spending time in reflection or on developing the philosophical basis of human rights as a universal and international issue. The failure to find the time for such deliberations left the regime without a widely accepted foundation. However, some have argued that in the prevailing political atmosphere, delay presented the danger of an embroiled philosophical impasse that would have inevitably paralysed any further progress towards fulfilling the promise of the Charter.

As the chairperson of the Commission, Mrs Eleanor Roosevelt thought that progress meant drafting.[46] The first session of the Commission requested that Mrs Roosevelt, Charles Malik (Rapporteur) and P C Chang, (Vice-Chair),[47] prepare a preliminary draft of a Bill that would provide a basis for further discussion.[48] Assisted by John Humphrey, the Director of the Division of Human Rights in the Secretariat, this small drafting group met only once at a 'tea party' arranged by Mrs Roosevelt on the Sunday immediately following the adjournment of the first session of the Commission. During this meeting it soon became apparent that deep philosophical differences existed between the members of the group, particularly between Malik and Chang, which made material progress impossible. Chang, who represented the 'positivist-pluralist'[49] approach to human rights and international law, was acutely aware of the overwhelming western influence in the UN and was determined that the Bill of Rights should reflect a wider approach.[50] At one point he recommended that Malik and Humphrey spend some time reading Confucius (who stresses the duties attached to the role allotted to the individual within society) before making any further contribution to the drafting process.[51] Malik, on the other hand, took a 'natural rights-universalist'[52] approach, making it unlikely that the two opposing sides would ever resolve their philosophical differences.

To resolve these difficulties Mrs Roosevelt suggested that the Secretariat prepare a draft Bill of Rights drawing freely upon documents already submitted to the Commission, like the Panamanian draft and other drafts submitted by individuals and organisations.[53] Only two of these drafts were not in English or from western democratic societies.[54] Bearing in mind the difficulties thrown up at the 'tea party', and true to the reputation Mrs Roosevelt was gaining for pushing ahead at all costs, she informed ECOSOC that she proposed to appoint a new Drafting Committee of eight, a proposal to which they willingly gave approval.[55] It was within this enlarged Drafting Committee that further differences began to emerge.

The failure to settle important questions concerning differing assumptions on basic philosophical issues, or even to articulate with any clarity the goals and objectives of human rights activity before drafting began, offered extensive possibilities for misunderstandings. At the first session of the Commission several representatives pressed for time to establish a broadly acceptable philosophical basis before entering the drafting process but they were unsuccessful.[56] Consequently, the UN and its human rights machinery 'largely pirouetted around a missing centre' instead of coming to grips with hard issues that demanded restructuring and rethinking established moral and social precepts.[57] Furthermore, this failure gave fuel to ideological conflicts during the preparation of the Declaration and impaired any real progress towards developing binding agreements later.

However, it should not be assumed that all UN representatives, or those employed at the Secretariat, remained unaware of the long-term problems presented by a failure to engage in the philosophical debate. During the preparation of the Declaration at least two attempts were made to encourage the Commission to reflect upon its task. The first was made in a paper presented by the United Nations Educational, Scientific and Cultural Organisation (UNESCO). This paper addressed fundamental questions like the nature of rights, the distinction between political and economic rights and the contribution of international law in providing safeguards.[58] The second was in a paper prepared by Charles De Visscher for the Secretariat and was widely circulated to members of the Commission.[59] De Visscher urged the Commission to avoid technical/legal discussion or to set goals prematurely. He exhorted the Commission to maintain its focus on changing social values and to seek ways of expressing them:

> What does this legal conscience of the civilised world look for today? Undoubtedly something more than technical improvements of rules whose formal validity only too frequently contrasts with their disregard in practice. Something more, too, than the proliferation of organisations and proceedings which can only have a beneficial effect in so far as they are supported and associated by a spirit of international solidarity.

He went on to argue that the history of humankind demonstrates that human values have always been sacrificed to political values, but points out that this need not be so in the new world order:

> It is a pure delusion to expect a better international order to emerge simply and solely as the result of the establishment of direct relations between states, since the state, as the historical centre of national exclusivism, must, by its own nature, constantly seek to strengthen its own power and

the unlimited extension of sovereignty. The establishment of an international order presupposes certain psychological and necessary human conditions.[60]

Such exhortations seem to have had little impact however. The sense of urgency over human rights, coupled with the fear of becoming enmeshed in philosophical arguments that promised no easy resolution, meant that the Commission felt unable to adopt such an approach. Having ignored the fundamental philosophical questions, the Commission set about the business of drafting.

THE COMMISSION ON HUMAN RIGHTS

In the two years between the first meeting of ECOSOC and the adoption of the Declaration at the third session of the General Assembly, there was extensive debate in the Commission, ECOSOC, the Third Committee of the Assembly and the Assembly itself, but it is difficult to detect any sharp distinctions between the first draft prepared for the Drafting Committee and the final document.[61] Although by any standards for negotiating an international agreement the passage of the Declaration was swift, three features of the new world order help to explain why there was even this small delay.[62] Firstly, the smaller nations were acutely aware that they were participating on equal terms with the great powers for the first time. This encouraged prolonged debate as the smaller nations exercised the rights associated with their new status. Secondly, the debating process provided a valuable period for all states to assess the demands that human rights imposed upon the formulation of foreign policy and the administration of international affairs.[63] As we shall see later, this period also alerted many states to the dangers of entering legally binding agreements on human rights. Lastly, following the horror of war, and the widespread violations of human rights that the war had brought, all UN members wanted to take the opportunity of speaking to all aspects of the Declaration and thus associate themselves with the ideas enshrined in the Bill of Rights.

During the early months of ECOSOC and the Commission several questions increased the tensions between the twin imperatives of universal human rights and international realism. The question of Commission membership was the first of these. Was the cause of universal human rights better served by a Commission of experts, as suggested at Dumbarton Oaks, or by a Commission consisting of state appointed delegates? At the first session of ECOSOC several members expressed the view that the important responsibilities given to the Council, and through the Council to the

Commission, could only be fulfilled by accepting new principles that would lead inevitably to infringing previously accepted standards of international behaviour. Independent experts should be appointed in recognition of these new principles, which were too important to be left exclusively to states. There would be times, according to one member, when ECOSOC would be 'led to discard old ideas and the old practices of national sovereignty'[64] and when, 'members, especially of the Commission on Human Rights, must feel free to raise questions which might embarrass governments'.[65] On another occasion the representative for the Lebanon argued that what he regarded as the greatest advances in human thought, Marxism for example, had derived from individuals free of the state. He considered that 'it would be ironic and cynical if members [of the Commission] were not free from control, direct or indirect, of governments', because 'governments are sometimes biased, and members must be free to criticise them'.[66]

Another group of states took the opposite view, favouring state representatives as members of the Commission. The USSR, supported by the Ukraine, argued that only by appointing states as members of the Commission could ECOSOC hope to fulfil its obligations. The weaknesses of appointing experts, according to Mr Feonov (USSR), were fourfold. Firstly, the UN was created to provide solutions for international problems in the spirit of compromise between states. This aspiration could not be achieved among experts whose philosophical approaches might on occasions be diametrically opposed. Secondly, experts could only express their personal views, which would need the support of governments before they could be successfully implemented. This would lead to a third difficulty, which was the danger that a Commission of experts would become a mere discussion group or 'talking shop' without authority or legitimacy. Lastly, in international law only governments could be parties to treaties. Therefore it was necessary to involve them directly and at all stages of the drafting process leading to new international law.[67]

The debate over membership concluded in the Nuclear Commission with the recommendation to adopt a procedure that allowed the appointment of nongovernmental representatives for the full Commission. However, this recommendation was rejected by ECOSOC at its second session, where it adopted a procedure that ensured membership of the Commission would consist of official representatives of states. As a concession to those who favoured nonstate members, ECOSOC decided that appointments would be made under consultation with the Secretariat before final confirmation by the Council. This was intended to ensure an 'equitable geographic distribution of seats, a balanced expertise in the various fields covered by the Commission and the highest quality of expertise'.[68] This system was never fully implemented. The Secretariat never looked deeply into nominations so that the qualities of many representatives often left much to be desired.[69] John Humphrey recalled some years later that the system was so poor that he had good reason to believe one successful nomination was a Nazi sympathiser.[70] The decision to ensure that state members retained control over the future of the human rights regime finally brought to an end some important aspects of the debate between realists and idealists over providing universal means for protecting human rights. It was symbolic of the supremacy of the self-interested state over the universal rights of the individual.

A further indication of the predominance of state interests over those of the individual is seen in the approach the Commission adopted when considering its own competence to respond to petitions and reports of violations. The Commission's terms of reference allowed it to deal with any other matter concerning human rights not specifically covered, including the 'punishment of certain crimes which must be considered as international, as they constitute an offence against all mankind'.[71] The Nuclear Commission on Human Rights first took the view that pending the establishment of an agency for implementation, the Commission on Human Rights should be recognised as qualified to aid the appropriate organs of the United Nations in the task defined under Articles 13, 55 and 62 of the Charter. These articles authorise ECOSOC to make recommendations for the maintenance of peace and security through the protection of human rights. At the first full meeting of the Commission this view was debated at length. Following that debate the Commission communicated to ECOSOC its revised view that it 'recognised that it [the Commission] has no competence to take any action in regard to any complaints concerning human rights'.[72]

However, the legality of this action has been called into question. The Charter acknowledges an obligation to promote human rights and instructs ECOSOC and the Commission to develop procedures for fulfilling this obligation. By renouncing the power to examine petitions the Commission denied its own legal status as an instrument for taking positive action for the protection of human rights, substituting instead the lesser authority of merely monitoring situations and making reports. Whether the Commission possessed such self-denying authority is unclear, but the decision restricted its future ability to act, even in cases where violations were well known and recorded.[73]

Following its denial of competence to deal with human rights violations, the Commission constructed a system that allowed it to receive petitions, but provided no further powers.[74] Briefly, this allowed the Secretariat to acknowledge communications, but to inform the authors when doing so that the UN had no powers to act. Following this, concerned countries were sent summaries with the authors' names removed. Finally, in a closed session the Commission considered a confidential list of communications. This procedure quickly led to the Commission merely noting the list and, as such, 'it was possibly the most elaborate wastepaper basket ever invented'.[75]

THE FORM OF THE BILL OF RIGHTS

Since the form of the Bill of Rights had a direct bearing on its content and language, important decisions had to be made before the debate over norms could begin. As mentioned several times already, the air of urgency that pervaded all discussions on the Declaration allowed little time for exploratory work or for settling philosophical differences. What was required was an unspecific Declaration that offered all countries an opportunity to accept internationally agreed norms without offending either domestic or international publics. Among areas of potential disagreement were the relative stress to be placed on individual or group rights, conflicts between the natural and positive law approach and the ever present tensions between the universal rights of the individual and the state's right to noninterference in domestic affairs.

Three options were available for the form of the Bill of Rights. First, it could take the form of a resolution of the Assembly, in which case it would be morally binding on all members, but would not be admitted as part of international law. Second, it could take the form of a convention, adopted by the Assembly and open to ratification by those governments who chose to accede to it. Third, it could be appended to the Charter, bringing it into the realm of international law and therefore making it legally binding on all UN members. Apart from the Panamanian proposal at San Francisco, the last option was never seriously considered or debated. Few countries, and certainly none of the major powers, were prepared to enter agreements that threatened the principle of nonintervention and thus provide the UN with legitimate authority to interfere in the domestic affairs of members. However, both the remaining two options found favour with substantial groups in the Commission.

A compromise solution proceeded along two tracks. The first track was to prepare immediately a Declaration outlining agreed norms for human rights in as broad terms as possible, so that no states would find difficulty in accepting it. This would be followed at a more considered and leisurely pace by a convention detailing specific rights that bound all signatories under international law.[76] This arrangement fulfilled the three central requirements; speed in response to public opinion, widespread acceptability, and a delay in embarking on binding international agreements with unknown consequences. During the debate on the Bill of Rights it became evident that methods of implementation represented a third area that required special attention. The final approach to emerge therefore took the form of a 'triptych':[77] a central panel represented by the Declaration, flanked by two side panels represented by the Covenant and Methods of Implementation. If speed was of the essence then this course of action was successful, since many years would pass between the approval of the Declaration and the Covenants, while Methods of Implementation, about which there still remains considerable apprehension, are at a very rudimentary stage of development.

Throughout the Commission debates there was concern over the nature and legal status of the Declaration. The doubts expressed by the United States' delegation at private meetings have already been mentioned in the last chapter. Presenting the draft Declaration to the Third Committee, Mrs Roosevelt emphasised that:

> the draft Declaration is not a treaty or international agreement and did not impose legal obligations; it was rather a statement of basic principles of inalienable human rights setting up a common standard of achievement for all the peoples of all the nations.[78]

Several other representatives agreed with this view including, for example, the UK[79] and Mexico.[80] Although accepting the nonlegal status of the Declaration, New Zealand, Denmark and the Netherlands emphasised that only when legally binding conventions were completed would the strength of the Declaration be fully realised.[81] Panama and several other South American countries continued to press for appending the Declaration to the Charter to give it greater status.[82] However, the exact status of the Declaration remained equivocal even to those closely involved in its drafting. For example, following a speech made at Ann Arbor, Michigan, in the summer of 1948, the head of the Division of Human Rights was criticised for suggesting that the Declaration radically altered traditional definitions of sovereignty. In his view the UN's human rights work was of a 'revolutionary nature' because, in effect, what was being proposed was some kind of supranational supervision of the relationship between the state and its citizens.[83]

France was the only major power to accept that the Declaration might have some status in international law. While acknowledging that it could not be seen as legally binding in the sense of positive law, René Cassin (France) argued that it gave moral direction to which all states would aspire and therefore acquired legal authority as the authentic interpretation of the relevant features of the Charter.[84] However, since no General Assembly resolution can establish legal obligation, no other representative agreed with this position and several, including the UK, explicitly rejected it. The UN's own journal also reflects the uncertainty over the status of the Declaration. In an article entitled 'An International Achievement', Charles Malik praised the Declaration as a 'genuine international product', which in his view expressed the fundamental rights and freedoms pledged in the Charter. However, although Malik was intimately involved in the drafting process, he stopped short of claiming any legal authority for the Declaration.[85]

It is no surprise then that in 1948 a wide range of views was expressed about the status of the Declaration under international law. In many ways the very acceptability of the Declaration depended upon its lack of clarity. The decision of the Commission to proceed with the Bill of Rights in the form of a triptych, to develop the nonbinding central panel independently of and prior to the two wings, and to respond to political and public pressures to produce some document with great haste, led inevitably to ambivalence. In short, the need to achieve as wide an acceptance as possible led to a document that was necessarily open to broad interpretation. Its lofty moral intentions, its quasi-legal language and its political mix of eighteenth, nineteenth and twentieth century values, had something for everyone. Even those who abstained in the Assembly could defend their position by arguing that it did not go far enough. Lawyers could argue endlessly about the interpretation of particular articles or the meanings of words, and politicians could use it as a battleground to promote their own brand of ideology, pointing to norms that placed their own state in a good light while castigating others for their failure to comply with those norms. Importantly for the international system, although states had agreed on a wide range of human rights norms, the principle of nonintervention had been maintained.

The remaining two parts of the Bill made unsatisfactory progress during the same period. The working group set up to prepare the Covenants continued to meet and produce drafts, but by the time the Bill was passed to the Assembly for its consideration it was generally accepted that only the Declaration could be considered in detail. Some Commission members did express the fear that if the Declaration was adopted in isolation then the Covenant would never be completed. This view was fuelled by the argument that the Declaration was a complement to the Charter and therefore placed an obligation of compliance on all member states.[86] The working group on questions of implementation made even less progress. There was a wide range of views on how best to implement human rights, including educational schemes to inform all people of their rights, expulsion from the UN for persistent violations, member state self-reporting systems and an Australian proposal that advocated the establishment of an International Court of Human Rights.[87] However, every suggestion received vociferous objections. The polarised East–West situation also helped to obstruct progress as neither side wanted an agreement that held implications for future foreign policy.

The final structure of the Declaration has often been described as a simple division between political and civil rights on the one hand, and economic, social and cultural rights on the other. Indeed, this division became the focal point for disagreements during the debates leading to the adoption of the Declaration and continued as such throughout the drafting process for the Covenants. At every opportunity the socialist states berated the West for their backwardness in promoting policies that matched the high standards set by the Commission and boasted of the superiority of their own political systems. For example, during the discussion on the article on standards of living, medical care and social services (Art. 25), the USSR compared its own willingness to redistribute wealth and provide social insurance for its people with that of western countries whom, it claimed, remained reticent in fully embracing such rights.[88] The division between political and economic rights remains popular today, but a closer examination of the Declaration reveals a somewhat more subtle categorisation.

Articles 1–3 express the rationale and central norms upon which those rights developed during the eighteenth and nineteenth century rested, including life, liberty, freedom and equality. Articles 4–14 define and clarify these norms. These may be sub-divided into civil rights, including equal recognition before the law, privacy and freedom from arbitrary arrest, and personal rights, such as freedom from slavery, torture and all forms of discrimination. Articles 15–21 deal with social institutions such as marriage, the family, property rights and freedom of thought and expression. In similar fashion to the way Articles 1–3 act as a general statement preparatory for detailing civil and political rights, Article 22 provides a basic statement for social, cultural and economic rights that are then defined in Articles 23–27. These include the rights to work, to fair remuneration, to participation in the cultural life of the community and to social security during times of economic distress. The final three Articles are general statements that attempt to clarify the duties inherent in the state-individual relationship. While this division may bring a little more clarity to understanding the Declaration, it is important to note that only Articles 22–27 deal with the group of rights of central concern to socialist and less developed states. The remainder are of an overwhelmingly political and civil nature and reflect the dominant view of the western majority in the Assembly.

Following the decision to ask the secretariat to prepare a draft based predominantly upon texts submitted in English and from western states, the Declaration came to be seen as a product of western capitalist democracies who prioritised political and civil rights over those of a social, economic and cultural nature. Furthermore, the natural majority of the West was further enhanced by the procedure adopted at the UN for translating debates and discussion papers between English and French, the two official languages. Drafts were invariably made in English and translated literally into French without great regard for the meanings given to important words and phrases.[89] During the debates consecutive translation was more usual than simultaneous translation. This prolonged the length of meetings, made speeches difficult to follow and often led to important issues remaining unchallenged because some representatives lacked an adequate understanding of the proceedings. These circumstances provided an advantage not merely to the West but more specifically to the English-speaking nations. Even René Cassin, the French representative, recalled that he was 'in a most embarrassing position and had to pass over, simply because I had not heard them, certain proposals and formulations of resolutions which did not correspond to my views'.[90] Moreover, these advantages were further enhanced by the easy acceptance of a western philosophical approach and the reluctance of states to accept human rights in a form that offered a challenge to the existing principles of international society. The norms that the Declaration articulates are certainly those of the West, but even in areas where western values might appear challenged, like that of social security or the equal right to government employment, definitions were reached that satisfied all sides.

CONCLUSION

At this distance it is difficult to gauge what level of interest the Declaration sustained outside those few professional diplomats who had been so closely involved in its development and drafting. On 13 December 1948, just three days after the adoption of the Declaration, an editorial in the *Times* reported the 'meagre' achievements of the Third Assembly. It is full of pessimism for the future of the UN. In the writer's opinion the General Assembly had degenerated into a forum for propaganda at a time when it should have been tackling the major political issues of the day. The article continues with the argument that the Assembly was intended to 'give the small powers an opportunity once a year to offer their views, to approve or to criticise [but] it was not imagined that they would be asked to sit in judgement on the great powers themselves'.[91] The Declaration, which for Mrs Roosevelt marked the Third Assembly as the 'Rights of Man [*sic*] Assembly',[92] hardly merits a mention. A few curt lines record that 'a bill of rights has been adopted by those nations who believe in them'.[93] It is a matter of conjecture how the author would react to today's Assembly, dominated as it is by a majority of less developed states who use the UN to press their claims for economic and social rights so vigorously. It is also a matter of conjecture whether this leader writer would find it as easy to dismiss the Declaration today.

This dismissive attitude was prevalent among some governments also.[94] In the UK neither Bevin nor Attlee showed any interest in human rights during the preparation of the Declaration, and it appears not to have been mentioned once the Third Assembly was over. Christopher Mayhew recalls that he was never briefed by the Foreign Office on how to react to human rights issues at the UN. Furthermore, the Declaration did not make any material differences to UK policy. Nor did it stimulate any discussion on constitutional or legal changes. Indeed, Mayhew could not recall any discussion on the consequences of the Declaration upon his return to London.[95]

Today this view cannot be sustained. The demand for human rights significantly conditions the conduct of international relations, because it has achieved a place in the day-to-day language and conduct of politics that cannot be wholly ignored by any international actor. States can no longer violate human rights and remain free of the disapproval of the international community; nor can they remain totally negative in their attitudes towards such matters as education or the health and general prosperity of their citizens. Of course, it cannot be said that simply by reaching formal agreement on a nonbinding Declaration, norms have somehow been 'created' as many authors try to assert. Indeed, judging by the numbers of political arrests, cases of suppression of ideas and religious beliefs, killings and instances of torture reported in many countries, there are considerable doubts that anything exists to which the word 'norm' might be properly applied. There still remains an obvious gap between what Watson has called 'real norms' as assessed from actual behaviour, and 'paper norms' as represented by the Declaration.[96] This raises important questions concerning the underlying reasons why states submit themselves to protracted negotiations if, from the onset, there is little intention to react to the new conditions that result. The self-imposed limitations of the Commission and ECOSOC, which supported the widely held view that universal principles had no place in an international system dominated by the self-interest of states, led to a carefully worded Declaration that gave witness to the political nature of the regime. The production, acceptance and publication of a document of any sort, whether it is legally binding or not, has little effect unless states are motivated to observe human rights through political and social means. The Declaration is a statement of intentions that has subsequently come to mean that states can no longer ignore their responsibilities for violations of human rights anywhere in the world. Despite the assertion of domestic jurisdiction, by accepting the Declaration, states recognised the universal nature of human rights and tentatively acknowledged that it was no longer exclusively within their concern.[97]

The General Assembly was, and remains, a political arena for 'statist logic',[98] which in its first few years was the logic of western states led by the United States. The universal nature of human rights contradicts this logic, but public opinion and ideological expediency forced the Assembly to concern itself with normative issues. While postwar rhetoric may have been strong, the advent of the Cold War provided the urgency that led to the Declaration and the attempt to satisfy the hopes and aspirations of the world's peoples. Fundamental disagreements were simply ignored in the haste generated by the political and social circumstances following the war. The consequences of this were felt during negotiations for the two Covenants and still present barriers to advancing the project of universal human rights today.

NOTES

1. See, for example, speech by Prime Minister Attlee, GAOR, 1st Assembly, 10 January 1946.
2. Evan Luard, *A History of the United Nations: The Years of Western Domination — 1945–55*, vol. 1, (Macmillan Press, London, 1982).
3. Resolution 217(III)A of the General Assembly, Third Session, 1948, adopted by 48 votes to 0, with 8 abstentions. See annex for text. The Universal Declaration represented one part of what became known as the International Bill of Rights. The other two components of the Bill were the legally binding Covenants and measures of implementation. The decision to go ahead with this arrangement was not reached until the Commission on Human Rights was convened. At that time it became obvious that the aim of achieving a legally binding agreement within such a limited time scale was not possible.
4. A Glen Mower, *The United States, the United Nations, and Human Rights*, (Greenwood Press, Westport, 1979).
5. See, René Cassin, 'Looking back on the Universal Declaration of 1948', *Review of Contemporary Law*, No. 1, 1968, pp. 13–26.
6. 'The Agreement to Establish the Preparatory Commission of the United Nations' is reprinted in The Royal Institute of International Affairs, *United Nations Documents 1941–45*, (OUP, 1946), pp. 191–3.
7. *Economic and Social Council — Official Records*, 1st year, 1st session, p. 163.
8. Procedures at the UN required that drafts of the Declaration be passed up and down a hierarchical ladder before a final vote was taken in the General Assembly. Each step of the ladder allowed further debate. The ladder ran as follows: Drafting or Working Group of the Commission for Human Rights;

Commission for Human Rights; ECOSOC; General Assembly; Third Committee of the General Assembly; General Assembly (for a final vote or to be returned to ECOSOC and the Commission).

9. GAOR, 3rd session, 3rd Committee, 183rd meeting, Yugoslavia, p. 915.
10. Mr Heffmeister (Czechoslovakia), GAOR, 3rd session, 3rd Committee, p. 69.
11. GAOR, 3rd session, Plenary, p. 869.
12. U N Kudryartsev, 'Human rights and the Soviet constitution' in, *Philosophical Foundations of Human Rights*, (UNESCO, 1986). See also, D A Kerimov (general editor), *Soviet Democracy in the Period of Developed Socialism*, (Progress Press, Moscow, 1979), esp. ch. VII.
13. Arie Bloed and Fried van Hoof, 'Some aspects of the socialist view of human rights', in Arie Bloed and Fried van Hoof (eds), *Essays on Human Rights in the Helsinki Process*, (Martin Nijhoff, The Hague, 1985), esp. ch. 3.
14. Antonio Cassese, *International Law in a Divided World*, (Clarendon Press, Oxford, 1986), pp. 113–4.
15. GAOR, 3rd session, 3rd Committee, p. 46, Polish representative.
16. Eleanor Roosevelt, *The Autobiography of Eleanor Roosevelt*, (Hutchinson, London, 1962), p. 249.
17. GAOR, 3rd session, 3rd Committee, pp. 408–9.
18. GAOR, 3rd session, 3rd Committee p. 430.
19. See, L Henkin, 'The United Nations and human rights', *International Organization*, 29:3, 1965, pp. 504–17.
20. See for example, briefing paper dated 24th January, 1947, The Papers of Eleanor Roosevelt, Roosevelt Library, Hyde Park, New York, Box no. 4592. This paper recommends that Mrs Roosevelt remain mindful of public opinion and urges her to show visible enthusiasm for completing a non-binding Declaration. It also notes the possible resistance to a binding treaty. In a telegram to Mrs Roosevelt dated 30th January 1947, the Department of State once again demonstrated its concern over engaging in discussions on implementation. Specifically, the Department of State was concerned by a UN working paper on implementation to which the USA had many objections. ibid.
21. The socialist states regularly taunted the United States over this issue, often quoting from United States law on equality or relating stories of the activities of the Klu Klux Klan. See, GAOR 3rd session, 3rd Committee, pp. 131–2 and 142.
22. The papers of Eleanor Roosevelt, Roosevelt Library, Hyde Park, New York, Box no. 4587.
23. Mower, op. cit., pp. 41–42. See also, Commission, 2nd session, summary records, E/CN.4/SR.25 for evidence of this.
    As a further example of the careful preparation conducted by the USA at the UN, see briefing paper giving a detailed biography of each of the members of the Commission. With the exception of Cassin, Malik and Chang, US opinion of the other members of the Commission was not high. For example, 'Hodgson (Australia) — Considered unreliable, prone to drink and possibly anti-United Nations and anti-United States.': 'Lord Dukeston (UK) — Ill informed, lacking ability and little experience.' ibid., Box no. 4594.
24. J Donnelly and R Howard, 'Human dignity, human rights and political regimes', *American Political Science Review*, 80:3, 1984, pp. 801–17.
25. Liberal ideas of freedom were a challenge to colonialism and therefore presented a difficulty for many European states. For example, Roosevelt often

reminded Churchill that the United States could not support Britain in any attempt to retain her colonies once the war was over. See, Eleanor Roosevelt, *As He Saw It*, (Hutchinson, London, 1968), pp. 34–7.

26. See remarks made by René Cassin and Charles Malik, GAOR, 3rd session, 3rd Committee, 137th meeting.
27. Charles O Lerche describes the US as being 'mesmerized' by the 'uniqueness' of the Soviet Union. See his, *The Cold War....and After*, (Prentice-Hall, Englewood Cliffs, NJ, 1965) p. 36. Mrs Roosevelt demonstrated her concern for the future of human rights in a political atmosphere dominated by the fear of communism in a letter to President Truman dated 13th November 1947. In this she expresses her fears that 'loyalty hearings' in the USA would damage the reputation of America in the field of human rights. See Box No. 4587, Roosevelt Library, op. cit.
28. Mower, op. cit., pp. 41–2.
29. See the minutes of the 4th meeting of the US delegation, 24th September 1948, *Foreign Relations of the United States*, (US Government Publishing Office, Washington, 1975, publication no. 8805), p. 291.
30. See, D D Raphael, 'Human rights, old and new', in D D Raphael (ed), *Political Theory and the Rights of Man*, (Macmillan, London, 1967), pp. 54–67.
31. Note that even the few concessions that were made were vigorously opposed by some sections of US society. For example, the American Bar Association conducted a campaign against any suggestion of what it called 'state socialism'. See speech by Frank E Holman, 'The greatest threat to our American heritage', *Vital Speeches of the Day*, XXIV, September 15th, 1953, pp. 711–7.
32. See, GAOR, 3rd session 3rd Committee, p. 43 for a refutation of the implications of Article 2(7) of the Charter by Mr De Leon (Panama).
33. Peru, supported by Cuba and Panama, proposed setting up a sub-committee instructed to examine and compare the draft of the Declaration with that of other declarations like the American Declaration of the Rights and Duties of Man. GAOR, 3rd session, 3rd Committee, 90th meeting.
34. D F Flemming, 'The Cold War origins and development' in, D Carlton and H M Levis (eds), *The Cold War Debate*, (McGraw-Hill Books, 1989).
35. Norman A Graebner, 'Cold War origins and the continuing debate: A review of current literature', *Journal of Conflict Resolution*, 13:1, 1969, pp. 123–32.
36. Unattributed article, *The Times*, 6 November 1944, p. 5.
37. John Lewis Gaddis, *The United States and the Origins of the Cold War*, (Columbia University Press, London, 1972), p. 355.
38. Telegram from Kennan to Secretary of State, 22nd February 1946, reprinted in, *Foreign Relations of the United States — 1946*, vol. VI, (Department of State publication no. 5470, 1979), pp. 696–709.
39. Lerche, op. cit., p. 19.
40. GAOR, 3rd session, 3rd Committee, 102nd meeting, pp. 142–3.
41. GAOR, ibid., 103rd meeting, p. 160.
42. Christopher Mayhew, Time to Explain, Hutchinson, London, 1987), p. 107.
43. This was the opinion John Humphrey held of both sides of the Cold War. See John Humphrey, *Human Rights and the United Nations: The Great Adventure*, (Transnational Press, Dobbs Ferry, 1984), p. 64.
44. Lord Mayhew, House of Lords, 5 July 1989.
45. Cassin, op. cit.

46. For example, Eleanor Roosevelt made a series of notes prior to the first meeting of the Commission one of which reads simply: 'The job is to complete a draft Bill in two weeks time'. See, Box No. 5487, Papers of Eleanor Roosevelt, op. cit.

47. As an indication of the control that the USA had over the proceedings in the UN it is interesting to note that Roosevelt, Malik and Chang were their preferred candidates for the posts they eventually held.

48. Report of the Commission, *ECOSOC—Official Records*, 2nd year, 4th session, supplement no. 3, Ch. 2.

49. By this I mean an approach that recognises cultural differences in viewing human rights and looks to positive international law in providing solutions.

50. It should be remembered that at this time the form of the Bill of Rights had not been agreed. Although Eleanor Roosevelt was under instructions from the Department of State to promote the idea of a nonbinding Declaration in preference to a binding treaty, this small drafting group were instructed to prepare a draft for a Bill of Rights. To many representatives at the UN, the term Bill carried normative meanings associated with binding international law.

51. For recollections of this meeting see Eleanor Roosevelt, *Autobiography*, op. cit., p. 29.

52. In contrast to the positivist-pluralist approach, this approach begins by recognizing the universal nature of humankind and attempts to define rights common to all humankind as a species.

53. At the time the draft presented by Panama was well developed and researched. It included comments pointing to rights already mentioned in the constitutions of a number of states, e.g., it noted that the right to free association was included in the constitution of 39 states. The Commission had already considered a proposal to ask the Secretariat to make a draft. However, this was rejected because it was considered too important a task to be divorced from direct involvement of Commission members. See, *Summary Records of the Commission*, E/CN.4/SR.12.

54. Included among these were drafts received from Irvin A Isaacs, Reverend Wilfred Parsons, Rollin McNitt, Viscount Shanky, Hersch Lauterpacht, H G Wells, and the American Law Society. The two drafts not in English were by Alejendro Alvares and Gustavo Gutieriz.

55. Resolution 46(V) of ECOSOC. The membership of this new group was Australia, Chile, China, France, Lebanon, the USSR, the UK and the USA. Roosevelt, in fact, had no authority to take such action, her decision being a 'dubious legal act' according to Humphrey, op. cit., pp. 29–30.

56. See, Commission, Summary Records, 1st Session, E/CN.4/SR.7 and SR.13.

57. Moses Moskovitz, *International Concern with Human Rights*, (Oceana Publications, Dobbs Ferry, NY, 1974), p. 161.

58. UNESCO, *The Grounds for an International Declaration of Human Rights*, (phil./10, Paris, 31st July 1947).

59. Mrs Roosevelt had certainly seen a copy. See her annotated copy Box No. 4595, Roosevelt Library, op. cit.

60. See document E/CN.4/40, 1st December 1947.

61. Compare the Declaration with the draft prepared by the French representative, René Cassin (document E/CN.4/AC.1/rev.1), reproduced in the *Yearbook of Human Rights for 1947*, (UN publication no. 1949.XIV.1), pp. 495–8.

62. Tony Evans, 'Human rights: A reply to Geoffrey Best', *Review of International Studies*, 17:1, 1991, pp. 87–94.

63. Humphrey, *The Great Adventure*, op. cit.
64. Mr Noel-Baker, UK representative, *ECOSOC–Official Records*, 1st year, 1st session, p. 18.
65. Mr Noel-Baker, *ECOSOC–Official Records*, 1st year, 2nd session. Report of the Nuclear Commission, p. 38.
66. Dr Charles Malik, representative of the Lebanon, *ECOSOC–Official Records*, 1st year, 2nd session, annex 4A, p. 14.
67. See, ibid., *ECOSOC–Official Records*, p. 13.
68. Resolution 2/9, *ECOSOC–Official Records* 1st Year, 2nd Session.
69. According to Hersch Lauterpacht the whole process was a 'formality'. see Hersch Lauterpacht *International Law of Human Rights*, (Archon Books, London, 1968), p. 255, footnote (A).
70. Humphrey, op. cit., p. 17.
71. *Yearbook of Human Rights for 1947*, (UN publication No.1949.XIV.1), pp. 422–3 for a brief history of this debate. Sub-para (e) was originally left out of the terms of reference offered by ECOSOC but the Nuclear Commission requested its re-introduction.
72. Report of the Commission, Supplement No.3, *ECOSOC — Official Records*, 2nd year, 4th session, resolution 75(V), pp. 5–6.
73. See, Lauterpacht, op. cit., pp. 228–31.
74. *ECOSOC — Official Records* 2nd year, 4th session, supplement No. 3, pp. 5–6.
75. Humphrey, op cit, p. 28.
76. Drafting Committee of the Commission, 1st session, 9th–25th June 1947, *Yearbook of Human Rights for 1947*, (UN sales publication no. 1949.XIV.1), p. 483.
77. Cassin, op. cit., p. 18. However, the term was first used by the Belgium representative. See, Commission Summary Records, E/CN.4/SR.25
78. *General Assembly — Official Records*, 3rd Committee, 98th meeting, p. 32.
79. ibid., 93rd meeting.
80. ibid., 90th meeting.
81. ibid., 98th meeting.
82. ibid., 90th meeting.
83. Humphrey, op. cit., p. 46.
84. op. cit., 92nd meeting.
85. Charles Malik, 'An international achievement', *United Nations Bulletin*, 4:1, 1949, p. 5.
86. Typical of this view was the response of the New Zealand representative. See, GAOR, 3rd session, 3rd Committee, p. 33.
87. CHR, Summary Records, 2nd session, E/CN.4/SR.27.
88. GAOR, 3rd session, 3rd Committee, 143rd meeting, p. 563.
89. For example, see the misunderstanding caused by translation of the term 'drafting group', *ECOSOC — Official Records*, 2nd year, 4th session, 69th meeting.
90. Cassin, op. cit., p. 15.
91. *The Times*, London, 13th December 1948, p. 5.
92. *United Nations Bulletin*, 4:1, January 1948, p. 5.
93. *The Times*, op. cit.
94. An examination of the *Yearbook on Human Rights* between 1948 and 1950 demonstrates how little immediate impact the Declaration had on international diplomacy. The UK, for example, fulfilled its obligation to produce an entry on its own reaction to the Declaration by producing a quasi-philosophical

article that many Third World states might easily have mistaken for self-satisfied, sanctimonious preaching.

95. Mayhew interview, op. cit.
96. J S Watson, 'Legal theory, efficacy and validity in the development of human rights norms in international law', *University of Illinois Law Forum*, vol.3, 1979, pp. 609–41.
97. See O Schachter, 'The twilight existence of non-binding international agreements', *American Journal of International Law*, 71:2, 1977, pp. 296–304.
98. Richard Falk, *Human Rights and State Sovereignty*, (Holmes and Meier, London, 1981).

4 Human Rights and Hegemony

The presence of a hegemon in regime formation is of central importance to regime theory.[1] The successful creation of a regime depends upon three factors. First, the hegemon must possess the capabilities to perform the necessary tasks associated with ordering international interactions. Besides having the necessary organisational skills, this also includes the availability of technological and material resources.

Second, even if these resources are available, the hegemon must be willing to commit them to building a regime. Assessing willingness presents a complex set of questions. Recognising its responsibilities and obligations as a dominant international actor, the hegemon may want to pursue a different set of aims and objectives in its foreign policy from those thought desirable by influential sections of its domestic populace. Therefore, the tensions between domestic and international policy become an important factor with regard to assessing the willingness of the hegemon to utilise its potential in forming and maintaining a regime.[2]

Third, although in some issues-areas the hegemon may possess sufficient power to exact obedience, capability and willingness alone may prove insufficient in the absence of deference from lesser states. Unless weaker states are prepared to defer to the hegemon by recognising its legitimate intellectual and moral leadership in ordering negotiating and bargaining processes, a regime may emerge with formal rules and organisational machinery, but with little commitment by regime members to implement the full extent of the obligations they have undertaken.

The formation and subsequent strength of a regime are dependent on the absence or presence of these three features. For example, if all three are present then a strong regime might be expected to emerge, whereas if none are present there seems little chance of regime formation. Between these two extremes exists a range of possibilities that tend towards the formation of a weak regimes. For example, a hegemonic state can probably form a coercive regime if it possesses both a strong will and the capability to impose rules and norms on others. Despite their coercive quality, regimes of this type may produce considerable compliance, particularly under conditions where no alternative is available for weaker states to achieve desired outcomes.

Similarly, both the hegemon and weak states may accept the need to form a regime in some issue-area, but fail in their efforts through the hegemon's lack of capabilities and resources. A third example would be the case where a hegemon has no desire to utilise its capabilities to form a regime — for example, because the advantages of doing so accrue almost exclusively to weaker states — but where the demand of weaker states requires some response from the hegemon.

This chapter will examine in more detail the will of the United States to engage in developing a human rights regime beyond the weakest of forms. Although the United States gave early support to building a human rights regime, this was conditioned on the proviso that the regime emphasised civil and political rights. However, as the Cold War began to emerge, foreign policy makers in the USA became increasingly aware that defining human rights in terms of civil and political rights alone was a further encouragement for less developed states to turn to the USSR for leadership. This left the United States in the position of perceiving a need to maintain the allegiance of less developed states, but unable to do so because of its liberal ideology. Thus, the United States became caught between the need to fulfil its new postwar role as the single most dominant state on the world stage and the demand of influential sections of its domestic population to maintain an international policy that reflected American ideology.

The decision to produce two legally binding Covenants rather than a unified Covenant including political, civil, social, cultural and economic rights was taken following the events described here. Therefore, the singular term Covenant is used in most cases.

HEGEMONY AND DOMESTIC POLITICS

As mentioned earlier, the concept of hegemonic stability has become the most widely accepted approach to explaining regime formation and change. During the early period in the development of regime theory the importance of domestic politics received considerable attention.[3] However, more recently those utilising regime theory have tended to lay less stress on domestic issues. Instead, recent literature favours a more statist approach that seeks to explain regimes by reference to the concept of unified, rational state actors. This approach accepts that although a hegemon may not be sufficiently powerful to predominate in every area of international exchange, and therefore may at times find that it is obliged to settle for cooperative arrangements that are less than satisfactory for its own perceived interests, nonetheless the presence of a hegemon is a necessary, if not sufficient, requirement for providing and maintaining the rules that facilitate bargaining and negotiating processes. The hegemon must not only bear the costs of maintaining rules but must also possess both the capability and the will to implement them by disciplining those who refuse to conform.

It follows from this that since all regime members are bound by the rules of a regime, including the hegemon, and legitimacy is determined by adhering to the rules, then the ability of the hegemon to deviate from the accepted order, and to exercise its power in pursuit of its own interests as needs or circumstances change, may be severely curtailed. Put simply, the rules of legitimate action may come to represent a barrier to the exercise of hegemonic power. To utilise the language of economic analysis so favoured by regime theorists, the hegemon is understood as the provider of public goods (e.g., order, openness, legitimacy) in an international market economy where the hegemon bears a disproportionate share of the costs. Over time the regime tends towards providing improved opportunities for less powerful states to gain access to goods previously denied to them. Consequently, the hegemon may no longer accept the costs of maintaining an order unsuited to its current interests. Thus, regime costs and the equalising effects of a regime lead to two possible consequences: either the hegemon is weakened relative to less powerful states or, alternatively, the hegemon will attempt to exert its power in defence of its own interests, weaken or dismantle the regime and initiate a period of less regulated competition.

This rather deterministic understanding of hegemonic stability provides a focus for criticism for important regime theorists like Robert Keohane. Keohane recognises that the nature of regime formation and maintenance cannot be understood fully without supplementing the crude power theory of hegemonic stability with a knowledge of domestic politics and social attitudes. He argues that as domestic actors within the hegemonic state become aware that a regime no longer fulfils their aspirations — perhaps because the regime has been used successfully by less powerful states to gain an advantage over the hegemon — then domestic interests attempt to mobilise public opinion in support of a foreign policy more in tune with their interests. In the words of Keohane:

> Hegemony is defined as a situation in which one state is powerful enough to maintain the essential rules governing interstate relations, and willing to do so. This interpretative framework retains an emphasis on power but looks more seriously than the crude power theory at the internal characteristics of the state. It does not assume that the strong state automatically creates incentives to project one's power abroad. Domestic attitudes, political structures, and decision making processes are also important.[4]

Such an approach to international regimes and hegemony blurs the distinction between international and domestic politics, and removes the emphasis on systemic factors when attempting to understand regime creation and change. Furthermore, with the continued growth of transnationalism and international institutions, domestic actors increasingly find that they must respond to political and economic environments beyond the direct control of the state. Domestic actors are rarely powerful enough, nor sufficiently well placed in their relationship with international institutions, to influence outcomes and must resort instead to gaining the ear of their own governments to be heard.

This understanding of regimes assumes that domestic interests are filtered through the hegemon's political and social institutions and emerge as a particular pattern of interests expressed as the norms and rules of an international regime. It is therefore important to understand how these organised interests behave in response to the growth of international institutions. Without taking account of domestic factors, international institutions, and organisations associated with regimes, could be understood incorrectly as independent variables enforcing rules with which domestic actors must passively comply. Such an approach assumes that domestic actors play no role in the formation or reformation of a regime. However, as Mary Ann Tetreault has observed, 'the impact of hegemony on the hegemon itself aggravates domestic economic conflicts and conflicts over strategic foreign policy', which for the United States, with its history of distrust of government, isolationism and liberal ideology, can often bring high political costs.[5] Although structure remains important it does so because it favours the promotion of some attitudes over others or opens channels of influence to some actors while closing them to others. It is, as Geoffrey Underhill has pointed out, not the structures of international or domestic politics that determines outcome, but the politics that takes place within those structures:

> It is political conflict, within domestic societies and among states in the international system, which ultimately determines the direction of international regime formation and change.[6]

For these reasons the remainder of this chapter will examine in greater detail the decision by the United States to withdraw from playing a full part in negotiations and discussions on forming a human rights regime. Events leading up to this decision demonstrate that domestic politics and political structures within the hegemon, together with the emerging postwar trend towards international institutionalism, all conspired to delay the creation of a strong human rights regime. In particular, domestic anti-human rights interests coalesced around the so called 'Bricker Amendment' to the constitution of the United States. This amendment is more often understood as an attempt to ensure that individual states (within the United States) retained their independence within the federal structure but, as we shall see, many supporters of Bricker saw human rights as a considerable threat to the policy of racial segregation maintained in many states. Furthermore, many domestic interests began to realise the economic consequences of accepting internationally recognised political and civil rights, particularly in the field of labour relations and foreign capital investments.

DOMESTIC POLITICS AND REGIME FORMATION

Since the early 1930s conservative leaders in the United States had become increasingly concerned over what they perceived as dangerous and unwanted incremental changes to the constitution. Pointing in particular to President Roosevelt's New Deal, conservatives claimed that these changes held important consequences for the American way of life, including the liberal economic system, government and society. Specifically, they argued that the rights of the states enshrined in the constitution were being increasingly eroded as the federal government sought to implement federal policies on economic and social issues. During the war years and immediately afterwards, these fears were exacerbated through policies like the racial integration of American troops abroad, the establishment of the Fair Employment Practices Commission, the report of the Commission on Civil Rights that proposed federal action to outlaw continued segregationist policies, and growing concern in Washington over segregated education. Against these moves, conservative leaders concluded that states' rights should be ardently defended 'as the only bulwark against an expansive federal government which would impose a host of liberal programmes, including the elimination of racial restrictions on marriage, property ownership, and education'.[7]

By the early 1950s, conservative concerns about the changing nature of both the constitution and long established domestic institutions were reinforced by new worries over substantive issues concerning America's evolving international role. As mentioned in chapter 3, isolationist elements feared that the role the United States was casting for itself in the new postwar international order, particularly the leading role undertaken at the United Nations, threatened the social and economic fabric of American society. Many conservatives were concerned that ratifying the Charter held far reaching political and social consequences for the United States. In particular conservatives noted that the UN Charter called for higher standards of living, improved conditions for economic and social progress, solutions to health and social problems and respect for human rights without distinction as to race, sex, language or religion. Although reassured at the time of the Senate hearings on the ratification of the Charter that Article 2(7) explicitly excluded any UN interference in domestic affairs, many remained sceptical. In particular, these sceptics emphasised that according to Article VI of the United States' constitution, a ratified treaty became the supreme law of the land and therefore predominated over any state law to the contrary. Thus, conservative sceptics argued that the Charter itself represented a considerable threat to the constitutional rights of the states to develop independent legal, social and economic policies free of federal interference.

Although the Charter was overwhelmingly approved by the Senate in 1945, conservative and isolationist arguments began to gain ground through the late 1940s and the early 1950s.[8] Against the backdrop of the Cold War, and more importantly the Korean war fought under the auspices of the United Nations, those who had consistently resisted the social and economic policies of Presidents Roosevelt and Truman began to form a coalition with those who saw the United States' new international role as a threat to the traditional American way of life. This coalition noted with some alarm several court decisions, which they claimed supported their assertion that the United States constitution was giving way to international treaty obligations. They cited, for example, *Oyama v California* (1948) where the Supreme Court overturned a Californian law forbidding aliens to own property, at least in part because Californian law was inconsistent with the UN Charter, a treaty to which the United States had acceded and which therefore took priority over state law.[9] In *Sei Fujii v California* (1951) the California District Court ruled that in adopting the Universal Declaration of Human Rights the United Nations had defined the rights and freedoms referred to in the Charter, including the right to own property, and therefore no state law limiting property rights on grounds of race remained constitutional.[10]

A third and crucial example that excited the attention of the coalition concerned President Truman's attempt to place privately owned steel mills under government control in order to avert a strike that threatened to interrupt arms production vital to the prosecution of the Korean war. Although the Supreme Court ruled that Truman's action was unconstitutional, the opinions of three dissenting judges were seized upon by the conservative coalition as further evidence of the potential for international entanglements to interfere with domestic policy. These dissenting judges argued that the UN Charter gave authority to the United States to take all necessary steps to respond to any aggression that threatened international peace and security. Furthermore they argued that the Charter was approved by Congress and, therefore, the President had an obligation to take whatever actions were necessary in fulfilment of American responsibilities, including actions designed to ensure the continuation of arms production.[11]

A further concern for conservatives was the failure of the United States to gain acceptance of a federal clause in the human rights Covenant. Such a clause would guarantee that in a federal system a Covenant could not be imposed upon constituent states unless they acceded to it independently through their separate legislative apparatus. Indeed, throughout the early period of the Commission both the Roosevelt and Truman Administrations had taken for granted that such a clause would be included.[12] During the 1950 Assembly attempts began to give substance to the clause in the following form:

(a) With respect to any articles of this covenant which the federal Government regards as appropriate under its constitutional system, in whole or in part, for federal action, the obligation of the federal Government shall to this extent be the same as those of Parties which are not federal States.

(b) In respect of articles which the federal Government regards as appropriate under its constitutional system, in whole or in part, for action by the constituent States, provinces, or cantons, the federal Government shall bring such provisions, with favourable recommendations to the notice of the appropriate authorities of the States, provinces or cantons at the earliest possible moment.[13]

Supporters of the clause attempted to confine their arguments to legal concerns, focusing on the difficulties federal governments would experience in enforcing international agreements that demanded legislation in areas for which constituent parts had exclusive responsibility. For the United States this included social, economic and — importantly for southern states with established segregationist policies — political and civil rights. Supporters of the federal clause warned that the failure to accommodate the constitutions of federal states would result in further delays and threatened to reduce the number of states that felt able to ratify the Covenant. Furthermore, they emphasised that momentum for reaching early agreement on the Declaration might be lost and never regained.

However, as early as 1950 it was clear that the majority in the Assembly would not tolerate any special considerations for federal states. For example, Mr Bolhari (Pakistan) noted with irony how on some issues the United States, representatives found no difficulty in presenting themselves as spokespersons for a unitary state, while on other issues they were transformed into representatives of a federal state with no authority to speak on behalf of all their peoples.[14] Similarly, Mr Altman (Poland) reminded federal states that under international law only states were subjects. He went on to argue that constitutional and domestic institutional arrangements were of no interest to the Covenant, which was a legally binding international instrument. He wondered if there was not some hidden motive behind attempts to include a federal clause. This motive, he insinuated, could be discovered by looking at the consequences of the Covenant for racist states like Georgia, Mississippi and South Carolina; states that were in most need of human rights legislation.[15] The Chinese representative, Mr P C Chang, expressed the majority view that the Covenant, like the Declaration, should be applied universally and free of restrictive impediments like the federal clause. He reminded those who asked for a federal clause of the paradox they were presenting:

> If a federal government did not consider itself competent to settle questions which were not strictly military or diplomatic, it was difficult to see where the responsibility for solving them lay. Furthermore, if the government maintained that such questions were the responsibility of its constituent parts, whether they were described as states, provinces or cantons, it might be asked why in those circumstances the responsible parts were not represented on the same footing as the federal government.[16]

Such opposition only added to conservative anxieties over human rights and gave fuel to the call for amendments to the constitution of the United States before further erosion took place. The federal clause was defeated at the tenth session of the Commission when the USSR introduced a proposal that upheld the universal nature of human rights and extended the provision of the Covenant 'to all parts of federal states without any limitations or exception.'

One of the most influential organisations that put its weight behind the growing coalition to stop further erosion of the constitution was the American Bar Association (ABA). The ABA had become one of the most outspoken campaigners against including any economic and social rights in the Universal Declaration on the grounds that this class of rights transgressed the traditional American concept of rights.[17] Having failed in the attempt to remove Articles 22–27 of the Declaration, the ABA was determined that the United States would either ensure that 'so-called economic and social rights continue to be excluded from the Covenant'[18] or, alternatively, that it would not ratify the Covenant at all. The ABA's arguments against expanding the treaty arrangements of the United States were fourfold. Firstly, under the Constitution treaties are enforceable throughout the country and potentially undermine the states' separate law making powers. To ratify a human rights treaty was therefore a challenge to existing state laws that discriminated on grounds of sex, race, colour, language, property, birth status or political opinion. For example, the ABA argued that laws relating to women, miscegenation, and even state laws designed to outlaw the communist party, would be rendered unconstitutional. Secondly, ratification of any human rights treaty would almost certainly lead to the annulment of United States' immigration and naturalisation laws, because every human being would have the right to asylum. Under those circumstances the United States would lose the right to determine who should or should not enter the country. Thirdly, a human rights treaty would empower the federal government to enact certain civil rights laws and other legislation that would not be enacted in the absence of such a treaty. Lastly, the proposals to include economic and social rights in any Covenant should be understood as a further attempt by communist states to ensnare the United States in a complex international legal system that sought to penetrate, influence and finally bring down the traditional social and political values for which America stood.[19]

Frank E Holman, the President of the ABA, often employed the racist card in his arguments against the United States ratifying any further international treaties that held implications for the social and economic life of the American people. With both the Covenant on Human Rights and the Convention on Genocide in mind, he warned that *Fujii v California* had already demonstrated the possibility that some agency of the UN — perhaps a future World Court — might easily nullify existing immigration laws and enable a multitude of Chinese, Indians and Indonesians to move from their over-populated countries to the United States. Furthermore, he argued that because the United States' constitution gave precedence to treaty over state law, then ratification of any treaty on genocide or human rights would authorise Congress to carry out legislation — including, say, an anti-lynching bill or other civil rights measures — that interfered in matters previously understood as in the control of the states. This, he argued, would allow civil rights activists and minority groups to claim that these international treaties superseded and invalidated segregation laws and all other discriminatory practices.[20]

These conservative fears fuelled the demand for a constitutional amendment that eventually took the form of a proposal placed before the Senate by John Bricker (Rep., Ohio) on 15 September 1951 known as the Bricker Amendment.[21] Scholars remain divided over the central issue that inspired Bricker and his supporters to propose a constitutional amendment. Tananbaum, for example, argues that although Bricker chose human rights as the focus of his attempt to restrict Presidential powers in the field of treaty making, his real target was the United Nations, which he and his supporters saw as a threat to sovereignty.[22] Tananbaum also distinguishes between Bricker's central concern to restrict the president's ability to make secret executive agreements (e.g. Yalta) without consulting, informing or gaining the approval of Congress, and the central concern of the ABA to protect the constitutional rights of the states from the consequences of both executive agreements and treaties.[23] Kaufman and Whiteman, on the other hand, argue that while there was increasing concern over the use of treaties as a means of enforcing domestic social and economic change 'the original impetus for the Bricker Amendment was a concern about the United Nations' human rights treaties.'[24] Whatever the original purpose of the Bricker Amendment it was instrumental in ensuring that the United States became more circumspect in its role as the moral leader of the world within the UN, and delayed indefinitely the development of a strong human rights regime.

THE BRICKER AMENDMENT

Between 1951 and 1953 Bricker produced several versions of his proposed amendment as he sought to gain the support of the widest possible coalition and thus ensure its success. All the versions followed a similar pattern:

Section 1:
A provision of a treaty which conflicts with this constitution shall not be of any force or effect.

Section 2:
A treaty shall become effective as international law in the United States only through legislation, which would be valid in the absence of a treaty.

Section 3:
Congress shall have power to regulate all executive and other agreements with any foreign power or international organisation. All such agreements shall be subject to the limitations imposed on treaties by this article.

Section 4:
Congress shall have power to enforce this article by appropriate legislation.[25]

By the time Bricker introduced the final version on 7th January 1953 the amendment was cosponsored by sixty-two Senators and its success seemed close.

The arguments presented by Bricker and his cosponsors reiterated closely the concerns of the conservative coalition that had been developing since the founding of the United Nations. Firstly, they argued that if the aim of the Covenant was to ensure greater protection of human rights then it fell far short of achieving this end. The proposed Covenant, they observed, was written in vague, inexact language and contained so many loopholes and possibilities for derogation that it promised a lower standard for the protection of human rights than currently existed in the United States. Furthermore, Bricker's supporters claimed that the proposed Covenant contained several articles that were frankly 'un-American', for example, the right of the state to suppress the free press during times of national crisis. A second group of arguments employed by Bricker and his supporters concerned legal aspects of treaty making and the social consequences of this for America. Citing cases like *Fujii v California*, *Oyama v California* and *Missouri v Holland*,[26] Bricker stressed the threat that a human rights Covenant posed to state laws, particularly in the area of race, colour, property and political opinion. Thirdly, Bricker and his supporters saw the inclusion of economic and social rights in the proposed Covenant as providing the possibility of extending the role of government to include every aspect of a citizen's life. Bricker asserted that although few would object to the legitimate aspirations of people to improve their social and economic conditions, aspirations were not rights that Americans could claim against their government. This led to a further argument put forward by supporters of Bricker. They argued that the proposed Covenant was a further manifestation of efforts by Soviet and other east European states to promote the virtues of communism, gain the support of underprivileged sections of the population and undermine the American political, social and economic system. George Finch, a member of the ABA, testified to the Senate hearing on the Bricker Amendment that:

> the United States should not participate in the negotiations of treaties, the effect of which would be to build around us a wall of socialistic and communist containment in anticipation of the withering away of our principles of human freedom and of the decay of the free institutions we have established to secure them. Are we so certain of our internal strength that we can resist indefinitely the communistic softening to which we are being subjected?[27]

The importance of the ABA has already been mentioned and this was reflected in the privileged position its members were afforded at the Senate hearings on the Bricker Amendment. For example, apart from the Chairman inviting them to sit at his table during the course of the proceedings, and the consultations that took place to ensure that meetings were timed to suit the diaries of ABA members, they were frequently allowed to question witnesses, a privilege more usually reserved for members of the committee. Furthermore, the proceedings were arranged so that at least one member of the ABA could testify after all those opposed to the amendment completed their evidence. This gave the ABA the advantage of responding to any arguments that opponents may have brought up during the hearing.[28]

Economic interests were also well represented at the hearings. The United States Chamber of Commerce, for example, argued that the proposed human rights Covenant would effectively destroy vital parts of America's free enterprise system and thus threaten the very existence of the United States. The National Association of Manufacturers stressed that the proposed Covenant would legitimate federal government interference in labour and management through the imposition of greater government controls. A further example is the testimony of W L McGrath, the United States Chamber of Commerce delegate to the International Labour Organisation (ILO). As an example of the dangers of engaging in an international organisation with economic implications, and as a warning of the outcome of ratifying a human rights Covenant, McGrath reported that the ILO was attempting to assume the authority to formulate and implement universal socialist laws on social and labour issues that it hoped to impose on all nations. As an example, McGrath cited the ILO's proposals for the treatment of women workers, which included maternity leave without distinction between legitimate and illegitimate births, free medical care and the right to one hour a day on full pay to nurse children.[29]

From the inception of the Commission, and particularly during its deliberations in preparation for the Universal Declaration, conservative sections of the American public had questioned the acceptability of the inclusion of rights on economic and social issues. Now that the time had arrived to give legally binding status to the rights first articulated in the Declaration, these conservative elements gained in strength. Such was the concern over human rights during the period of the Bricker Amendment that Congress sought clarification and reassurance whenever any issue came up for debate that bore any implications for human rights. For example, the reference to the Declaration in the preamble to the 1952 treaty of peace with Japan led Congress to ask the architect of the treaty, John Foster Dulles, for confirmation that it would not commit the United States to any specific actions whatsoever.[30] Supporters of the Bricker Amendment promised not only to challenge any further United States' involvement in developing a human rights regime, but also to constrain the executive in performing its responsibilities in the field of foreign policy. If the Bricker Amendment were to succeed, its potential for placing the United States in a subsidiary role, as little more than an observer in the new world order, was immense. When Republican Dwight D Eisenhower replaced Harry S Truman as President in 1953 he had won conservative support on promises and statements made during his Presidential campaign. These included a pledge to continue to uphold the constitutional principle of separation of powers, his acknowledgement that Democratic Presidents Roosevelt and Truman had sought too much power for the Presidency and his expressed desire to restore the constitutional balance between the President and Congress. The problem for the new administration then, was how to deliver these promises without damaging the position of the United States in the United Nations and its new status in the postwar world.

HEGEMONY, BRICKER AND THE HUMAN RIGHTS REGIME

Eisenhower remained reluctant to take any firm action against the Bricker Amendment, even in the face of a growing realisation that vital planks of United States postwar planning could not have been achieved under Bricker. On advice from his constitutional lawyers, Eisenhower began to understand that had Bricker been in force in 1945 United States membership of both the UN and NATO would have been in doubt. Stated concisely, the Bricker Amendment posed a series of interrelated questions for Eisenhower: 1) was it possible to appease conservative leaders and 2) defeat the Bricker Amendment, while simultaneously 3) retaining Presidential treaty making powers and 4) the status of the United States as the moral leader of the new world order? This was no small task since the United States had already demonstrated to the international community the importance it attached to human rights through the lead it had taken in the Commission, including the appointment of an internationally respected person as its representative, in the figure of Eleanor Roosevelt. The growing dissatisfaction of many less developed states over the United States' position on such matters as economic and social rights, coinciding as it did with the introduction of the Bricker Amendment, added further complexity to the situation.

Furthermore, although most states denied the validity of the Universal Declaration as positive international law following its approval, it became increasingly cited in constitutions and official documents. This aroused fears that the Declaration was rapidly assuming the character of customary law, applicable to all members of the international community, whether or not they were involved in its drafting or voted for it in the General Assembly. Thus, to withdraw entirely from the drafting debate on the Covenants held the possibility that the United States would find itself required to adhere to international law for which it had no responsibility. Eisenhower's new approach to human rights in the UN was already beginning to take shape during the last days of the outgoing administration. Assistant Secretary of State for UN Affairs Hickerson called for a review of the United States' position on human rights that would be responsive to two important needs:

a) to the need of maintaining United States' leadership in rallying and strengthening the free peoples of the world; and

b) to domestic criticism of specific actions taken or contemplated in the promotion of human rights in the United Nations, particularly with respect to the proposed Covenants on Human Rights.[31]

Noting conservative reaction within the United States, Hickerson was at pains to assert that leadership in human rights 'offered a significant factor in the Cold War'. He argued that withdrawal from the Covenant debate would seriously weaken the moral leadership of the United States, to the extent of offering the USSR a significant opportunity for exploitation. Furthermore:

[s]hould the United States abandon the Covenants, it is certain that before completion, the texts would substantially deteriorate and articles would be included utterly unacceptable to the United States. The Covenants will no doubt serve as accepted standards of conduct after their approval by the UN, whether the United States does or does not ratify them.[32]

In a further memorandum Hickerson recommended three possible ways forward.[33] Firstly, he urged the administration to undertake a campaign designed to promote the argument that international law was not the best way of promoting human rights. Secondly, he suggested that other means of promoting human rights should be encouraged, including a system of self-reporting on human rights progress in each country. Thirdly, Hickerson recommended the appointment of a rapporteur with the responsibly to receive reports, to report progress on human rights and to offer advice on human rights developments. Furthermore, he recommended that these objectives might be achieved by adopting a two-track policy: 1) formally announcing that the United States did not intend to ratify the Covenants and 2) undertaking a programme to actively promote 'other' methods of improving human rights behaviour. These suggestions were discussed in Cabinet during mid-February 1953, within the context of the Bricker Amendment debate. The new policy to emerge from these discussions was finalised in time for the ninth session of the Commission, a year before the Bricker Amendment was voted on in the Senate.[34]

During the Senate hearings on the Bricker Amendment, officials of the Eisenhower administration made no attempt to defend the development of a human rights regime in the United Nations. Indeed, it was considered essential that the administration should demonstrate to the Senate that the President had no intention of signing any Covenant on human rights or any other treaty that might have implications for economic, social and political affairs. On 18th February 1953 Secretary of State John Foster Dulles announced that the President was 'committed to the exercise of the treaty-making power only within traditional limits' and therefore had no intention of asking Congress to ratify any treaty on human rights. Dulles continued by affirming that the United States remained committed to the cause of human rights but would pursue this cause through 'persuasion, education, and example rather than formal undertakings'.[35] Thus, Congress had no cause for concern that the treaty making powers of the President would be used to implement domestic economic and social change.

This new policy was transmitted to the Commission during the second day of its ninth session by Mrs Lord, Eisenhower's choice to replace Eleanor Roosevelt.

> The climate of world opinion does not yet seem favourable to the conclusion of the Covenants in the United Nations. The Covenants will not have the expected effectiveness in the field of human rights. For these reasons, my government has concluded that in the present stage of international relations it would not ratify the Covenants.[36]

However, in order to avoid excluding itself entirely from the debate on the Covenants, the statement goes on to remind members that the Covenants will be 'looked upon as a more precise and definite statement of the principles embodied in the Universal Declaration of Human Rights, irrespective of their ratification or non-ratification.'[37] In this way the United States reserved the right to continue with its contribution to the drafting process, while forcefully asserting its resolve to avoid any legally binding consequences.

In place of a commitment to ratify the Covenants, Lord announced a proposal for a so-called 'Action Plan' in an attempt to fulfil Hickerson's second requirement that the United States retain the moral leadership of the free world. This was presented as a more efficient method of securing improved standards of human rights conduct than the legal approach that the Covenants represented. The Action Plan was in three parts. The first proposed the appointment of a rapporteur who would be charged with the responsibility of consulting governments, nongovernmental organisations and specialised agencies, and presenting reports on various aspects of human rights. The second proposed a system of annual reports on human rights to be prepared by each member government, which would be considered by the Commission. The last facet was a proposal to establish advisory services on specific aspects of human rights. Included here was a scheme for providing visiting experts who would assist governments in making legal and institutional changes in fulfilment of human rights norms, international seminars on specific aspects of human rights, educational scholarships, and training abroad for government officials and diplomats.

The United States' new policy achieved its domestic aims in that the Bricker Amendment was defeated in February 1954, thereby preserving the treaty making powers of the President. However, the aim to retain a dominant position within the human rights debate was less successful. The formal declaration that the United States would not ratify the Covenants offered the USSR and its allies an opportunity to seize the initiative in the human rights debate. In the Cold War environment of the 1950s, the blunt statement that no intention existed to ratify the Covenants, even before their final form was known, made any United States' contribution less consequential. Once the influence of the United States was withdrawn, the vacuum was quickly filled by Eastern bloc and less developed states who were able to promote their own particular interests.[38] Over the next decade United States' involvement in the Covenant debate oscillated between total disinterest and cautious contributions motivated by an awareness that legally binding agreements were likely to become accepted standards whether the United States contributed to them or not. In this way the idea of human rights, adopted by the United States as a symbol of its moral superiority after 1945, became divorced from its postwar architect and began to develop an independent character that increasingly reflected the interests of socialist and less developed states.

CONCLUSION

One United States' official, who was a close observer of the debates surrounding the Bricker Amendment, has remarked that 'Seldom in human history was so much risked by so many for so little cause'.[39] Had the Bricker Amendment been adopted by the Senate then it would have been difficult, perhaps impossible, for the President to negotiate agreements with other countries over a wide range of common interests, including security and economic cooperation. As Dulles and Eisenhower saw it, if the Bricker Amendment had been successful then other governments would have called into question the competence of an administration made impotent by the obligation to seek the approval of all its constituent parts before a treaty could come into force.[40] However, the growing fear of 'socialism by treaty',[41] coupled with the experience of McCarthyism, left the incoming Eisenhower administration with few options. A failure to defeat Bricker offered the prospect of a further period of isolationism, lasting damage to the new found international prestige of the United States and less chance of entering markets important in guaranteeing the economic future of Americans.

However, the price paid for defeating Bricker was the administration's promise to withdraw from further meaningful negotiations on the development of a strong human rights regime. Publicly, the USA's withdrawal from the Covenant debate was presented as simply a new approach adopted by the incoming administration. Moreover, the new administration argued that its approach was intended to make progress in the field of human rights in a way that the Covenants could not hope to achieve.[42] However, as Kaufman and Whiteman have shown in their analysis of testimony given in the Senate hearings on the Bricker Amendment, fifty percent of all testimony given was concerned with the consequences of entering into any agreement on human rights whatsoever, whether legally binding or not.[43]

The majority of UN members did not entirely accept the official rationale for the United States' new approach to human rights. Mrs Lord reported that Sweden, India, Chile and Uruguay all interpreted the new policy on human rights as a response to Bricker, rather than a new approach adopted by the incoming Eisenhower Administration. She also reported that although many members of the UN were unhappy with the development of the Covenants, and reserved the right not to ratify, few thought it expedient to withdraw before knowing their final form and content.[44] Noting that among these were the USSR and the UK, Mrs Lord expressed concern that the United States ran the risk of becoming increasingly isolated on human rights issues and feared that this might have repercussions for the future of the United States within the UN.

This chapter set out to examine the role of a hegemon in regime creation. Regime theory argues that the creation of a regime depends upon the will and the capabilities of a hegemon. However, as Keohane has pointed out, neither willingness nor capability can be properly understood without supplementing the crude state power theory model of hegemony with an analysis of prevailing domestic politics and social attitudes. Domestic actors are often aware that demand for an international regime may mean a government agreeing to norms and rules that place restrictions on their ability to pursue their interests. When this occurs, domestic actors utilise their political and economic resources to ensure that any regime that does emerge is of the weakest kind.

The role of the United States in negotiations to create a human rights regime explains the importance of domestic politics within a hegemonic state. During the war years the United States government had put forward the idea of a future new world order that would place human rights at its centre. This left a powerful demand for human rights once the war was over. The United States' government also saw an opportunity to augment its new role as global hegemon by taking the lead in building a human rights regime and thus establishing its moral authority. However, the United States — or more correctly its government and administration — failed to confine the scope of human rights to prevailing social values. Caught between powerful domestic interests and international demand for a human rights regime, the administration sought a compromise. That compromise meant that the necessary hegemonic authority to establish a strong human rights regime was denied.

NOTES

1. Stephen Haggard and Beth A Simmons, 'Theories of international regimes', *International Organisation*, 41:3, 1987, pp. 419–517.
2. Geoffrey R K Underhill, 'Industrial crisis and international regimes: France, the EEC and international trade in textiles, 1974–84', *Millennium*, 19:2, 1990, pp. 186–190.
3. See, for example, Peter A Gourevitch, 'The second image reversed: The international sources of international politics', *International Organisation*, 32:4, 1978, pp. 881–911, and Robert O Keohane and Joseph S Nye, *Power and Interdependence: World Politics in Transition*, (Little Brown, Boston, 1977).
4. Robert O Keohane, *After Hegemony: Co-operation and Discord in the World Political Economy*, (Princeton University Press, Princeton, 1984), pp. 34–5.
5. Mary Ann Tetreault, 'Regimes and the liberal world order', *Alternatives*, vol. 13, 1988, p. 19.
6. Underhill, op. cit., p. 189.
7. Natalie Hevener Kaufman and David Whiteman, 'Opposition to human rights treaties in the United States: The legacy of the Bricker Amendment', *Human Rights Quarterly*, 10:3, 1988, p. 310.
8. Eleanor Roosevelt's personal notes demonstrate how acutely conscious she was of conservative reaction to human rights throughout her period as the chairperson of the Commission, particularly in the area of economic and social rights. See, for example, notes prepared for her speech to the Third Committee of the General Assembly, 6th session, delivered on 5th December 1951. In this speech she attempted to set out US objections to including economic and social rights on the grounds that universal implementation was unachievable, that specifying the nature of such rights was impossible and that procedures used for receiving petitions on political and civil rights were inappropriate for economic and social rights. Papers of Eleanor Roosevelt, Hyde Park, New York, box no. 4587. For an earlier example of this concern see the

memorandum of a conversation between Roosevelt and her advisers, 3 July 1947, in the same box.

9. Supreme Court, *Oyama v California*, 332 US 633 (1948).
10. *Sei Fujii v State of California*, 217 Pac. (2nd) 481 (1950).
11. *Youngtown Sheet & Tube Co., v Sawyer*, 343 US 667–710 (1952). See also Duane Tananbaum, *The Bricker Amendment Controversy: A Test of Eisenhower's Political Leadership*, (Cornell University Press, Ithica, 1988). Tananbaum cites this case as of particular significance in drawing together the conservative coalition.
12. Several references to the importance of the federal clause can be found. See, for example, 'Dept of State Instructions to the US Delegation', April 1951 *Foreign Relations of the United States — 1951*, (US Government Printing Office), pp. 734–5.
13. This was the preferred text of the USA during the Commission 6th session in 1950. Several other texts were also presented.
14. GAOR, 5th Session, 3rd Committee, 292ed meeting, p. 135.
15. GAOR, 5th Session, 3rd Committee, 293rd meeting, p. 141.
16. P C Chang, GAOR, 5th Session, 3rd Committee, 292nd meeting, p. 138.
17. See, for example, letter to Eleanor Roosevelt from William Ransom, 4 May, 1946, Papers of Eleanor Roosevelt, op. cit., box no. 4587.
18. Letter to Eleanor Roosevelt enclosing the report and recommendations of the ABA's Committee on the United Nations, ibid. box no. 5487. This report also argues that the USA must make it clear that the Covenant would not be self-executing, that a federal clause must be included, that no international court of human rights could be tolerated and that any complaints system would exclude individual petitions.
19. See, Tananbaum, op. cit., ch. 3.
20. Frank E Holman, 'Giving America Away', 1st October, 1951, *Vital Speeches of the Day*, vol. XVI, pp. 748–53; and 'The greatest threat to our American heritage', September 15th, 1953, *Vital Speeches of the Day*, vol. XXIV, pp. 711–17. Tananbaum, op. cit., deals extensively with the role of the ABA and its campaign to resist any attempt to alter the US constitution by means of treaty. According to Tananbaum the slogan of this campaign can be summed up as 'Save the United States from Eleanor Roosevelt'.
21. Bricker had at first proposed that the Senate adopt a resolution that would have required the President to announce that the Covenant on human rights was unacceptable and that the United States was to withdraw form all further discussions on the Covenant.
22. Tananbaum, op. cit., ch. 2.
23. William Manchester, *The Glory and the Dream: A Narrative History of America — 1932–1972*, (Bantam Books, New York, 1975), pp. 674–77 and Arthur M Schlesinger, *The Imperial Presidency*, (Andre Deutsch, London, 1974), pp. 150–53.
24. Kaufman and Whiteman, op. cit., p. 311.
25. For a contemporary analysis in support of Bricker see George A Finch, 'The need to restrain the treaty-making power of the United States within Constitutional limits', *American Journal of International Law*, 48:1, 1954, pp. 57–82.
26. *Missouri v Holland*, 252 US 416 (1920). This case concerned an attempt by the federal government to introduce federal legislation to protect certain species of migratory birds. At first, this federal law was ruled unconstitutional

by the courts. However, by entering into a treaty with Britain to protect such birds a new statute had been enacted. The Supreme Court upheld this new legislation on the grounds that Congress had the right to pass all laws necessary and proper for discharging its constitutional responsibilities as the national government. Thus, since the President and the Senate had the power to make treaties it was incumbent on the courts to uphold them.

27. Quoted in Kaufman and Whiteman, op. cit., p. 327.

28. ibid., p. 321.

29. Tananbaum, op. cit., pp. 84–5.

30. See, memorandum of telephone conversation between Dulles and officer in charge of the UN Cultural and Human Rights Affairs, 8 February 1952, *Foreign Relations of the United States — 1952–4*, (US Government Printing Office, Washington), 1979, p. 1536.

31. See, Memorandum by Hickerson, 9th February 1953 in, *Foreign Relations of the United States — 1952–4*, (US Government Printing Office), 1979, pp. 1542–6.

32. ibid.

33. Memorandum by legal adviser (Phleger) and Hickerson to the Secretary of State, 11th February, 1952, *Foreign Relations of the United States — 1952–54*, Vol.III, (US Government Printing Office, Washington, 1979), pp. 1549–54.

34. See, memorandum by Secretary of State, 20th February 1953, *Foreign Relations of the United States — 1952–54*, vol. III, (US Government Printing Office, Washington, 1979), p. 1555. See also memorandum from Assistant Secretary of State (Sandifer) to the Director of the Office of UN Economic and Social Affairs (Kotschnig), ibid., p. 1554–5. This memorandum transmitted the proposed new policy on human rights to United States officials at the UN.

35. John Foster Dulles, *Foreign Relations of the United States, 1952–54*, (US Government Printing Office, Washington, 1979), vol. 3, pp. 1549–54.

36. Statement made by Mrs Lord before the Commission's 9th session, Geneva, 8 April 1953.

37. ibid.

38. See, John Humphrey, *Human Rights and the United Nations: The Great Adventure*, (Transnational Publishers, Dobbs Ferry, NY), 1984, pp. 176–81.

39. Interview with Covey Oliver, University of Prince Edward Island, Canada, 19 July, 1990. Covey Oliver used the term 'Bicker Amendment' on many occasions during the interview.

40. Manchester, ibid., p. 675.

41. Dwight D Eisenhower, *The White House Years: Mandate for Change — 1953–56*, (Heineman, London, 1963), p. 278.

42. See telegram to Mrs Lord from the Acting Secretary of State to the Consulate General at Geneva, 10th April 1953, *Foreign Relations of the United States — 1952–54*, (US Government Printing Office, 1979), p. 1575.

43. Kaufman and Whiteman, op. cit. In their analysis of American attitudes to human rights, Kaufman and Whiteman use text analysis to compare arguments against US involvement in 1953 to those offered in 1979 at the time of Carter's attempt to gain acceptance of the Covenants. They find that over 93% of the arguments used in 1953 appeared in the 1979 hearings.

44. Telegram from Mrs Lord to Department of State, 8th April 1953, *Foreign Relations*, ibid., p. 1574.

5 The International Covenants on Human Rights

A brief look at the *Yearbook on Human Rights* for the years immediately following the Third Session of the General Assembly gives an insight into how the Declaration was viewed by many states and with what significance they viewed it. Many influential members of the UN used their entries within these volumes to emphasise their historic record of concern for the legal protection of human rights. For example, in 1949 the United Kingdom submitted legal essays on the 'Writ of Habeas Corpus'[1] and an essay entitled the 'Current Safeguards for the Defence in English Criminal Proceedings' in 1951.[2] Other similar essays all designed to point to positive aspects of existing human rights arrangements are not too difficult to find.[3] Mr Chang (China) was particularly impressed by these high standards, often remarking that if all the speeches and claims made in defence of human rights records at the UN could be believed, then there was no need to continue with developing an International Bill of Rights.

Entries under the names of many other states, however, display a greater awareness of the norms articulated in the Declaration. This is particularly noticeable in the new constitutional arrangements of those states that suffered political upheaval during the Second World War. In this category are Czechoslovakia,[4] Poland,[5] and the Federal Republic of Germany,[6] all of whom made specific constitutional arrangements in response to the Declaration. Further evidence of the emergence of human rights norms can be seen in treaties and agreements adopted by intergovernmental organisations that specifically invoked the Declaration. These include the recommendations of the 1951 West Indian Conference, which called for the 'continued and accelerated implementation, wherever necessary in Caribbean Territories, of the principles and objectives set forth in the Declaration of Human Rights',[7] the Treaty of Peace with Japan, which commits Japan to promoting 'the principles of the Charter of the United Nations' and 'to strive to realise the objectives of the Universal Declaration of Human Rights',[8] and the preamble to the European Convention on Human Rights, which acknowledges the aims of the Declaration.[9]

121

The fourth part of General Assembly resolution 217 called for the publication and dissemination of the Universal Declaration among all peoples throughout the world.[10] Work began on translations of the original English and French texts into other languages in response to this. Materials were prepared for use in schools, including pamphlets, posters, discussion guides and films, and radio and television programmes. The specialised agencies of the UN and nongovernmental organisations were supported in their efforts to promote the Declaration, and 10 December was declared Human Rights Day, celebrated both at the UN headquarters and in individual countries.

UN officials, diplomats and interest groups closely involved in the progress of the Bill of Rights were undoubtedly more aware of the Declaration's significance than those concerned with other UN interests. However, enthusiasm for the Declaration at the Secretariat was tempered by the thought that, although it represented an early landmark in the process of improving human rights throughout the world, it remained nonetheless a non-binding instrument.[11] The discussions to develop the norms expressed in the Declaration into legally binding rules, which were begun and continued in parallel with the Declaration debate in the Commission and ECOSOC, now became the focal point for developing the human rights regime. Although two legally binding Covenants were successfully drafted, and attracted the required number of ratifications to become operative by 1976, the Declaration remains the most often quoted and widely known document in the field of human rights and is increasingly accepted as a source of international law.[12]

The short time it took to prepare the Declaration can be contrasted with the lengthy and detailed negotiations that preceded the Covenants. For several years the draft Covenant prepared by the Commission during 1947 and 1948 moved to and fro between the Assembly, the Third Committee, ECOSOC and the Commission, but little progress was made. From 1955 an article-by-article debate began, occupying the majority of the Third Committee's time through many sessions. In 1966 this debate concluded with two draft Covenants, one on civil and political rights and the other on economic, social and cultural rights.

As discussed earlier, regime theory assumes that regime building requires the active involvement of a hegemon with both the will and the capability to structure and enforce regime rules. It has also been argued that in the case of human rights the United States possessed neither of these capacities. This chapter will continue with this argument. It will examine the failure of the United States and its allies to confine the definition of human rights within their own interests. Four features help explain why the Covenant was so delayed in its completion.

Firstly, the United States and other western states believed that the Universal Declaration already demonstrated sufficient progress in human rights to reassure international publics that humanitarian issues were now central to the new world order. Therefore, the need to make haste in drafting international law was less compelling. Furthermore, Eleanor Roosevelt was under instructions from the Department of State to avoid reaching any conclusions on the Covenants throughout her period of office as Chair of the Commission.[13] This reflected the United States' difficulty in accepting that certain rights, like the right to work and to social security, were legitimate claims that belonged in any human rights treaty at all. It also suggests that early progress in the area of human rights was dependent on accepting a statement of norms that allowed wide interpretation.

Following from this is a second feature concerning detailed and legally binding agreements. While the human rights debate in the UN remained at the level of broad generalities, offering all states something but stopping well short of articulating specific rules, few states found reason to withdraw their support for its aims. During the Declaration debate the focus remained upon a small number of key issues that suggested several possible approaches. Among these were the legal status of the Declaration, questions concerning intervention and the legitimate inclusion of economic rights. The task the Commission and the Third Committee assumed for itself was to find a form of words that reconciled divergent proposals. No concerted effort was made to find wide agreement on new approaches that made the Declaration less open to interpretation. Instead, compromise solutions were sought using the existing positions of members as the building blocks from which general statements could be drawn. By the time the debate moved to the Covenant, powerful interests had begun to understand more fully the implications of developing human rights law and the limitations that such law would impose upon both their domestic and international policies. Consequently, states became more reticent about making the move from general statements on human rights to legally binding obligations. In short, human rights were of value to all states during the period of postwar reconstruction, provided their substance remained ambiguous and indeterminate. When the time came to flesh out the bones represented by the Declaration, to define specific rights and impose specific duties upon states, the enthusiasm and commitment of many to move beyond general expressions of human rights to legally binding rules tended to evaporate.[14]

The third feature that distinguishes the debate leading to the Declaration from that on the Covenants concerns the role of less developed states. The new role of less developed states as international actors within the forum of the UN gave them their first opportunity to exchange views with one another, to identify common interests and to attempt to promote coherent, unified policies that served these interests. This opportunity was further strengthened as South American states, particularly those who were founder members of the UN, realised that they also had many interests in common with more recent members. Many South American states had been independent since the early nineteenth century, but following early progress towards development, had been in economic decline for much of the twentieth century. The experience of the South American states on the international stage further encouraged a collective consciousness among the less developed states and promoted them to press for including rights that the West rejected. Furthermore, several South American states were involved in the preparation of the Bogota Declaration of Human Rights and were therefore well informed of the issues.

Mrs Lord, the USA's representative on the Commission from 1953, was certainly aware of the inexperience of many representatives of less developed state. During the first weeks of her term of office she sent a memorandum to the Department of State expressing the view that often new members seemed unaware of important issues. She also noted how reticent many less developed state representatives were to express the views of their country or to participate fully in the debates. Consequently, Mrs Lord planned to use their difficulties to make important statements in the hope that they would not respond, and thus, through their silence, gain agreement on issues that might otherwise be rejected.[15]

The fourth feature that distinguished the two debates is the numerical advantage of less developed states at the UN as decolonisation gained momentum during the 1950s and 1960s. This allowed the collective consciousness of less developed states to gain in authority in the Assembly. It meant that the West's conception of human rights could be challenged in two broadly defined areas. Firstly, less developed states pressed for group rights as opposed to individual rights. In the Covenants this took the form of resistance to the inclusion of a colonial clause and to demands for the right to self-determination. Secondly, less developed states demanded that the scope of the Covenant should expand beyond traditional ideas of civil and political rights and include economic rights also. Both issues had come up during the Declaration debate, but once the discussions turned to legally binding Covenants that imposed duties on all states, the aspirations of the growing coalition of less developed states demanded greater attention. The socialist states gave the fullest support and encouragement to less developed states in their pursuit of these issues. However, it is important to note that the interests of the socialist states were largely concerned with Cold War considerations.

Three specific debates exemplify these four features. These are the debate over including both civil and political rights and economic and social rights in a single Covenant; the debate over including an article on self-determination in both Covenants; and the so-called colonial clause introduced by the colonial powers in an attempt to exclude colonial territories from the obligations defined by the Covenant. These particular debates have been selected because of their importance to the interbloc political and ideological struggle that characterised most of the activities of the United Nations during the period. Judging from the numerous sessions devoted to them, they were also considered important at the time. In each of these debates the four features described above are present. Although sometimes one feature would take precedence over the others, collectively they challenged the concept of human rights that western states, and particularly the United States, envisaged as a prerequisite for the new postwar order. These debates further weakened the resolve of the United States and other western states to promote the cause of human dignity. Importantly, although the preparation of the Covenants required eighteen years, the arguments developed during the early years, particularly those introduced at the Third Committee of the Fifth Assembly, remained remarkably unchanged throughout the period.

THE BIFURCATION OF THE COVENANT

Articles 22 to 27 of the Universal Declaration, which describe economic, social and cultural rights in the broadest possible terms, were included in the Declaration only after a lengthy, hard fought debate. Western states had come to accept this class of rights with two provisos. First, less developed states had to acknowledge that methods of implementation appropriate for civil and political rights were inappropriate for economic and social rights. If the West did accept economic and social rights as legitimate claims, this was on the understanding that implementation depended upon the availability of resources and that it would be gradual. Secondly, the Declaration was understood as a non-binding agreement that did not impose a duty on the rich to help the poor in their struggle for economic development. However, as the debate turned from the Declaration to the Covenant both provisos were challenged increasingly. Indeed, the debate over including economic, social and cultural rights in a single Covenant became one of the most politically charged and emotive issues during the early years of developing a human rights regime.

As we saw in chapter 3, the United States had come under attack during the Declaration debate whenever the question of economic and social rights arose. More specifically, three problems surfaced that required urgent attention as the debate turned to preparing a legally binding Covenant. First, as the imperatives of the Cold War emerged, maintaining moral leadership within the UN was acknowledged as an essential requirement of United States' foreign policy. This was of particular importance as both the United States and the Soviet Union sought to win the hearts and minds of peoples living in less developed states. Yet for historic and ideological reasons to do with liberalism and isolationism, the United States was unable to fully support the inclusion of economic and social rights within either the Declaration or the Covenant. Consequently, many questioned the United States' claim to moral leadership within the United Nations. Secondly, it was already clear by 1948 that less developed states provided both the physical and ideological space upon which many future Cold War battles would be fought. It was therefore essential for the United States to present policies that went some way towards meeting the claims of less developed states for economic progress. Thirdly, and often at variance with the first two requirements, the United States' administration needed to reassure domestic publics that its commitment to human rights did not extend to economic and social rights for reasons exemplified by the Bricker Amendment.

At first the United States was slow to grasp the importance of these issues. For example, in a 1950 memorandum entitled 'Postmortem on the Third Committee', Deputy Director Green of the United States Office of UN Economic and Social Affairs recorded the changing character of the Assembly.[16] This memorandum recorded the surprise of the United States' delegation that less developed states attached such high importance to the Third Committee's economic and social responsibilities. It continued by accusing less developed states of failing to understand the political significance of the Cold War and of expressing themselves in 'emotional' terms rather than applying 'political reason'. According to Green, the Third Committee was 'something of a safety valve for emotions stifled in the two political committees',[17] where questions of security predominated and where the role of less developed states was less easily defined. Unless the United States was prepared to listen to the demands of less developed states, and accommodate them wherever possible, Green concluded that the USA was in danger of losing its moral authority within the UN. This concern became a central issue in communications and meetings between government officials and members of the United States' delegation to the UN during the following year. The changing character of the Third Committee was clearly a shock and seen as a threat to the aspirations of the United States.[18]

Work on the Covenant had continued in parallel to the Declaration debate from the first session of the Commission. In response to part E of General Assembly resolution 217 (III) that adopted the Declaration, the Commission decided at its fifth session to 'complete the draft Covenant on human rights' and requested the Secretary-General 'to transmit the draft Covenant and draft measures of implementation to Member Governments for their comments'.[19] This draft contained some 26 Articles and alternatives exclusively concerning civil and political rights. Although additional articles concerning economic, social and cultural rights had been submitted to the Commission by several states — notably the USSR — they were not considered because of the constraints of time. However, acknowledging that the Covenant was intended to provide for the realisation of the general norms laid out in the Declaration, including economic, social and cultural rights, the Commission requested the secretariat make a survey of all UN organs and specialised agencies with responsibilities for matters within the scope of Articles 22 to 27 of the Declaration. The purpose of this survey was to provide a basis for informing the Commission during its further deliberations on economic and social rights.

The question of including economic, social and cultural rights arose again at the Commissions's sixth session[20] and at ECOSOC's eleventh session.[21] During these sessions opponents of including economic and social rights in the Covenant reiterated the arguments used during the preparation of the Declaration: first, the claim that this class of rights were not fundamental rights; second, the argument that the economic and social welfare of the citizen remained the responsibility of each state; and third, that international law was an inappropriate way of protecting economic and social rights.[22] However, while these three arguments provided the pretext for many speakers, Cold War and ideological conflicts provided the impetus for much of what they said.

As argued earlier, much of the argument in support of economic and social rights offered by the USSR revolved around the distinction between understanding human rights as a point of 'departure' or 'arrival'. The USSR pointed out that General Assembly resolution 217(III)E called for a single Covenant on human rights that reflected the principles enshrined in the Charter. To exclude the rights expressed in Articles 22 to 27 of the Declaration meant that the Covenant would be less effective than the Declaration, which they argued was in any case an incomplete statement of rights. Furthermore, the representative of the USSR argued that a Covenant legitimising rights exclusively of a political and civil nature would be seen by the socialist states and many others as a 'step backwards', because these states already guaranteed economic and social rights in their constitutions to higher standards than proposed at the UN.[23]

Although representatives of the socialist states expressed themselves forcefully over the inclusion of economic and social rights, their accusations directed at the West were nothing compared to those levelled by representatives of many less developed countries. Less developed states accused the West of avoiding their international obligations to help the underprivileged by denying the legitimacy of economic and social claims. Moreover, they argued that western states, who had already achieved relatively high standards for civil, political and economic rights, would be placing the onus for change exclusively on the shoulders of those whose present level of development was rudimentary. Typical of this type of riposte was that of Mr Noreiga (Mexico), who argued that western states had lost sight of their history.

> Those who wished to postpone such action [to include economic, social and cultural rights] until some unspecified time, took as narrow a view of human needs as the Europeans of the Victorian era, who failed to look beyond their tidy and orderly world and to see the misery and subjugation of other people.[24]

The representative of Saudi Arabia (Mr Baroody) played a particularly prominent role in criticising the West. He claimed that the West had hidden ulterior motives for excluding economic, social and cultural rights from the Covenant and warned of the dangers of excluding certain rights:

> It is not surprising that most of those who took that cautious position were representatives of colonial Powers. It was plainly not in their interest to accelerate the implementation of an effective Covenant, since the result in dependent territories might be to awaken that population from its lethargy. Hence, the representatives of countries which themselves enjoyed the exercise of economic, social and cultural rights were unwilling to extend the benefits of those rights to populations which lived and laboured in a morass of backwardness.
> If colonial peoples, which were already seething with unrest, were given a Covenant guaranteeing political rights without providing economic and social security, they would revolt and fight and would die fighting so that those who came after them might at least live on terms of equality with their fellow men. It would be a tragedy if reform could be obtained only through revolt.[25]

Similarly, Mr Kyali (Syria) wondered whether behind the advice of patience [offered by western states] in respect of granting those rights there did not lurk the fear that their inclusion in the draft Covenant and implementation might make the future position of certain colonial Powers rather difficult

> The opposition of some Powers to the inclusion of articles on essential economic, social and cultural rights arose either from a superiority complex or from a keen sense of selfish colonial interest.[26]

For the United States, such attacks on western values were particularly disturbing, because they allowed the Soviet Union the luxury of sitting back and watching the less developed states do their Cold War work for them.[27]

In an attempt to satisfy both sides of the argument, several states promoted the possibility of drafting two separate Covenants, one on civil and political rights based on the draft before the Committee, followed by a second instrument on economic rights that could be added later.[28] However, this was unacceptable to many who feared that the cause of economic, social and cultural rights would become marginalised or lost forever if they were not enshrined in a single Covenant.[29] Several draft resolutions were placed before the Third Committee at the Fifth Assembly. These included the joint resolution of the Philippines and Syria, which called for 'the consideration of additional instruments and measures dealing with economic, social, cultural and other rights not included in the draft Covenant',[30] and that of Greece and New Zealand calling for a separate instrument dealing with economic, social and cultural rights that would be considered only after the completion of the draft before the Committee on political and civil rights.[31] However, the final resolution was unequivocal in accepting the equal importance of both sets of rights. Following the Third Committee's recommendation, the General Assembly adopted resolution 421 (V). Part E of that resolution reads:

> Whereas the Universal Declaration regards Man [*sic*] as a person, to whom civil and political freedoms as well as economic, social and cultural rights indubitably belong.

> Whereas, the enjoyment of civic and political freedoms and of economic, social and cultural rights are interconnected and independent...

> (b) Calls upon the Economic and Social Council to request the Commission on Human Rights, in accordance with the spirit of the Universal Declaration, to include in the draft Covenant a clear expression of economic, social and cultural rights in a manner which relates them to the civic and political freedoms proclaimed by the Draft Covenant.[32]

This was perhaps the first occasion that less developed states, with the support of the socialist states, had succeeded in turning an Assembly decision against the wishes of the United States. The result caused considerable reverberations both at the UN and among domestic publics, particularly in the United States. This decision not only added to existing domestic tensions, manifest in the Bricker Amendment, but gave further impetus for a radical reappraisal of United States' policy on human rights at the UN. Furthermore, it did nothing to enhance the role of moral leadership that the United States sought to assume within the United Nations. Throughout 1951, Mrs Roosevelt, in consultation with the Department of State, the President and her UN advisers, sought to develop a new policy that satisfied the three aims outlined at the beginning of this section, i.e., moral leadership, support from less developed states and avoidance of domestic criticism. Importantly, and to stress the point again, these aims were understood as imperatives of the Cold War, rather than arguments over building a human rights regime.[33]

During the early months of 1951 it became clear that United States' policy on economic and social rights was an increasing handicap to achieving its aims. In September of 1951 the Department of State prepared a policy paper on the United States' response to the inclusion of economic, social and cultural rights in a single Covenant. While continuing to stress that including economic and social rights would both delay the completion of the Covenant and cause political difficulties at home, the proposed new policy appeared to accept the majority view in the Assembly:

> To press for the separation of those provisions in the face of majority opposition in the Assembly would only invite a great deal of ill-will against the United States and rebound unfavourably with respect to the general political position of the United States *vis-à-vis* other countries, particularly in the case of the many underdeveloped countries urging the inclusion of these provisions in the Covenant.[34]

This new policy did not however diminish the energy with which the United States pursued its preferred goal of reversing Assembly resolution 421 (V). Between the Fifth and Sixth Sessions of the Assembly, these efforts succeeded in shifting the majority in favour of drafting two Covenants. Pressure began to build for this shift at the Seventh Session of the Commission in April and May 1951 when, following the completion of articles on economic, social and cultural rights, attention turned to methods of implementation. As several western states had argued earlier, it emerged that methods of implementation appropriate and acceptable for articles concerning political and civil rights were inappropriate for articles on economic, social and cultural rights. This realisation brought further unsuccessful attempts to gain approval for asking the Assembly to reconsider its decision to include both political and economic rights in a single Covenant.[35]

However, a further attempt to reverse the Assembly's decision was successful at the Thirteenth Session of ECOSOC.[36] Noting the difficulty the Commission had encountered in devising machinery for the implementation of both sets of rights in a single Covenant, a resolution was proposed jointly by Belgium, the United Kingdom and the United States that ECOSOC:

> (3) invite the General Assembly to reconsider its decision in resolution 421(V) to include in one Covenant articles on economic, social and cultural rights together with, civil and political rights.[37]

Although the USSR opposed this resolution, proposing instead an alternative that asked the Assembly to confirm its policy to draft a single Covenant, it was passed by ECOSOC by 11 votes to 5 with 2 abstentions. At the Third Committee all the old arguments were rehearsed again. A number of representatives, including the USSR, Iraq, Pakistan and Yugoslavia, questioned the legality of ECOSOC's request to have the Assembly reconsider a resolution already adopted at a previous session. Mr Altof Husain (Pakistan) alleged that certain members of the Commission, 'representing countries whose point of view had not been adopted by the majority of the Third Committee, had tried once more to make their views prevail'.[38] As on so many other occasions during the decade that followed the end of the Second World War, the debate shifted quickly away from requirements for the protection of human rights towards the imperatives of the Cold War. Accordingly, Mr Vllrich (Czechoslovakia) pointed to the United States' House Committee on Un-American Affairs as an example of why the United States was reluctant even to accept a Covenant on civil and political rights.[39] He charged the United States with 'restricting the exercise of civil and political rights on the one hand and economic, social and cultural rights on the other, in furtherance of its preparations for war'.[40] Similarly, Mr Kasov (Byelorussia) and Mrs Domansk (Poland) accused the United States of denying civil and political freedoms for its own people by attempting to bifurcate the Covenant, calling it a 'trick to prevent the proclamation of economic, social and cultural rights which constituted the basis of civil and political rights'.[41]

By the end of the debate it was clear that the previous year's majority in favour of a single Covenant had been overturned. The draft resolution proposed by the Third Committee, which was finally adopted by the Assembly on 4 February 1952, requests ECOSOC to ask the Commission to draft two Covenants, which should be submitted simultaneously for consideration at its seventh session of the Assembly.[42]

This resolution set the seal on important aspects of the International Bill of Rights and was influential in determining the character of the debate for many years. For the United States in particular, the separation of economic and social rights from civil and political rights went some way towards achieving its policy aims both within the UN and at home. Although many political problems lay ahead, the United States and its western allies judged that the bifurcation of the Covenant would help clarify their arguments against including economic and social rights in any legally binding form at all. Important in this respect was a belief that arguments against acknowledging the legitimacy of economic and social rights — qualitative differences, economic rights through self-help, and the inappropriateness of international law for promoting economic rights — could be better pursued once formally separated from civil and political rights. Although the less developed states had not achieved their aim of giving economic rights equal weight to political rights in a single Covenant, the United States' acceptance of a separate Covenant for economic rights tacitly promised some progress towards tackling the problems of poverty and underdevelopment. Thus, the United States maintained the role of moral leadership within the UN, at least temporarily.

SELF-DETERMINATION

The central purpose of the UN was to avoid future conflicts involving territorial claims of sovereignty over other countries, such as those made by Nazi Germany during the Second World War. Under the heading 'Purposes and Principles', Article 1(2) of the Charter states the rationale for the United Nations, which is to develop friendly relations among nations based upon respect for 'equal rights and self-determination of peoples'. Referring to the international trusteeship system, Article 76 calls for 'progressive development towards self-determination or independence'. However, although the principle of self-determination informed all aspects of the United Nations, important questions concerning how to determine when a people had a right to self-determination, or who should decide when this point had been achieved, were left largely undebated. The San Francisco Conference had seen a brief discussion of the issue, and a further opportunity had been presented during the General Assembly debate over disposing of the former Italian colonies of Libya and Somaliland, but no conclusions had been drawn. Indeed, the final decision to grant independence to Libya gave little attention to such questions as the social cohesiveness of the people or their economic or political ability to sustain independence. Instead, as one author expressed it, the Assembly was motivated by political concerns so that paradoxically 'self-determination was arranged from the outside'.[43]

The question of self-determination had arisen periodically during the Declaration debate but had not become a major issue. The Declaration does not mention self-determination and therefore its heightened importance as the drafting of the Covenants proceeded left many representatives unprepared. For the newly independent and less developed states who identified with countries that remained under the colonial control of European powers, self-determination, along with economic and social rights, became the single most important political issue during the Covenants debate. Thus, attempts to clarify the meaning of self-determination and its parallel concept the 'rights of peoples', became an unintended political consequence of concern over international human rights.[44]

At the 311th meeting of the Third Committee, a joint proposal by Afghanistan and Saudi Arabia calling for the Commission to 'study ways and means which would ensure the right of peoples and nations to self-determination' was adopted by 31 votes for to 16 against with 5 abstentions.[45] Of the sixteen states that voted against nine were west European and four were previously colonies of the United Kingdom possessing strong white, Anglo-Saxon governments. No European country supported the proposal. Introducing the resolution, Mr Baroody (Saudi Arabia) articulated the views of many less developed states:

> The first eighteen articles of the draft Covenant defined the rights not of individual man, but of man as a member of society ...
> Some non-self-governing peoples lived in ignorance of the very existence of such a right; other[s], more politically conscious, were being deluded by promises of independence to be achieved at some indeterminate date under the guidance of colonial Powers. It was, however, not in the interests of the colonial Powers to celebrate the implementation of human rights in the territories under their administration, since they feared that their own economies might suffer thereby.[46]

For the next five years self-determination became a recurring theme in the Assembly, the Commission and ECOSOC. Three broad and overlapping areas of argument were used by those opposed to the inclusion of an article on self-determination: these were legal/technical, political and economic.

Technical arguments stressed that the Bill of Rights was an attempt to protect the rights of the individual. Therefore, while not necessarily denying that self-determination was a legitimate right that could be claimed collectively by some peoples, it was an inappropriate right to include in the present Covenant. If the focus of the Bill now shifted to collective rights then many states, principally the colonial powers and those inhabited by several national or ethnic groups, would not ratify the Covenant. This would disappoint the hopes and expectations of individuals throughout the world and risk devaluing the progress that the Commission had achieved in the past, including the Declaration.[47] Self-determination was therefore more appropriately dealt with in the Trusteeship Council and the Fourth Committee of the General Assembly, which under the Charter were responsible for Non-Self-Governing and Trust Territories.

Secondly, and following from the above, further technical objections concerned the imprecision of definitions for such terms as 'self-determination', 'peoples' and 'nations'. Mr Corley Smith (UK) thought that the term self-determination lacked clarity and doubted whether it could ever have the same meaning in both English and French. In any case it was, he believed, a serious error to assume that a collective principle like self-determination could be transformed into an individual right merely to accommodate the current Covenant. Such an attempt would imply that 'each human being should thus have the right to self-determination regardless of the consequences for others'. The natural conclusion to this would be anarchy since it entailed the *reductio ad absurdum* that each individual could claim to be a sovereign state.[48] The representative of the United States supported this view and argued that while the Charter gave expression to self-determination as a collective principle, it was not intended that this should be understood as an individual right. Furthermore, she argued that self-determination and self-government were not synonymous. Self-determination meant a shared experience for the common good, including a shared financial burden in providing such things as roads, schools and the means to make and enforce the law. To conceive of self-determination as synonymous with self-government 'was to mistake the form for the substance and [this] might jeopardise the very rights which were to be promoted'.[49]

Arguments of a more political nature concerned confusion over exactly which peoples could claim the right to self-determination. Three possibilities existed: Trust Territories as defined by the Charter; Colonial Territories currently governed by metropolitan powers; and ethnic peoples currently incorporated into an existing state. Examples of the first group included the relationship between Togoland under UK administration and Cameroon under French administration; of the second, the relationship between Kenya and the UK; and of the third, the integration of Latvia and Lithuania into the constitution of the USSR. This question was never fully explored for its technical significance in a legally binding international Covenant. Instead, the distinctions among the three possible categories of peoples presented further ground for fighting political battles in the Cold War.

These battles were fought on the distinction between self-determination as an internal (the right to secede) or external right (the right to be free of colonial rule).[50] Internally, many states feared that including a right to self-determination would legitimate claims for independence by ethnic minorities and secessionist groups within existing state borders.[51] For example, the USSR supported an exclusively external view of self-determination, arguing that the Soviet people had achieved the objective of self-determination and had used that right to become part of the multinational state of the Union of Soviet Socialist Republics.[52] Furthermore, the USSR and other east European states accused the United States of 'trying to stifle movements for national independence' by all possible methods, including the use of force such as that seen in Korea.[53]

Externally, although accepting that self-determination was central to the existence of the UN, the colonial powers took a narrow view and were reluctant to apply the principle beyond Europe. This was contrary to the broader view held by many non-European states who understood self-determination as a universal principle that supported their call for decolonisation. Defending their narrow view, colonial powers argued that many peoples who might benefit from a right to self-determination were not yet ready to control and administer their own affairs. Since the Covenant would express universal rights and also demand universal and immediate implementation, the right to self-determination was therefore inappropriate.[54] Furthermore, the colonial powers argued that the prerequisites of all other rights were political and civil freedoms, and these were therefore prior to the goal of self-determination.[55] Crucially, at both the internal and external level, those against including self-determination asked how the UN would respond to conflicts involving the claim of self-determination. In an internal dispute over self-determination, would the UN's duty be to enforce a return to the *status quo*, or to challenge the existing order, support the right of secession and threaten the domestic jurisdiction of a member state? In similar fashion, externally, what action would the UN anticipate taking against a state that refused to grant independence to one of its colonies?[56] Those opposed were careful not to reject self-determination as an important political principle with 'strong moral force' and an important place within the new postwar international order. However, they argued that as a political principle it required political means to ensure that it was maintained and enforced. The achievement of self-determination was therefore a complex and diverse issue that would cause increased conflict if it was expressed as a legal right. Self-determination should therefore be subordinated to more important principles of the UN, for example, the maintenance of peace and security.[57]

While technical and political arguments were prominent during the debate over self-determination, economic arguments were the cause of most concern for western industrialised countries. In 1952 Chile had successfully introduced an additional paragraph to draft Article 1 of the Covenant that gave all peoples the right to dispose of their natural resources as they saw fit:

> The right of the peoples to self-determination shall also include permanent sovereignty over their natural wealth and resources. In no case may a people be deprived of its own means of subsistence on the grounds of any rights that may be claimed by other states.[58]

Although this paragraph was presented as an attempt to establish the sovereign right of a people over natural resources, industrialised states thought they detected a more sinister motive that threatened their economic well-being: an attempt by national governments to legitimate the nationalisation and state control of important extraction industries. To accept the paragraph, opponents argued, would imply the Assembly's endorsement of the right to expropriate capital investment without compensation. This was contrary to all that the UN stood for in developing the global economy and would surely affect the current trend towards increasing cooperation on economic development. In a world where autarky was an impossible goal, opponents argued that any reduction in economic cooperation, particularly in the area of international capital investment, could only be damaging for both developed and less developed countries alike.[59]

None of these arguments impressed supporters of self-determination. They argued that the distinction drawn between collective and individual rights was illusory, for self-determination was a 'prerequisite for the exercise of all other rights'.[60] Why, they asked, should arguments concerned with definitions be so important during the debate on self-determination when, on other occasions, such difficulties were brushed aside. For example, in preparing other articles for the Covenant no member had insisted on exact legal definitions for 'fair-wages', 'social security' or 'adequate standard of living' More tellingly, the Charter itself did not offer any help in defining nebulous concepts like 'peace keeping' or 'aggression', which were integral concerns of the UN. Furthermore, the Charter had been drafted and ratified without thought for perfecting the single, most important legal concept upon which the UN was founded: that of the state.[61] To resist the inclusion of self-determination was to misunderstand the new postwar international order where peoples 'seemed to know, without legal counsel, that they were, in fact, nations and thus entitled to have a say in their own dealings'.[62] Third

World states further accused the industrialised colonial powers of attempting to maintain their international political status,[63] a status which depended upon maintaining a supply of cheap raw materials, together with strategic bases throughout the globe that ensured continued control of the sea.[64]

Although opponents dominated the early days of the debate, from 1952 it became increasingly obvious that an article on self-determination would be included in both Covenants. At the Seventh Session of the Assembly, resolution 637 C (VII) requested ECOSOC to instruct the Commission to 'continue preparing recommendations concerning international respect for the right of peoples to self-determination'. Acknowledging this resolution, at the Eighth Session of the Assembly, the Third Committee considered a further resolution sponsored by twenty states calling for self-determination to be the first article in each of the proposed Covenants. Resigned to their defeat, opponents of self-determination made no contribution when this resolution was debated: it was a silence that several speakers noted with some satisfaction.[65]

When the article-by-article debate on the Covenants began during the tenth session of the General Assembly in 1955, few believed that it was possible to resist the inclusion of an Article on self-determination. However, this did not stop the Third Committee from devoting a further twenty-six meetings to debating the proposal and rehearsing all the arguments again. Those opposed emphasised that including self-determination would jeopardise the whole Covenant, that it did not constitute an individual right, that it was not a right but a principle, and that the Covenant should reflect only those norms set out in the Declaration, which itself did not refer to self-determination. Supporters acknowledged that although self-determination was a collective right, it was nonetheless a prerequisite for the enjoyment of all other rights. They also reminded opponents that the Eighth Session of the Assembly had decided that self-determination should be included. By way of concession, supporters stressed that the Article was not concerned with secessionist groups, or the terms 'peoples' and 'nations', but with gaining independence for colonial peoples.[66]

After further attempts at delaying the formal acceptance of the Article — including the suggestion that self-determination was better dealt with in a separate protocol or covenant and that another working group should be set up to study its nature, scope and limits — the Article was finally brought to a vote. The adoption of the Article, which became Article 1 in both Covenants, represented a major victory for less developed states in their attempt to use the human rights debate at the UN as a means to achieving political ends.[67] For those who opposed self-determination as a right, the defeat was a further reminder that the UN could not be always relied upon to legitimate the preferred goals of the powerful.

THE COLONIAL CLAUSE

If the attempt by the less developed states to initiate a norm of self-determination was seen as an explicit assault on colonial states and the colonial system, then the colonial clause was an attempt to preempt such a threat.[68] The colonial clause sought to confine implementation to signatories of the Covenant, explicitly excluding all other territories that were under their jurisdiction, including Colonial, Trust and Non-Self-Governing Territories. With the mood in the Assembly already growing avowedly anticolonial by 1950, the colonial clause offered even greater opportunities for less developed and socialist countries to denounce colonial powers. The United Kingdom (the original sponsor of the clause) and France were criticised for attempting yet again to maintain their economic prosperity by 'dictating their prices to colonial peoples', forcing them to 'sell their valuable raw materials for a song',[69] and 'perpetuating the myth of self-government'.[70] France in particular was subjected to severe criticism for its constitutional arrangements with Algeria and Morocco.[71]

Three reasons were presented for including a colonial clause. First, it was argued that the colonial powers held 'paternal responsibilities' in relation to their colonies. Conscious of these responsibilities, and diligent in fulfilling them, colonial powers felt an obligation to prepare colonial peoples for independence, but this would take time. Therefore, the criticism often levelled that the sole purpose of the clause was to avoid implementing the Covenant in colonial territories for reasons of self-interest were unfounded. Proponents of the clause did not deny self-determination as a principle of the postwar order. They did however recognise that to implement the principle without thought for education, or for developing the necessary institutions to support it, would represent a negation of their responsibilities. Therefore, it was simply a distraction to engage in questions to do with normative issues, like the rights and wrongs of colonialism. Of greater importance were questions to do with how best to move from the present colonial system to one that fully integrated colonial territories into the society of states. Supporters of the clause argued that their intention was simply to facilitate this process.[72]

A second and related argument in support of the colonial clause concerned the purpose of the Covenant. According to supporters of the clause this was to improve existing standards of human rights. To achieve this required a Covenant that made demands upon the resources of all signatories, not one that could be readily embraced simply because its provisions aimed at the lowest common denominator. Although standards were improving in the colonies and dependent territories, supporters of the clause argued that it would be many years before either economic or social conditions in the least developed countries would approach the levels proposed in the draft Covenant. To avoid drafting a document that provided for the most meagre standards, the present draft required a colonial clause to allow developed states to ratify, while also giving less developed countries time to realise their aspirations. In short, the Covenant should be applied immediately and in its entirety in those countries where suitable conditions already prevailed, but should be introduced by degrees in those countries that the Charter recognised as presently unfit for full independence.[73]

Opponents of the colonial clause were less than impressed by these arguments and suggested that the true motivation behind the clause was less noble. They claimed to detect an underlying current of racism that supporters attempted to dignify by labelling it the 'level of civilisation' argument. Opponents argued that the spread of imperial power during the nineteenth century had been considered synonymous with the spread of civilisation. This link, which was reinforced by the colonial clause, had become so favoured that the term 'native' was now widely understood to mean non-European. But as Mr Chang (China) reminded the European colonial powers, their superior civilisation had done little to support peace and security throughout the world during the twentieth century:

> Civilisation had largely meant European rule. A reaction to that attitude had begun to develop by the early twentieth century and, after two world wars, the world ought to have a different idea of the meaning of civilisation. It was true that there were different degrees of technology and other forms of advancement but, as the Charter clearly showed, that did not mean that less-developed areas were to be exploited by outsiders.[74]

Furthermore, opponents noted that colonial powers often emphasised the heavy responsibilities that the burden of administrating Non-Self-Governing Territories had placed upon them. Colonial powers had expressed their paternal concern for their charges, a concern that emphasised the duty they accepted to nurture the less fortunate to a point of international maturity where they might, at some future time, achieve full independence. However, opponents of the clause rejected these claims and pointed to the enormous advantages colonial powers gained from continuing their existing relationships with their colonies. Apart from the obvious economic benefits afforded by colonialism, colonial powers also acquired important political benefits that helped enhance and maintain their existing power and political status. With more than a hint of irony in emphasising this point, Mr Chang (China) acknowledged the enormous burden so unselfishly accepted by the colonial powers. Indeed, he recognised it as a double burden, for not only did colonial powers have to accept costly responsibilities for those unable to care for themselves but 'they also suffered because [this] power corrupted them'.[75]

The third set of arguments presented by supporters of the clause was concerned with democratic rights: that the Covenant should recognise the right of colonial peoples to ratify the Covenant for themselves once they had achieved independence. The representative of the United Kingdom emphasised how much his government had achieved in advancing its policy to introduce responsible self-government in the colonies. In particular he emphasised the setting up of legislative bodies and institutions that provided a measure of local autonomy in domestic matters. However, he reminded the Third Committee that the realm of international politics remained, at present, the reserve of the UK. Therefore, if the UK, or any other colonial power, exercised its prerogative and ratified a legally binding international agreement that required application in dependent territories, this would be depriving those territories of the right to decide matters that could directly affect their domestic social and political institutions. Thus, those who objected to the inclusion of a colonial clause were demanding that dependant territories should not be afforded autonomy, but should instead continue to have important international issues decided for them. The only alternative to the inclusion of a colonial clause was for colonial powers to consult and come to agreement with all their dependent territories before ratifying the Covenant. Such delays were incompatible with the urgent need to establish clearly defined international human rights and could easily be avoided by agreeing to insert a colonial clause.[76]

A second argument relating to democracy and the right of colonial peoples to participate in the preparation of international agreements, had parallels with those arguments put forward to oppose the Articles on self-determination. This argument pointed to Chapters XI and XII of the Charter, under which administrating powers were called upon to be sensitive to the varying levels of development in Trust and Non-Self-Governing Territories. Nothing in these Chapters suggested that international agreements entered into by administering powers should be applied unilaterally to these territories. Indeed, Article 73 called upon the administering powers to take regard of the distinctive cultures of Trust and Non-Self-Governing territories. Since the proposed Covenant would have profound effects on the domestic life and culture of many countries, supporters of the colonial clause argued that colonial and non-self-governing peoples should be provided with the opportunity to determine for themselves whether to ratify it after they had achieved full statehood.[77]

Opponents of the clause were quick to see the irony in the concern of the colonial powers for the democratic rights of people in colonised countries. They noted that during the debate on self-determination, colonial powers had attempted to reserve for themselves the right to determine when a territory was ready to achieve full independence. Indeed, they had vigorously deflected all suggestions that colonial peoples themselves might be consulted through democratic processes. Opponents of the clause therefore asked why in opposing self-determination, colonial administrations denied the duties imposed upon them in the Charter, while in proposing the colonial clause these duties were rigorously upheld?

Furthermore, opponents claimed that constitutional and democratic arguments were being exaggerated in support of outmoded concepts of international relations that discriminated against colonial peoples. Opponents argued that since the end of the Second World War the entire concept of sovereignty had been rethought, modified or even revolutionised. They reminded champions of the colonial clause that the UN was built upon principles that explicitly recognised the international nature of social, economic and human rights. These matters were now accepted as vital to the pursuit of international peace and security. Consequently, many of these issues were no longer exclusively within the domestic jurisdiction of the state. Therefore, as the Charter made clear, it was not the preserve of colonial powers to determine just when certain principles of the new world order should be applied, but rather the concern of the international community as a whole.

The final resolution to emerge from the Third Committee of 1950 (later to become Assembly resolution 422(V)) gave clear and unequivocal instructions to the Commission to complete a draft Covenant. Unlike resolution 421(V), which asked for further 'study' to ensure 'ways and means' of including in the Covenant articles concerned with self-determination, economic, social and cultural rights and the possibility of including a federal clause, resolution 422(V) refers an approved wording back to the Commission. What emerged was a resolution diametrically opposing the intentions of the United Kingdom and other colonial powers. Rather than a colonial clause it was an anticolonial clause:

The provisions of the present Covenant shall extend to or be applicable equally to a signatory metropolitan State and to all the territories, be they Non-Self-Governing, Trust or Colonial Territories, which are being administered or governed by such metropolitan State.[78]

By the Twenty-First Session of the General Assembly, which adopted the two Covenants, the colonial clause was perceived as unnecessary by most members of the UN. At that Session the views of the Assembly reflected the advances made in dismantling colonial empires as the process of decolonisation progressed. International opinion had shifted such that at the 1411th Meeting of the Third Committee Mrs Dmitruk (Ukraine) was able to propose that explicit recognition of universal application was no longer required and that the colonial clause should be deleted.[79] Furthermore, it was argued that to give special mention to colonialism in any form at all represented an undesirable institutionalisation of a fast decaying norm. Importantly, the Assembly had previously adopted the Declaration on the Granting of Independence to Colonial Countries and Peoples, which repudiated the existence of any legal right of some states to govern others.[80] This, and the growing acceptance of a norm of self-determination, made even an anticolonial clause redundant. When it came to the vote Ukraine's proposal to delete the clause was accepted unanimously.

CONCLUSION

On 22 December 1966, under the headline 'UN Progress in Non-Political Field', the London *Times* announced the adoption of the two Covenants. This newspaper article shows little understanding of the nature of the debate at the UN:

> The twenty-first session of the United Nations General Assembly, which has just ended, had at least three positive achievements to its credit. None of them was political, but that does not detract from their significance.[81]

This passage shows that the writer understood the field of international human rights as apolitical and confined to legal and philosophical fields. It is evident from the debates described above that such a view cannot be sustained. By 1950, and throughout the period when the Covenants were under discussion, human rights activity in the UN was a major focal point for the Cold War. In the words of Evan Luard, commenting on the 1960 Assembly:

> Instead of the UN being used as the forum where world leaders could seriously discuss serious issues, it presented the spectacle of a bear-garden, where representatives of the great nations of the world scuffled and jostled and abused each other.[82]

In the context of the Cold War ideological struggle developing within the United Nations, colonialism, self-determination and the rights to economic and social welfare were fundamental issues to be exploited at every opportunity.

The policy aims of the United States remained largely unsatisfied. The most pressing issue for the United States' administration, exemplified by the Bricker Amendment, was to find a satisfactory response to public disquiet over the administration's policy in favour of greater involvement in international affairs. The failure to gain acceptance of a federal clause discussed in chapter 4 and the potential threat of nationalisation implicit in self-determination, did nothing to strengthen the hand of the United States' Government in persuading the American people that an even deeper involvement in international affairs was desirable. Although the bifurcation of the Covenant offered the opportunity to accentuate traditionally held beliefs about civil and political rights, at the expense of devaluing economic and social rights, this proved insufficient to reassure influential sections of the American public that the Covenants did not represent a threat.

Withdrawing from the Covenant debate in order to appease public opinion jeopardised international aspects of United States' policy. Within the context of the Cold War, the United States' success in reversing the Assembly's decision not to produce two Covenants and its support of the colonial clause, did nothing to promote better relationships with less developed states. By 1965 UN membership had increased to 119. Of these, nearly eighty had recently emerged from foreign domination.[83] In announcing that it had no intention of signing the Covenant, thereby leaving the formation of a human rights regime leaderless, the United States provided less developed and socialist states with an opportunity to promote values that were contrary to the idea of being an American.[84] Both sides of the Cold War grew to realise that the Commission and the project of universal human rights provided a suitable vehicle for conducting ideological disputes, particularly in the context of Africa and Asia. The United States' failure to provide direction for the human rights regime became a crucial factor in strengthening the Soviet hand.[85]

By the time the two Covenants came before the Third Committee for their final reading in 1966, there was little support for the colonial clause or opposition to including self-determination as a right. Following the initial disputes over these issues, the colonial powers had come to realise that the newly independent states would be obliged to continue many of their existing economic ties if they hoped to achieve the levels of development to which they aspired. The change from a colonial to a noncolonial international system did not bring the disruption that many feared. The colonial powers soon discovered that they could develop new relationships that some have called 'economic imperialism'.[86]

NOTES

1. *Yearbook on Human Rights for 1949*, (UN, New York), pp. 229-34.
2. *Yearbook on Human Rights for 1951*, (UN, New York), pp. 359-64.
3. For example, France, pp. 92-95; USSR, pp. 354-6, which also includes a report on the success of the latest five year economic plan; and Israel, pp. 122-29, all found in the *Yearbook on Human Rights for 1951*, (UN, New York).
4. *Yearbook on Human Rights for 1950*, (UN, New York,), pp. 53-6.
5. ibid., pp. 173-7.
6. *Yearbook on Human Rights for 1951*, (UN, New York), pp. 99-105.
7. West Indian Conference, Curacao, 27th November — 8th December, 1950.
8. Treaty of Peace with Japan, done at the city of San Francisco, 8th September, 1951.
9. Convention for the Protection of Human Rights and Fundamental Freedoms, signed in Rome 4th November, 1950.
10. General Assembly resolution 217(III) D, 10th December, 1948.
11. Interview with John Humphrey, McGill University, Montreal, Canada, 2nd October, 1989. Although during the adoption debate most representatives had been careful to remind the world that their countries did not consider the Declaration legally binding in any way, a few acknowledged its importance and potential as a source of law. Humphrey himself and the French representative Rene Cassin were in this category.
12. R Ramcharan, *The Concept and Present Status of International Protection of Human Rights*, (Nijhoff, The Hague, 1989).
13. See for example, Department of State briefing paper to Mrs Roosevelt, undated but in her personal files for 1947, (box no. 4592, Roosevelt Library, Hyde Park, NY); telegram from Department of State (30-1-47) urging Mrs Roosevelt to defer discussion of issues of implementation, (also in box no. 4592); and notes from Department of State advisers during the first session of the Commission, impressing on Mrs Roosevelt that the Declaration was the prime objective and urging her to defer all other issues as far as possible (box no. 4594).
14. Oran Young, 'The politics of international regime formation: managing natural resources and the environment', *International Organisation*, 43:3, 1989, pp. 349-75. Borrowing from James Buchanan's concept of the 'veil of uncertainty', Young argues that the move from vague principles to binding agreements brings new information that often increases doubt in the minds of regime members.
15. 'Communications from Mrs Lord to the Deptartment of State', 28 April 1953, in *Foreign Relations of the United States — 1952-54*, (US Government Printing Office, 1972), pp. 1575-7.
16. Memorandum to David H Popper, principal executive officer of the US Delegation to the Assembly from Deputy Director Green, *Foreign Relations of the United States — 1950*, (US Government Printing Office), pp. 575-8.
17. ibid., p. 578.
18. See, for example, *Foreign Relations of the United States — 1951*, (US Government Printing Office), the views of Mrs Roosevelt in 'Memorandum of conversation by James Simsarian', 29 May 1951, pp. 740-4; and, 'Positional papers prepared by Dept of State for UN delegation', 28 September 1951, p. 753.

19. See, *Yearbook on Human Rights for 1949*, Commission on Human Rights, 5th Session, 9 May to 20 June, 1949, pp. 330-2.
20. Commission 6th Session, 27 March to 19 May 1950.
21. ECOSOC, 11th Session, 5 July–9 August, 1950.
22. GOAR, Third Committee, 5th Session, 288th meeting: respectively, the UK, p. 107; Canada, p. 174; and the UK, p. 174.
23. See ECOSOC, Official Records, 11th Session, 1950, p. 175 and p. 144.
24. ibid., p. 178.
25. GAOR, Third Committee, 1950, p. 187.
26. ibid., p. 189.
27. See memo by Green, op. cit.
28. See speeches of the representatives of Brasil, USA and the UK, (297th meeting) and India, (299th meeting), GAOR, 5th Session, 3rd Committee.
29. The representative for Uruguay brought even greater confusion to the discussion by proposing three separate covenants: i) rights inherent in the person (life): ii) political rights: iii) economic, social and cultural rights. This proposal was not received with great enthusiasm. ibid. p.128.
30. UN Doc. a/C.3/L.71/Rev.1
31. UN Doc. a/C.3/L.83
32. General Assembly Resolution 421(V) adopted by 38 votes to 7 with 12 abstentions.
33. *Foreign Relations of the United States — 1951*, vol. II, (US Government Printing Office, Washington), 'Positional paper prepared by Department of State for the US delegation to the 13th session of ECOSOC', 29 June 1951, p. 744.
34. 'Positional paper prepared by Deptment of State for UN delegation to 6th Session of the Assembly', September 28th 1951, in *Foreign Relations of the United States — 1951*, (US Government Printing Office), p. 756.
35. *Yearbook on Human Rights for 1951*, (UN, New York), 1953, p. 525.
36. ECOSOC, 13th Session, 30 July to 21 September 1951.
37. ECOSOC resolution 384(XIV), *Yearbook on Human Rights for 1951*, (US Government Printing Office), p. 480-1.
38. GAOR, 6th Session, 3rd Committee, 362nd Meeting, 1951, p.92.
39. During her chairmanship of the Commission, Eleanor Roosevelt was often preoccupied with these 'loyalty hearings' because of the potential damage they could cause to the reputation of the United States in the UN. See her letter to President Truman dated, 13 November 1947, box no. 4587, Papers of Eleanor Roosevelt, Roosevelt Library, Hyde Park, New York.
40. GAOR, 6th Session, Third Committee, 366th Meeting, 1951 p. 118.
41. ibid., 168th meeting, Kosov (p. 127), Domansk (p. 130)
42. General Assembly resolution 543(VI).
43. Clyde Eagleton, 'Self-determination in the United Nations', *American Journal of International Law*, vol. 47, 1953, p. 89.
44. See, J Crawford, 'The rights of peoples: Some conclusions' in J Crawford, (ed) *The Rights of Peoples*, (Clarendon Press, Oxford, 1988), p. 159-75.
45. This resolution later became section D of General Assembly resolution 421(V), 4 December 1950.
46. GAOR, 5th Session, 3rd Committee, 309th Meeting, p. 240.
47. GAOR, 10th Session, 3rd Committee, for examples of this type of argument; Sweden, p. 86; China p. 89; and Belgium p. 94.
48. GAOR, 6th Session, 3rd Committee. 401st Meeting, pp. 329-30.

49. Mrs Roosevelt, GAOR, 7th Session, 3rd Committee, 1953, 447th Meeting, pp. 174-5.

50. GOAR, Mr Beaufort (Netherlands), 7th Session, 3rd Committee, 447th Meeting, p. 171.

51. P G Lauren, *Power and Prejudice: The Politics and Diplomacy of Race Discrimination*, (Westview, Boulder, 1988) ch. 6 and Antonio Cassese, 'The self-determination of peoples' in Louis Henkin (ed) *The International Bill of Rights*, (Columbia University Press, NY, 1981) pp. 92-113. Both use a similar classification of 'internal' and 'external' self-determination.

52. USSR, GAOR, 10th Session, 3rd Committee, 646th Meeting, p. 108-9.

53. Mr Kiselyov (Byelorussia), GAOR, 7th Session, 3rd Committee, 444th Meeting, p. 153.

54. See comments by Mr Soudan (Belgium), ibid, p. 242-3.

55. Comments by Mr Cassin (France), ibid., 311st Meeting, pp. 246-7.

56. Evan Luard argues that from 1955 the UN role did in fact shift from peace keeping and the maintenance of peace to one of actively bringing about change. See his *A History of the United Nations: The Age of Decolonisation*, (Macmillan, Basingstoke, 1989)

57. Speech by the representative of the UK, GAOR, 10th Session, 3rd Committee, 642nd Meeting, p. 90-1.

58. UN Doc.E/CN.4/L.24

59. See, for example, Mrs Lord (USA), GAOR, 10th Session, 3rd Committee, 646th Meeting, pp. 109-19 and 676th Meeting, p. 262.

60. Representative of Chile, GAOR, 10th Session, 3rd Committee, 645th Meeting. p. 103-4.

61. See, contribution by representative of Pakistan, GAOR, 7th Session, 3rd Committee, 448th Meeting, p. 180 and that of Mr Begum Liaquat Ali Kalm (Pakistan), p. 179.

62. Representative of the Philippines, GAOR, 7th Session, 3rd Committee, 453rd Meeting, p. 216.

63. Mr Frontaura Argandona (Bolivia), GAOR, 7th Session, 3rd Committee, 450th Meeting, p. 197.

64. Mr Baroody (Saudi Arabia), ibid., p. 168.

65. Resolution a/C.3/L.371/res.1. For comments on the silence of the colonial powers see Mr Abdel Ghani (Egypt), GAOR, 8th session, 3rd Committee, 525th Meeting, p. 241; and Mr Baroody (Saudi Arabia), p. 247.

66. *Yearbook of the United Nations — 1955*, (UN, New York), pp. 153-56.

67. A/C.3/L.489 adopted by 33 votes to 12, with 13 abstentions.

68. See GAOR, 5th Session, 3rd Committee, p. 160-1 which emphasises such a link.

69. Mr Baroody (Saudi Arabia), GAOR, 5th Session, 3rd Committee, 296th Meeting, p. 164.

70. Mr Bokhari (Pakistan), GAOR, 5th Session, 3rd Committee, 291st meeting, pp. 159-61.

71. By 1950 the membership of the Assembly included a large bloc of Arab and Muslim states who were in regular contact with Algerian and Moroccan leaders. During the debate on the colonial clause, members of this bloc would often read out extracts of communications from these leaders detailing the contempt with which France treated its north African colonies. Vociferous among those who spoke regularly against the colonial clause were

Afghanistan, Egypt, Ethiopia, Iraq, Lebanon, Pakistan, Saudi Arabia, Syria, Turkey and the Yemen.

72. This and the remaining issues presented in support of the colonial clause were most forcefully expressed by the representative of the UK. See, for example, GOAR, 5th Session, 3rd Committee, 294th Meeting, p. 150-1.

73. For an example of this type of argument see Mr Moody (Australia), GAOR, 5th Session, 3rd Committee, 294th Meeting, p. 154. This was a curious argument that seemed to suggest that the Covenants should be applied only in areas where the standards it sets out had already been achieved. It is open to the criticism that was often levelled by the USSR, that western states saw human rights as a point of 'arrival' rather than a point of 'departure'.

74. Mr Chang (China), GAOR, 5th Session, 3rd Committee, 295th meeting, p. 159.

75. ibid., p. 159.

76. See speech by UK representative, op. cit., pp. 150-1.

77. See, for example, speeches by Mr Lesage (Canada), p.159, and Mr Soudan (Belgium), p. 161, both in GAOR, 5th Session, 3rd Committee, 295th Meeting.

78. Adopted as General Assembly resolution 422(V) 4 December 1950, by 36 to 11 with 8 abstentions.

79. GAOR, 21st Session, 3rd Committee, 1411th Meeting, p. 195.

80. Resolution 1514(XV), 1960. Text in Ian Brownlie, *Basic Documents on Human Rights*, (Clarendon Press, Oxford, 1981), pp. 28-30.

81. The *Times*, Thursday, 22 December 1966, p. 8, emphasis added.

82. Evan Luard, *A History of the United Nations: The Age of Decolonisation — 1955–1965*, (Macmillan, Basingstoke, 1989), p. 128.

83. Luard stresses the importance of this for self-determination and economic rights. ibid. p. 17.

84. Louis Henkin, 'The United Nations and human rights', *International Organisation*, 19:3, 1965, pp. 504-17.

85. Luard, op. cit., ch. 20.

86. Sally Morphet, 'Article 1 of the Human Rights Covenant: its development and current significance', in Dilys Hill (ed), *Human Rights and Foreign Policy*, (Macmillan, Basingstoke, 1989).

6 Implementation and Foreign Policy

The previous chapters have focused upon the way that the idea of human rights was kept alive in the General Assembly, Councils, Commissions, Committees and Working Groups of the United Nations. However, for much of the period between 1945 and the early 1970s human rights remained a 'minority' interest.[1] Beyond those engaged directly in the debate on the Bill of Rights, or those involved in special interest pressure group politics, there is little evidence that the idea of human rights achieved the status of a social institution such that it affected the day-to-day conduct of international politics.[2] For most of the period the international political agenda was dominated by military security and economic interests. This was so even before the United States withdrew formally from the debate on human rights and left the regime without hegemonic leadership. In the early postwar period, these interests focused upon economic reconstruction and the political consequences of an emergent East–West ideological struggle. Later, the mutual apprehension and mistrust of the Cold War gave focus to security issues at the expense of all other considerations, including human rights. The United States adopted a policy of 'containment' and gave support to any government, totalitarian or authoritarian, provided it was avowedly anti-communist.[3] During the late 1960s and early 1970s the energy crisis, nuclear disarmament and détente were the central concerns of international politics. However, the end of the Vietnam war, followed by the collapse of détente, provided the catalyst for questions about the paucity of moral content in United States' foreign policy. By early 1975 even Secretary of State Henry Kissinger, a man with little previous enthusiasm for human rights as a foreign policy aim, was showing some concern for the issue.[4]

The final paragraph of the preamble to the Universal Declaration of Human Rights recognises the duty of 'every individual and every organ of society' to promote respect for human rights by progressive measures, both 'national and international'. This obligation is restated in Article 2 of the Covenant on Economic, Social and Cultural Rights, but not the Covenant on Civil and Political Rights, which calls upon signatory states to take constitutional measures for the protection of human rights. The purpose of this chapter is to examine attempts within the United Nations to provide methods of implementation that demanded attention both nationally and internationally. No detailed analysis of these measures will be made here. This is a task already undertaken elsewhere in a growing body of literature.[5] However, in order to complete the task of understanding attempts to build a human rights regime it is necessary to examine the options for implementation considered by the United Nations.

This will be done in two ways. The first will examine progress in completing the third panel of the triptych of the Bill of Rights. This panel was intended to provide international measures to implement human rights, which are the decision-making procedures of the regime. Methods of implementation received little attention during the lengthy debate over standard setting, as represented by the Declaration and the Covenants. The Commission accepted that implementation could not be fully considered until legally binding rules were finalised, although it accepted that the strength of the regime would depend on successful methods of implementation. However, as the debate on the Covenants drew to a conclusion attention turned from standard setting to implementation.

Secondly, foreign policy provides an important insight into the way states have reacted to attempts to build a human rights regime. The foreign policy of the USA is of particular significance because hegemonic leadership is crucial for regime building. The Presidency of Jimmy Carter coincided with the shift of emphasis from standard setting to implementation. Although human rights were given a central place at the level of political rhetoric, Carter's human rights policy found both its inspiration and final demise in three areas familiar to earlier Presidents: a concern for reinforcing and legitimating the moral standing of the United States, domestic attitudes and economic interests.

INTERNATIONAL IMPLEMENTATION OF HUMAN RIGHTS

As discussed in chapter 3, at its second session the Commission on Human Rights decided to proceed with the work of preparing an International Bill of Rights in the form of a triptych; a Declaration, a legally binding Covenant and measures for implementation. A drafting committee had been appointed which was subsequently divided into three working groups, each given the responsibility of developing proposals for one panel of the triptych. The working group on implementation soon came to the conclusion that the question of implementation was more closely related to the preparation of one or more Covenants than to the Declaration. They reasoned that while the Declaration would take the form of a recommendation of the Assembly, and would not therefore be enforceable, the Covenant would be legally binding on all signatories. Therefore, at the early stage of developing a Bill of Rights, which focused almost exclusively on the Declaration, the best that the working group could hope to achieve was to articulate general principles in preparation for more substantive proposals once the form and content of the Covenant were known. Even this was premature for some members of the working group. For example, the Ukrainian representative withdrew from the group, on the grounds that it was futile to consider implementation until the rules provided by the Covenant were well established.[6]

Of the three panels of the Bill of Rights, the one on methods of implementation was the least debated in all of the relevant UN organs. Although in part this was for the reason pointed to above, it was also caused by the constraints of time. Almost invariably during the early years, the agendas of those UN organs concerned with human rights were so overfull that only the most pressing items were debated. This meant that items under methods of implementation were frequently deferred from year to year. Furthermore, and perhaps most important, many countries remained reluctant to consider the problems presented by implementation. As noted earlier, the United States had consistently warned its representatives on the Commission to avoid discussion of implementation,[7] while the socialist countries had always pursued a policy that confined implementation to the level of the state.

Finally, one further complexity added to the problems of developing methods for implementing human rights. As noted in the last chapter, the rationale for bifurcating the Covenant rested largely on the difficulty of devising implementational procedures appropriate for both sets of rights. Today, authors who address the problem of implementation tend to confine themselves to civil and political rights, ignoring socio-economic rights completely or at best giving them cursory attention only.[8] Indeed, many of these authors do not see the necessity of mentioning that their focus is confined to civil and political rights. This suggests that bifurcation has indeed led to forfeiting the unity of human rights and that the fears of many less developed countries have been realised.

Before anything could be agreed on methods of implementation four general questions were considered. First, what form should methods of implementation take? Should they, for example, be dealt with in separate articles within the Covenants, a separate protocol annexed to the Covenants, or an instrument needing separate ratification altogether? Second, would only states have the right to initiate proceedings under the Covenants or would such rights be extended to individuals and groups? Third, under what circumstances would proceedings be activated? Finally, what machinery should be established to deal with reported violations of human rights and what powers should such machinery be given?

In answer to these questions, several proposals were made in the interval between the resolution on the Declaration and the beginning of the debate that considered the two Covenants article by article. Three possibilities were considered: judicial proceedings through a Court of Human Rights, arbitration conducted by a High Commissioner for Human Rights acting under the authority of the General Secretary, and monitoring procedures.

Judicial proceedings

Many of those engaged in developing the human rights regime came from a legal background. It might therefore seem natural for them to turn to judicial processes for resolving disputes. It should also be noted that twelve of the original eighteen members of the Commission had legal training. However, the proposal to establish an International Court of Human Rights found few supporters. Proposals for a Court were put forward on several occasions during the Declaration debate, but were never fully discussed. Most states remained suspicious of setting up any adjudicatory machinery with potentially higher authority than the state, even though the Declaration was not intended to be enforceable international law. Although both sides of the Cold War pointed to Article 2(7) as the reason for resisting a Court, their real concerns were less noble. Western states feared they would become subject to inspection themselves, particularly as the majority in the Assembly grew increasingly in favour of less developed countries. The racist policies of many southern states in the USA and the colonial record of many European states would therefore become exposed to criticism. For the USSR and its socialist allies, a Court offered the possibility of exposing the excesses of Stalinism and opening the communist system to public scrutiny.[9] The last serious attempt to promote the idea of a Court was made by Australia during the Fifth Session of the Commission held in May and June 1949. Although the only vociferous objectors were the socialist countries, who reiterated their disapproval of all attempts to undermine the authority of the state with any international machinery for implementation, the relative silence of other states indicates what little enthusiasm they had for creating a Court.[10]

Adjudication of human rights cases through a Court could have taken one of two forms: criminal or civil. The Nuremberg and Tokyo trials, which were being conducted during the early period of the human rights debate in the Commission, must have suggested to those considering methods of implementation just how much confidence they could place in judicial processes. Three closely linked categories of crime were considered at

Nuremberg: crimes against peace, war crimes, and crimes against humanity. The first two categories represented crimes that broadly affected the interests of the state. The third category was distinguished from the other two because it recognised that state officials could not treat their own citizens, or those of other countries, as they pleased and remain free of legal proceedings. This might have suggested to some observers that international society had tacitly signalled its intention to widen its traditional and legitimate area of concern. However, the limits of that concern can be judged by noting that only two Nuremberg defendants were found guilty of crimes against humanity only.[11]

A further insight into how a Court might work was offered by the European Court of Human Rights, which was set up as the Covenant debate began. However, by 1966 this Court had heard only two cases so that the consequences of implementing human rights through a judicial system remained unclear.[12] Even if this one available example of a regional court had shown that adjudication was a viable means of resolving some cases of human rights violations, it is doubtful whether expanding the principle to the global level would have found favour at the UN. The political nature of human rights, particularly when associated with collective rights like the right to self-determination, left both lawyers and governments uneasy: lawyers because any confusion between law and politics was thought detrimental to the judicial process, and governments because they saw any weakening of the principle of nonintervention as destabilising.

Although some have claimed that the failure to create an International Court of Human Rights left all attempts to establish effective methods of implementation impotent and 'headless',[13] the difficulty of separating the legal from the political aspects of human rights meant that establishing a Court was never seriously considered. As we shall see in later sections on foreign policy, the degree of interest a state takes in the human rights record of another state is inspired by political not legal considerations. That is to say, while a state may resort to extravagant rhetoric, and on occasions take vigorous action because of an adversary's record on human rights, in the case of allies or those who demand an uncontentious relationship as the price of maintaining some form of strategic advantage, turning a 'blind eye' is the common reaction. It should therefore be asked whether an international Court would have retained any authority given the complex philosophical, political and legal nature that human rights developed in the UN.

Arbitration

Several forms of arbitration were discussed for settling disputes over human rights during the Covenant debate. The most radical of these was the attempt to create the position of United Nations High Commissioner for Human Rights. During the first few years of the Commission the idea of establishing the office of High Commissioner for Human Rights was particularly attractive because no machinery existed to deal with the burgeoning number of petitions that continued to flood the Secretariat. There was therefore an urgent need to establish some means of dealing with these. It was proposed that the High Commissioner would have similar powers to those held by the High Commissioner for Refugees. However, finding a satisfactory definition of a refugee had proved contentious. In the face of disagreements over rights, particularly over political and economic rights, the task of defining the role of a High Commissioner promised further antagonism. Furthermore, the High Commissioner for Refugees was given powers that many saw as legitimising intervention in the domestic affairs of the state. Therefore, to offer similar powers to a High Commissioner for Human Rights represented far reaching reforms of the international system, and few showed any enthusiasm for that. The socialist states argued that the creation of a High Commissioner for Refugees offended against the rules of international society. They also argued that the powers of the High Commissioner were ineffective and would contribute towards the perpetuation of a refugee problem, rather than solve it.[14] During the meetings of the Third Committee held in 1950 there was general agreement that the central principle of the human rights regime would be that states remain the primary actors for ensuring high standards of human rights.[15] Where disagreements did occur they focused on whether methods of implementation should be included in the Covenant or drafted as a separate protocol.

Three familiar arguments were used against the appointment of a High Commissioner. Firstly, Article 2(7) of the Charter states that nothing in the Charter 'shall authorise the United Nations to intervene in matters which are essentially within the domestic jurisdiction of any state or shall require the members to submit such matters to settlement under the present Charter'. Secondly, the Charter, taken as a whole, required a collegiate body in the exercise of its powers, not a single individual. Thirdly, although Nuremberg and Tokyo had tacitly accepted the individual as a subject of international law, many states continued to view this as a singular exception, not to be extended beyond its immediate application. Those opposed to creating a High Commissioner argued that neither the individual holding the post of High Commissioner nor the individual petitioning the High Commissioner could be recognised as subjects under international law. Although the objectors to creating a High Commissioner presented their arguments as though defending the principles of international law, the true motivation for rejecting the idea was political. As Roger Stenson Clark has noted, had the

Assembly taken the centrality of human rights in the Charter seriously, the case for reforming the existing international legal system, and for creating the office of High Commissioner, could have been made.[16]

Although these three arguments formed the basis for defeating the idea of a High Commissioner, there was a fourth reason that made agreement on any form of implementation unlikely. This was that little agreement could be found on the best way to implement human rights, even among those states who accepted the legitimacy of intervention on grounds of human rights and supported placing the individual at the centre of international law.[17] Apart from the proposal to create a High Commissioner, the Commission and the Third Committee were also considering a wide range of other possibilities. These included the proposal to create regional courts, self-reporting procedures covering all or part of the Covenant, systems of diplomatic negotiation over human rights disputes, and empowering the proposed Human Rights Committee to collect information through the initiation of their own enquiries prior to carrying out enforcement procedures. The failure to resolve differences over the best way to proceed meant that no overall majority could be reached even by the most earnest advocates of implementation. With proponents divided, opponents to any but the weakest form of implementation found no difficulty in defeating any measure that promised an extensive reform of existing principles of international law and society.

On 20 December 1993 the Assembly adopted resolution 48/141, creating the post of High Commissioner for Human Rights. This followed a recommendation of the 1993 Vienna Conference on Human Rights. The first holder of this post is José Ayala Lasso. Although the new High Commissioner is active in finding solutions to some known cases of gross violations, it is too early to assess the effectiveness of the new post. However, the early evidence suggests that the role may lack the necessary resources and support to fulfil the high hopes of Vienna. This will be discussed in the final chapter.

Monitoring

Successful monitoring involves gathering, collating and evaluating information in preparation for making recommendations on ways of improving human rights conditions. As discussed in chapter 1, the possibility of fulfilling these functions was hindered from the outset when the Commission decided that it had no authority to take action on individual human rights complaints. However, as the debate on implementing civil and political rights continued, it became clear that for implementation to have any meaning at all, powers to investigate violations and complaints had to rest with some authority.

As with so many other important issues related to the Covenant, it was the Third Committee of the Fifth Assembly in 1950 that laid the foundation for all future debate on the issue of implementation. Excluding the socialist states, who remained implacable in resisting any form of intervention on human rights matters,[18] agreement was soon reached to establish a Human Rights Committee consisting of eighteen members charged with monitoring progress on implementing the Covenant on Civil and Political Rights. Under Article 28 of the Covenant, these members would be elected by secret ballot from a list of persons nominated by state parties to the Covenant, be of 'high moral character and recognised as competent in the field of human rights'. Article 31 calls for consideration of the geographical distribution, the representation of different forms of civilisation and the principal legal systems when determining membership. The Committee should be given responsibility for reviewing reports, which parties to the Covenant on Civil and Political Rights would undertake to submit on the measures adopted, and progress made, in ensuring the implementation of rights set out in the Covenant. Furthermore, under Articles 41 and 42 it was proposed that an optional provision should be made to enable any state party to the Covenant to initiate a complaint against another state party if both states had previously accepted the competence of the Committee.

Although agreement on the responsibilities of the Committee was reached without too much argument, many states pointed to the consequences of confining the Committee's work to state reports and communications alone. They argued that the Covenant, and the Declaration before it, dealt almost exclusively with the relationship between the state and its citizens. However, now that the Commission was considering methods for implementing the Covenant, these were confined to state-to-state relationships. This left the individuals and groups of individuals who were the real victims of human rights violations with no access to machinery for implementation.[19] As a compromise between those who defended the traditional right of a state to uphold the principle of domestic jurisdiction and those who accepted the legitimacy of human rights as an international concern, the United States, supported by several other countries, proposed that a separate Optional Protocol be drafted that permitted individuals to submit petitions for consideration by the Committee.[20]

The plan to establish the Human Rights Committee survived the early debates on implementation and the Committee has subsequently become the principal instrument for implementing the Covenant on Civil and Political Rights. However, an understanding of the procedures that the Committee has developed since its inception is more revealing than a mere listing of constitutional obligations.[21] Although McGoldrick has argued that since it began its work the Committee has 'established itself as a respected body of independent, highly qualified members who have attracted consistent praise for the serious and constructive nature of their deliberations',[22] it has achieved far less than many enthusiasts have argued. For example, under Article 41 of the Covenant on Civil and Political Rights, state parties contract to submit reports on their existing human rights practices within one year of ratification and after that whenever the Committee so requests. While many states have fulfilled this requirement on time, many others are less diligent. In some cases the reports have been less than revealing when they are eventually submitted. The report of Guinea claimed that 'citizens of Guinea felt no need to invoke the Covenant because national legislation was at a more advanced state',[23] while Bulgaria, equally blandly, claimed that all the rights incorporated in the Covenant were enshrined in national law.[24] A further example is that of India, which needed seven reminders of its obligation to report under the Covenant before finally responding in 1989, four years late. The failure of India was particularly worrying because of widely reported violations of human rights in the Sikh community. Indeed, when the report was submitted it included information on special laws relating to Sikhs that the Committee saw as an attempt to derogate from Article 6 of the Covenant, the right to life. The failure to submit reports on time so hampers the work of the Committee that the Assembly regularly passes resolutions urging state parties to the Covenant to honour their obligations.

A further weakness is that the Committee is still not in agreement over the meaning of Article 40(4) of the Covenant, which calls for the Committee to make 'general comments' on progress in implementation. Some argue that this permits the Committee to make detailed comments on each of the reports submitted by state parties, thus enabling it to point to failures and areas of concern that need action before further reports are requested. This interpretation would allow the Committee to make specific recommendations on the law and practice of state parties. Others interpret 'general comments' in narrower terms to mean assessing the effectiveness of existing international procedures for implementing human rights. In this interpretation remarks on specific reports would be expressly forbidden. It is this second, narrower meaning that has thus far found favour with the Committee. As might be expected, this view has meant that the Committee does not offer any formal evaluation, comment or constructive criticism on the measures taken within particular states in compliance with the Covenant. Instead, it confines itself to making general recommendations intended to offer state parties guidelines on methods of more efficient reporting procedures. Furthermore, the optional provisions that allow states to submit complaints about the human rights activities of other state parties to the Covenant have never been invoked and are likely to remain unused.[25]

At first the Committee was further restrained by its inability to conduct follow-up monitoring of the limited recommendations it could offer. The results of the Committee's deliberations and recommendations therefore remained unknown. In 1992 the Committee decided to include a request for follow-up information, which must be included in subsequent state reports. The contribution that this will make remains unclear, but since states do not always fulfil their obligation to report in the first instance, it is difficult to see how the request to provide more information will improve matters.

The Committee's role under the Optional Protocol may deserve a greater measure of optimism. By 1991 the Committee had received 472 communications relating to 36 states and offered a 'view' on 125 of the petitions set before it. The term 'view' is used because the Committee has no authority to compel compliance with the Covenant. However, although these 'views' have resulted in a few states altering their domestic practices, it must be kept in mind that so far only 74 states have ratified or acceded to the Optional Protocol. It should also be noted that most of those states that have accepted the more effective procedures offered by the Optional Protocol are perhaps least in need of them. For example, one success claimed by the Committee refers to changes in the Dutch social security system following a case where several individuals were refused benefits.[26] In the final analysis, McGoldrick has observed that 'it must be frankly admitted that compliance with the [Human Rights Committee's] views by States parties has been disappointing', particularly where serious violations are the subject of communications.[27] Furthermore, the number of cases that come before the Committee represent only a small percentage of the total number of petitions received by the UN in any year.[28]

Although the Committee can be said to have achieved a status such that many states now accept its independence, and its operating procedures have stimulated at least some minor alterations in state practice, its contributions towards the promotion and protection of human rights in countries where gross violations remain common may fairly be said to be 'more than a whimper' but 'less than a roar'.[29] Given the commitment that state parties undertake under Article 2(2) of the Covenant 'to take the necessary steps, in accordance with its constitutional processes and with the provisions of the present Covenant, to adopt legislative and other measures as may be necessary' to give effect to the Covenant, the Committee's achievements seem relatively small. As one author has recently concluded, although the Committee has made some progress:

> [m]any of the changes are only minor alterations to domestic human rights machinery needing extensive overhaul. Others appear largely gratuitous or are presented in such vague terms that it is unclear whether the changes will actually further the Covenant, despite the assurances of the government. ... In areas of judicial usage of the Covenant, the fact that only eight countries report the application of the Covenant in case law is especially disappointing.[30]

To repeat, it was realised early on that methods of implementation appropriate for civil and political rights were inappropriate for economic, social and cultural rights. Although the UN has always been careful to stress the indivisibility of rights, at least in the legal-formal sense, as implementation gained in importance this principle became increasingly strained. As suggested in chapter 5 on the decision to bifurcate the Covenant, disagreements over prioritising one set of rights over another were nothing new. On the one hand the industrialised western states were not fully committed to giving equal weight to political and socioeconomic rights, while on the other socialist and most of the less developed states were attempting to undermine the formal equality given to the two classes of rights in favour of socioeconomic rights.[31]

Like the Covenant on Civil and Political Rights, state parties to the Covenant on Economic, Social and Cultural Rights are contracted to furnish periodic reports, not to a committee of experts, but to the ECOSOC. The procedure adopted by the Council to deal with these was initially to set up a Sessional Work Group of state representatives and to phase reporting in three stages over a six-year cycle.[32] To augment this procedure the working group were permitted to invite observers from specialised agencies, other Council members, state parties and other states who expressed an interest. The Covenant on Economic, Social and Cultural Rights is distinguished from that on Civil and Political Rights in two important ways that make the task of international monitoring less effective. Firstly, Article 2 of the Covenant on Economic, Social and Cultural Rights calls for 'progressive' as opposed to immediate implementation of the rights it establishes. Secondly, no procedures exist for individual complaints such as provided by the Optional Protocol. These distinctions mitigate against effective international monitoring and mean that the Covenant has even weaker powers of implementation than those provided in the Covenant on Civil and Political Rights.

More recently, ECOSOC resolved during its 1985 session to set up a Committee to help the Council in assessing reports on economic, social and cultural rights, including the submissions of specialised agencies. The new Committee is also required to formulate suggestions and recommendations of a general nature.[33] This Committee started to consider working methods and procedures when it first met in 1987. Although the Committee began the study of reports during its first meeting, it is still at the stage of defining the standard procedures that it will adopt. It therefore remains to be seen whether this new Committee will improve the monitoring capabilities of the Council and give state parties greater guidance on economic and social issues.[34]

Following the recommendations of the 1993 Vienna Conference on Human Rights, the new Committee began the work of devising indicators to measure progress in the realisation of economic, social and cultural rights during its 1994 meeting. It also began consideration of an optional protocol to the Covenant that would allow individuals to submit communications for its consideration. However, the new Committee suffers the same problems as the Human Rights Committee and has already had some difficulty in persuading states to submit reports on time and in sufficient detail. Furthermore, the new Committee is a committee set up by ECOSOC, not a 'treaty body' like the Human Rights Committee, constituted under Article 28 of the Covenant on Civil and Political Rights. Therefore, the new Committee will have even less independence and authority than its counterpart on civil and political rights.[35]

While acknowledging that many states pay only lip-service to obligations undertaken internationally to implement human rights, many human rights enthusiasts believe that '[n]evertheless amazing progress has been made, notably in the United Nations'.[36] However, while enthusiasm may be a prerequisite for developing arrangements for the protection of human dignity, claims of 'amazing progress' seem premature. Many states are far from prompt in fulfilling reporting obligations. Those reports submitted are often sketchy, vague and full of generalised statements. In states where serious violations are known to occur reports are often evasive, and neither the Human Rights Committee nor ECOSOC has the formal powers necessary to make further investigations. The annual report of the Human Rights Committee remains restricted to making general comments rather than specific recommendations. Furthermore, specialised agencies and nongovernmental organisations, who have detailed knowledge of human rights conditions in particular states and could therefore make an invaluable contribution to the quality of reports, play a minimal formal role in the proceedings.[37] In the absence of any judicial powers, binding decisions, enforcement powers, or the authority to make specific recommendations, the only authoritative procedure left is that of persuasion. Consequently, the impact of the Committee, such as it exists, 'lies in its moral and legal authority as a respected and independent human rights body'.[38] Finally, both the Human Rights Committee and the Committee on Economic, Social and Cultural Rights have found it necessary to reduce the number of meetings they hold because of lack of resources. Although the Charter identifies the protection of human rights as a central aim of the UN, only 0.7% of its budget is devoted to human rights activities.[39] Antonio Cassese's pessimistic assessment of implementation does seem apposite:

> So long as there is not a collective sense of solidarity and no joint interest in respect for fundamental standards of behaviour on human rights, the prospect for a satisfactory implementation of the whole body of law concerning crimes against humanity remains poor.[40]

POLITICAL IMPLEMENTATION OF HUMAN RIGHTS

With this in mind it should be questioned whether the resources available for the international protection of human rights is best utilised to support quasi-legal, formally constituted standing bodies with few powers. Although by its nature the United Nations inevitably turns to formal-legal means in its attempts to enforce the obligations undertaken by its members, current methods of implementation have sometimes been supplemented by the less judicial and more political practice of deprivation. Deprivation is administered on a case by case, *ad hoc* basis rather than through established standard procedures for dealing with human rights violations.

The best known attempt to use deprivation for securing human rights is the case of South Africa, to which the Assembly has devoted considerable energy and many resolutions opposing that country's policy of apartheid. Beginning in 1956 with the establishment of the UN Commission on the Racial Situation in the Union of South Africa, the Assembly sought to secure the support of members in isolating South Africa from the rest of the international community. This was on a voluntary basis at first, but after 1977 sanctions were mandatory on all UN members. UN specialised agencies were invited by the Assembly to 'take the necessary steps to deny technical and economic assistance to the Government of South Africa' and 'to take active measures, within their fields of competence, to compel [South Africa] to abandon its racial policies'.[41] At the forefront of these efforts was the World Bank and the International Monetary Fund (IMF). However, these organisations were either incapable or unwilling to utilise their potential for depriving South Africa of vital economic support. Although the World Bank and the IMF attempted to defend their position because under their constitutions they were obliged to consider requests for assistance on purely economic reasoning alone, most of the Assembly refused to accept such a view. However, other agencies were more willing to comply with the Assembly's wishes. For example, the World Health Organisation resolved to expel any member state that contravened humanitarian principles, and the United Nations Educational, Scientific and Cultural Organisation (UNESCO) withdrew all further assistance from South Africa. Furthermore, the Assembly, ECOSOC and the Commission attempted to exclude the South African government from international trade in almost all sectors, particularly the arms trade.[42] Despite this effort and persistent pressure from the Commission and the Assembly, French, German and other banks continued to give credits to South Africa and even to increase them to make up the shortfall created by UN agencies.[43]

The success of deprivation as a means of protecting human rights is unclear. First, during the same period that the Assembly attempted to isolate South Africa, little attempt was made to vilify any other country where serious violations of human rights were known to have taken place, for example, in Cambodia and Indonesia. This led many commentators to speculate that most less developed states in the Assembly were more interested in using apartheid as a racist 'trump card' in their struggle to assert their authority by shaming wealthy ex-colonial states into increasing their economic support for development assistance. Secondly, the success of deprivation depends largely upon the willingness of developed states, who trade with the target state, to discontinue their existing economic relationships. The response of many developed states was inconsistent and erratic in South Africa's case. For example, the policies of the United Kingdom, and to a lesser but still important extent the United States, fluctuated between compliance with and opposition to the Assembly's wishes.[44] Incredibly, the United Nations did not withdraw $250 million in pensions funds in South Africa until 1985.[45] Thus, deprivation is difficult to assess as an alternative to legal-formal means of protecting human rights. Although some scholars have argued that deprivation threatened South Africa with expulsion from international society in 1975,[46] others have claimed that deprivation contributed little as a tool in the protection of human rights.[47]

The optimism shown by many commentators makes it difficult to offer an assessment of current arrangements for implementation. Optimism springs in part from the fact that many authors, for example Opsahl, come from a legal background and are therefore impressed with the legal-formal approach that the UN adopts. Such an approach ignores important political questions and overlooks the continuing reports of human rights violations in states that are parties to the Covenants. The increasing number of ratifications and accessions to the Covenants may be an important step in signalling that human rights are increasingly gaining acceptance as a legitimate issue of concern for the whole of the international community. However, the high optimism of some authors would perhaps be better reserved for a time when international actors demonstrate through their actions a willingness to promote and implement human rights. The tendency of most states to accept a formal commitment to human rights by acknowledging the existence of international law, while simultaneously rejecting all but the weakest and unchallenging methods of implementation, does not inspire confidence. As Donnelly asserts, 'the move to implementation or enforcement involves a major qualitative jump that most states strongly resist — usually successfully'.[48]

While international publics seek ways of expressing their commitment to human rights through the activities of nongovernmental organisations, the media and domestic political processes, a state's response can be assessed through the importance it affords human rights in its foreign policy. While the United States continued to maintain its policy of not ratifying any legally binding commitment to human rights, it attempted to promote itself as the foremost exemplar of human rights. Therefore, US foreign policy on human rights remains an important indicator of how seriously states take their commitment to human rights. It is to this that we must now turn. The Presidency of Jimmy Carter is of particular interest here because it demonstrates the difficulties governments have in fulfilling their duties as protectors of the national interest while simultaneously attempting to respond to the growing pressure to accept responsibility for promoting the human dignity of peoples everywhere.

FOREIGN POLICY, DOMESTIC POLITICS AND HUMAN RIGHTS

Policy makers in the United States and elsewhere have long held that a government's obligations are confined to its own peoples and territory.[49] This has been interpreted to mean that the civil and political rights of the citizens of other states should play no part in foreign policy calculations. Furthermore, this has been understood to absolve rich states from a duty to help poor members of international society in their struggle for economic development. However, a growing consciousness that we now live in an increasingly interdependent world, encouraged by the rise of transnational communications, has increased the demand for action on human rights. This has meant that while governments might prefer to invoke traditional reasons for conducting foreign policy, unimpaired by moral concerns for the destiny of the world's peoples, it is now impossible to escape the human rights implications of foreign policy. For example, while in 1973 Secretary of State Henry Kissinger was offering the view to the Senate Committee of Foreign Relations that he believed it dangerous for the United States to make the domestic policy of other countries a direct objective of American foreign policy, the House Foreign Relations Sub-Committee was preparing a report regretting that human rights played so little part in foreign policy calculations.

Attempts to reconcile the tensions between traditional foreign policy concerns and the demand for human rights are instructive when considering the importance that states attach to human rights. As John Vincent has argued, today 'when reference is made in contemporary international politics to the notion of international legitimacy, something more is meant than a 'kings peace' of sovereign states maintained by refraining from intervention.[50] These tensions are reflected at both the domestic and international level. While it is difficult to maintain a clear distinction between these two levels, attempting to do so helps give an insight into how seriously governments take the international obligation to promote human rights in other countries. For governments of powerful hegemonic states, particularly those like the United States, with its historic commitment to the cause of human rights, the demand to take action against those who violate human rights comes from both their own publics and those in other countries.

A recurrent theme of this book has been the historic need felt by the American people to project their own ideological and moral superiority into almost every aspect of international politics. At the time the Covenants were reaching the necessary number of ratifications to enter into international law, the prestige, status and self-esteem of the American people were at a particularly low ebb following defeat in Vietnam and the aftermath of Watergate. With the growth of the civil rights movement, these factors encouraged significant sections of the American public to press for greater consideration to be given to human rights in foreign policy.

Following the end of the Vietnam War both domestic and international publics began to question foreign policy actions that lacked moral content.[51] Many people saw the Vietnam war as an abdication of American moral leadership and a denial of the values upon which the ideological battles of the Cold War had been fought. This stimulated a debate about the nature and purpose of foreign policy in a democratic state with responsibilities and obligations in almost all regions of the globe.[52] In the United States this raised questions about the relationship between the executive and the legislature, where the legislature were more in tune with generally held societal values. President Carter attempted to articulate these worries when he claimed that the Vietnam war had produced a profound moral crisis, 'sapping worldwide faith in our own policy and our system of life'.[53]

Secondly, the Watergate affair demonstrated that those entrusted with preserving and promoting the values of freedom and democracy throughout the world were also corrupt. How then could any United States government justify its role as the defender of human rights and the enemy of corrupt and unjust regimes throughout the world? Importantly, how could the United States claim moral and ideological superiority against the communist world when its own leaders were exposed as equally unscrupulous? Domestic publics began to question cherished beliefs about being American in a way unknown in postwar years; even though the power of public opinion and a free press proved sufficient to bring down the holder of the most powerful office in the world. In short, the American people came to believe that 'Watergate was something done to people by government out of control'.[54] Thus, Watergate raised questions about ethical behaviour at all levels of government. Congressional legislation on human rights was 'founded partly on negative reactions to Nixon and Kissinger' but also 'on negative reactions to the global containment of communism in Vietnam.'[55] This being said, enthusiasm for human rights as a legitimate foreign policy concern during the 1970s was not confined to the United States alone. As Mazrui has argued, the American people's demand for human rights in this period also reflected changes in normative expectations within all western publics in favour of higher standards of integrity from governments and their officials.[56]

Thirdly, several US interest groups campaigned for United States' action on human rights in several areas of the world. The reasons behind such action have been looked at earlier in chapter 2, where the tensions in United States' political culture between liberalism and rights claims were discussed.[57] These tensions were reflected in the House Foreign Relations Sub-Committee on International Organisation, sitting in late 1973. This Sub-committee noted that the Administration's attitude towards moral considerations in foreign relations did not reflect the central concerns of significant sections of the American public:

> The human rights factor is not accorded the high priority it deserves in our country's foreign policy. Unfortunately, the prevailing attitude has led the United States into embracing governments which practice torture and unabashedly violate almost every human rights guarantee pronounced by the world community. ... [The] consideration of human rights in foreign policy is both morally imperative and practically necessary.[58]

Such support for human rights eventually led to the policies of linking aid and trade with human rights, which are discussed below.

Two brief examples will illustrate how the links between domestic politics, human rights and foreign policy were exploited by important domestic lobbies. First, as James Mayall has pointed out, Carter was the first American President to owe a political debt to black voters.[59] Attracted by Carter's civil rights credentials, black voters and other civil rights activists, expected the debt to be repaid. In particular, Carter was expected to take foreign policy action on apartheid in South Africa. However, disillusionment soon set in, though Carter had given a central place to human rights in his presidential campaign. Upon gaining office the Carter Administration showed ambivalence on the imposition of sanctions and failed to influence the policy of international banks.

A further example is seen in legislation enacted by Congress that linked the granting of certain types of foreign aid to improvements in human rights in communist countries, particularly the USSR. The Jewish lobby was successful in promoting the importance of United States–Israeli relations, generally as a Middle East question but more specifically for protecting the interests of the Jewish people everywhere. In response to this lobby Congress passed two Bills aimed at putting pressure on the USSR to ease its restrictions on the rate of Jewish emigration so that by 1988 over 25,000 were allowed to leave.[60] The first of these was the Jackson–Vanik amendment (Title IV of the Trade Act, 1974). This forbade the granting of Most Favoured Nation status and Export–Import Bank trade credits and guarantees to countries with non-market economic systems if the president believed that the policies of such countries denied citizens the right to emigrate. The second Bill, which became known as the Stevenson Amendment, placed an annual limit of $75 million on trade credits granted to the USSR by the Import–Export Bank, again in an effort to force a change in emigration policy. Therefore, while Jackson-Vanik offered incentives to improve emigration policy, the Stevenson Amendment offered nothing.

It is clear that Carter's campaign to become President was influenced by public demand that the United States give greater attention to international human rights, although scholars are not in agreement that public opinion plays any part in the formulation of foreign policy.[61] This is clear when examining the history of Carter's policy on human rights. Instead of being the well developed and prepared policy it purported to be, it seems to have emerged very late in the nomination process for the Democratic candidacy. During the discussions of the Democratic platform drafting committee the advisers to both Jackson and McGovern, the other two candidates in the race for the Democratic nomination, tabled proposals that featured human rights.

Both proposed that, in future, foreign aid be conditional on potential recipients demonstrating progress in the field of human rights, with McGovern targeting right wing dictatorships and Jackson socialist and communist governments. Carter's advisers, on the other hand, appear to have been somewhat neutral, 'giving the impression of not having heard very much about the matter [of human rights] before and not having any particular views'.[62] According to Daniel Moynihan, Jackson's representative on the committee, the result was a compromise where each side agreed to be against the dictators that the other side disliked the most.[63] Therefore, Carter seems to have played a minimal role in the evolution of a the Democratic party's human rights foreign policy.

This left the Carter Administration with a popular policy, strong on rhetoric and generalisations, but less than fully developed. This often led to members of the Administration making contradictory statements on the conduct of diplomacy, so that other countries remained confused over American intentions and were often unable to give their full support. Similarly, distinguished career diplomats remained uncertain of their role and unable to develop programmes for implementing policy. Furthermore, the rhetoric of human rights exposed the difficulty of responding to demands inherent in the traditional role of the state while simultaneously responding to public feeling over the rationale for the founding of America itself. This was a problem that Eisenhower would have readily recognised. These contradictions and tensions remained unresolved because the Carter Administration had given so little thought to human rights in foreign policy before taking office.

FOREIGN POLICY, HUMAN RIGHTS AND INTERNATIONAL ACTION

John Vincent has identified three factors that mitigate against a successful human rights foreign policy. These are the need to ensure security, the imperative to prevent any one issue from impeding the normal processes of diplomacy and the economic imperative, particularly the need to continue trade.[64] Carter soon found that all three of these factors took priority over his human rights aims and restricted his ability to act.

The low self-esteem engendered by Vietnam and Watergate also brought increasing fears that other countries would perceive the United States as weakened and morally bankrupt. These perceptions were heightened further as the period of containment and confrontation that characterised the Cold War moved to a period of détente, including the tacit acceptance of the USSR as an equal partner in global affairs. Equality, after all, drew attention to the fact that the United States was not the single most powerful state. The central symbol of this equality was the SALT agreement that would leave both sides with roughly equal capabilities in nuclear weapons. Accordingly, a strong human rights policy became an attractive idea for asserting the moral superiority of American ideology. It avoided further perceptions of decline and showed that an arms control agreement had been negotiated from a position of strength.[65] In the words of Warren Christopher, spoken towards the end of Carter's Presidency, human rights 'gives us a way of taking the ideological initiative, instead of merely reacting'.[66] Sensitive to the view that the USSR was an equal partner in world affairs, Carter denied any 'relationship between the human rights decision ... and matters affecting our defense or SALT negotiations'. Furthermore, he asserted that there was no 'connection between the two in the minds of the Soviets'.[67]

Two methods for promoting human rights through foreign policy were emphasised by Carter: security assistance and economic aid. The first of these sought to invoke the provisions of Section 502B of the Foreign Assistance Act (FAA), which proscribes security assistance to 'any country the government of which engages in a consistent pattern of gross violations of internationally recognised human rights'. Following the 1974 report of the House Sub-Committee on International Organisation, which expressed concern over foreign governments using security assistance to oppress their peoples, Congress sought through 502B to amend the FAA and make security assistance conditional on a government's human rights record. The wording of 502B drew significantly from the language of existing international law on human rights. This was done deliberately to stress that the USA was merely implementing internationally accepted norms and thus avoid the criticism that it was imposing its own will on others.[68] Only under 'extraordinary circumstances' that threatened the national interest could the President continue assistance to a country despite known violations of human rights. Furthermore, the President retained the power to lift the prohibition on arms sales when he judged that a country's human rights record showed 'significant improvements'. Hence, 502B was an attempt to solve some problems familiar to supporters of the Bricker Amendment: finding a balance between the preservation of Presidential powers in foreign policy and the United States' historic concern for human rights.

However, conscious of the needs of security and trade, the drafters of 502B included several loopholes where Presidential discretion could be exercised in legitimately disregarding its provisions. First, the term 'consistent patterns' of violation allows the interpretation that if a government shows some progress in improving existing measures for protecting human rights, 'patterns' of violations were no longer 'consistent' and therefore not within the requirements of 502B. For example, the killing of over a hundred thousand people during the Indonesian invasion of East Timor, and the imprisonment of countless thousands more, was not defined as a 'consistent pattern' of violations because Indonesia promised to release all the prisoners within three years. Secondly, the notorious 'extraordinary circumstances' condition provides an opportunity for the President to avoid the application of 502B on grounds of national interest and the strategic necessity to support a government known to engage in gross violations. Examples where 'extraordinary circumstances' have been invoked include South Korea and the Philippines. Thirdly, 502B requires that security assistance be withheld from countries the 'government of which' engages in human rights violation. This has been interpreted as though the government must authorise the violations; thus absolving those adjudged not completely in control of the activities of their military or police. Lastly, exactly what assistance can be defined as a 'defence article' and therefore within the terms of the Act remains open ended. This meant that the Department of Commerce, charged with the task of classifying equipment as either military or civilian, has often undermined the intentions of 502B.[69]

In practice, while 502B may demonstrate continued interest in finding ways of implementing human rights, the traditional view prevails that a state's social and political environments remain a domestic affair. From the beginning the response to 502B was disappointing, principally because of the attitude of Secretary of State Kissinger towards human rights. Later, Congressional supporters of 502B grew more sceptical about the possibility of compelling the US government to comply. This was for two reasons. First, in common with past Presidents, Carter soon came to understand that naming the perpetrators of gross violations through refusing export assistance, or the 'exceptional situation' provision, was not compatible with maintaining diplomatic and foreign policy flexibility. Second, as the chill of the Cold War increased during the mid-1970s, the need to maintain strategic relationships with client states, unhindered by complex domestic issues of human rights, again became an imperative of foreign policy.[70] Applying the letter of 502B meant publicly castigating allies or potential allies by refusing security aid on grounds of human rights, risking important strategic relationships, and damaging diplomatic ties important to the conduct of the Cold War.

For all the rhetoric of the Carter Administration, human rights quickly resumed a secondary place in foreign policy.[71] As for 502B, it was never applied with any rigour to deny security assistance to potentially friendly (i.e., anti-communist) countries. Indeed, even when Carter's Secretary of State, Cyrus Vance, did fail to approve security assistance, he was careful to avoid any suggestion that this was in response to 502B. For example, the

Department of Commerce classified $25 million worth of helicopters as civilian aid, although they were used for military purposes by the Guatemalan Air Force.[72] The existence of 502B is therefore largely symbolic. The most successful outcome of 502B is the requirement to prepare Country Reports. The significance of the Reports is that they offer those with an interest in human rights a focus for arguments over United States' support for human rights violators.[73] However, 502B has made little contribution towards promoting rights, except perhaps as a political symbol that the United States retains its historic interest in internationally recognised human rights. Importantly, Country Reports reflect the ideological limitations on US attitudes towards human rights by their failure to mention economic and social rights.[74]

A second method for promoting human rights that received some attention in United States' foreign policy is the link between economic aid and a country's human rights. This has taken one of two forms: bilateral and multilateral.

Bilaterally, Congress made a further amendment to the Foreign Assistance Act in 1975 that restricted economic assistance to any country that displayed a 'consistent pattern of gross violations of internationally recognised human rights' unless 'such assistance will directly benefit the needy people in such country'.[75] However, as with security assistance the impact of these restrictions has been limited and the amendment has been invoked rarely. For example, although the United States Agency for International Development (AID) supported a policy of applying human rights criteria to economic assistance, this policy has not been implemented.[76] Again, although this offers an increased profile on which human rights activists can focus, bilateral economic restrictions on aid do not seem to have brought any real results.

Attempts to link multilateral aid to human rights have already been mentioned above. Although Section 701 of the International Financial Institutions Act requires United States' representatives to institutions like the International Bank for Reconstruction and Development, the International Development Fund and the Inter-American Development Bank to vote against loans to governments engaged in gross violations of human rights, exceptions can be made in cases where aid is judged to benefit a needy community directly. Two factors militate against the United States achieving results from this requirement. First, the constitutions of the international banks allow them to take decisions on loans on economic grounds only. Secondly, even when United States' representatives have voted against loans to countries that are known violators of human rights they have usually found themselves in the minority and therefore unable to influence decisions.[77]

Carter's human rights policies remained unfulfilled for four reasons. First, he soon discovered that the interests of human rights frequently conflicted with other, more traditionally held views of the purpose of foreign policy, like security and trade. He also discovered that human rights interfered with diplomacy, and the United States' ability to maintain or create friendly relations with other countries. Second, at a time in the history of the United States when national confidence and self-esteem were low, placing human rights at the top of the foreign policy agenda seemed an attractive option. However, as both Roosevelt and Eisenhower had discovered before, support for human rights could not be reconciled with ideological imperatives. Third, the policy of trading off aid for improvements in human rights seemed to many a case of 'moral imperialism' that did nothing to cement important strategic relationships with less developed countries. Fourth, and following from the last point, there remained an inherent contradiction in attempts to promote political and civil rights through withholding aid, which many less developed states saw as a right that placed a duty on the rich to assist the poor.[78]

CONCLUSION

This chapter has attempted to examine the development of decision-making procedures in the creation of a human rights regime. It set out the options discussed by the Commission on Human Rights. An examination of these options showed that although many states were prepared to engage in drafting nonbinding declarations, and following protracted negotiations to enshrine those standards in international law, they remained irresolute when determining methods of implementation. Four reasons can be identified for this reluctance. First, the principles of the regime — including the state as the central actor, non-intervention and domestic jurisdiction — mean that no authority higher than the state will gain legitimacy. Second, although states acknowledged that enforcement procedures for international law remain weak, they nevertheless recognised international law as an important institution of international society. Therefore, entering into binding agreements that would almost certainly be ignored by the majority presented the possibility of weakening a prized international institution. The only possible way of avoiding this was to agree to the weakest form of implementation. Third, while in formal terms political and socio-economic rights are indivisible, industrialised western states stressed the former while the majority of states in the General Assembly increasingly stressed the latter. This increased uncertainty over the nature of rights and caused confusion and conflict over which sets of rights should be implemented. Fourth, strong regimes emerge in response to perceived conflicts of interest where outcomes remain confused and uncertain. These conditions encourage states to negotiate and bargain in processes of regime building. However, through these processes states may begin to gain a greater insight into the issue that the regime is intended to order, i.e., the advantages and disadvantages of entering into a regime become clearer. Accordingly, attempts to build a regime may never succeed beyond processes for determining principles and norms because increased awareness of the issue makes states reluctant to accept binding rules and decision-making procedures.

Taking the United States as potentially the most influential member of the human rights regime, the second part of the chapter looked at the problems states have in attempting to promote internationally recognised standards of human rights through their own foreign policy. While some success can be claimed by the Carter Administration in elevating human rights in the consciousness of international publics, in all other areas success was at best limited. The underlying reasons for this can be found in several familiar difficulties that formed the core of the debate on human rights since the issue first came to prominence in the United Nations. These difficulties include finding a set of generally accepted norms that do not privilege one set of rights over another, reconciling universal and international principles and identifying appropriate methods for promoting human rights within foreign policy. As discussed above, Carter's human rights policy was largely the outcome of domestic politics. It resulted in an open ended, declaratory policy lacking in detail and with little substance.

At the end of the Carter Presidency American pride received a further blow as a result of the Iranian Revolution, which was a consequence, in part, of the inconsistent application of human rights policy.[79] The image of a weak and impotent America, graphically portrayed in the photographs of Carter at his Oval Office desk as he devoted the last remaining days of his Presidency to the task of gaining the release of the Teheran hostages, did little to win the admiration of either domestic publics or foreign governments. Similarly, as the SALT negotiations showed increasing signs of failure, and confusion grew over Carter's vacillations in using human rights as an instrument of stick and carrot diplomacy, the Administration looked increasingly weak and indecisive. Like other Presidents before him, Carter's attempt to develop an exemplary model of foreign policy that took full account of the demand for human rights failed to inspire confidence.

NOTES

1. Daniel P Moynihan, 'The politics of human rights', *Commentary*, 64:2, August 1977, pp. 19-26.
2. The *Department of State Bulletin*, for example, shows the following number of headings under human rights for the early 1970s: 1971 (8); 1972 (4); 1973 (4); 1974 (7); 1975 (11); 1976 (5). However, for the year 1977 there are 26 main headings and over 20 sub-headings.
3. David P Forsythe, *Human Rights and World Politics*, (University of Nebraska Press, Lincoln, 1989), ch. 5.
4. Karl E Birnbaum and Ingo Peters, 'The CSCE: a reassessment of its force in the 1980s', *Review of International Studies*, 16:4, 1990, p. 309.
5. See, for example, Dominic McGoldrick, *The Human Rights Committee*, (Clarendon Press, Oxford, 1991); M E Tardu, 'United Nations responses to gross violations of human rights: The 1503 Procedure' *Santa Clara Law Review*, vol. 20, 1980, pp. 553-601; B G Ramcharan, 'Implementing the International Covenants on Human Rights', in B G Ramcharan, *Human Rights: Thirty Years After the Universal Declaration*, (Nijhoff, The Hague, 1979), pp. 159-95; Dana Fisher, 'Reporting under the Covenant on Civil and Political Rights: The first five years of the Human Rights Committee', *American Journal of International Law*, vol. 70, 1982, pp. 142-53.
6. See letter to Mrs Roosevelt, 6 December 1947, Roosevelt Library, Hyde Park, New York, box no. 4588.
7. See, for example, letter to Mrs Roosevelt from Durward V Sandifer, Chief of the Division of International Organization Affairs, 29 January 1947; telegram from Department of State, 30th January 1947, both in box no. 4592, Roosevelt Library, ibid.
8. A typical example of this is Dorothy V Jones, *Codes of Peace: Ethics and Security in the World of Warlord States*, (University of Chicago, Chicago, 1991).
9. Philip Alston, 'The Commission on Human Rights', in P Alston (ed), *The United Nations and Human Rights: A Critical Appraisal*, (Clarendon Press, Oxford, 1990), pp. 126-210.
10. *Yearbook of the United Nations — 1948-49*, (Dept of Public Information, UN, New York), p. 539.
11. Antonio Cassese, *International Law in a Divided World*, (Clarendon Press, Oxford, 1986), pp. 288-91. The two found guilty of crimes against humanity at Nuremberg were Streicher and Schriach.
12. These are known as the 'Lawless' case (ECHR), series A, at 1, (1961), and the 'De Becker' case (ECHR), series A, at 1, (1962).
13. A Glen Mower, 'Implementing United Nations Covenants', in A A Said (ed), *Human Rights and World Politics*, (Praeger Publishers, New York, 1978), p. 112.
14. For a report on the final debates on the High Commissioner for Refugees and the 'Status of the Office of the United Nations High Commissioner for Refugees' see *The Yearbook of the United Nations — 1950*, (Department of Public Information, New York, 1951), pp. 581-87.
15. GAOR, 5th Session, Third Committee, 300th Meeting.

16. For a full account of the debate to create a High Commissioner for Human Rights see Roger Stenson Clark, *A United Nations High Commissioner for Human Rights*, (Nijhoff, The Hague, 1972), ch. 5.

17. For examples of such arguments see GAOR, Eight Session, Third Committee, 522nd meeting.

18. For an example of this, see the remarks of Mr Panyushkin (USSR), GAOR, Fifth Session (1950), Third Committee, 300th Meeting, p. 194.

19. For example, Mrs Lindstrom (Sweden), p. 191, Mr Pratt De Maria (Uruguay), p. 192, and Mrs Menon (India), p. 198, all in GAOR, Third Committee, 300th Session, 1950.

20. See speech by Mrs Roosevelt (USA), GAOR, 1950, Third Committee, p. 191-2.

21. In 1976, just prior to the first meeting of the Human Rights Committee, a method of implementation known as the 1503 procedure was put into place. Under this procedure complaints of violations received by any UN body were presented in summary form to a working group. If the working group accepted that 'consistent patterns' of 'gross violations' are taking place they can recommend a 'thorough study'. The differences between this procedure and the Optional Protocol are twofold. First, the 1503 procedure remains at the level of a report while the Optional Protocol is intended as an attempt to redress a violation. Second, the 1503 procedure focuses on 'persistent patterns' of 'gross violations', not on the cases of individuals. Now that the Committee is functioning the 1503 procedure is less significant. See, M E Tardu, op. cit.

22. McGoldrick, op. cit., p. 98. See also Torkel Opsahl, 'Instruments of implementation of human rights', *Human Rights Law Journal*, 10:1, 1989, pp. 13-33, and Fischer, op. cit.

23. Report of the Human Rights Committee, UN doc. A/39/40, 1985, para. 139. See also *Review of the International Commission of Jurists*, No. 33, 1984, p. 39. The Committee has repeatedly asked the government of Guinea to send a representative so that their report could be considered, but went ahead following the failure of the fifth request.

24. Report of the Human Rights Committee, UN doc. A/34/40, 1979, para. 112.

25. McGoldrick, op.cit., p. 50.

26. UN Doc. CCPR/C/SR.861 (1988).

27. McGoldrick, op. cit., pp. 202-6.

28. Tardu, op. cit. While Tardu estimates that the number of complaints received at the UN in 1971 was in the region of 20,000, in 1990 Bert Ramcharan estimated that this had increased to about 35,000. Interview, University of Prince Edward Island, Prince Edward Island, Canada, 20th July, 1990.

29. Tom Farer, 'The United Nations and human rights: More than a whimper, less than a roar', *Human Rights Quarterly*, vol. 9, 1987, pp. 550-86,

30. Cindy A Cohn, 'The early harvest: Domestic legal changes related to the Human Rights Committee and the Covenant on Civil and Political Rights', *Human Rights Quarterly*, 3:3, 1991, p. 32.

31. David Forsythe, 'Socio-economic human rights: The United Nations, the United States, and beyond', *Human Rights Quarterly*, 4:4, 1982, p. 434.

32. For a description of early progress on implementing economic, social and cultural rights see Ramcharan, op. cit. The recommended stages for submitting reports relate to specific Articles: i) Articles 6-9; ii) Articles 10-12; and iii) Articles 13-15.

33. ECOSOC res. 1985/17, 28th May, 1985.

34. John Carey (ed), *United Nations Law Reports*, (Walker and Co., New York, 1987), pp. 47-50.
35. *Review of the International Commission of Jurists*, No. 40, 1988, p. 22,
36. Torkel Opsahl, 'Instruments of implementation of human rights', *Human Rights Law Journal*, 10:1, 1989, p. 33.
37. Fischer, op. cit., pp. 146-7, argues that the Committee could not achieve what little it has achieved without the informal consultations with non-governmental organisations that many Committee members enjoy.
38. McGoldrick, op. cit., p. 102.
39. Opsahl, op. cit.
40. Cassese, op. cit., p. 293.
41. UN. Doc. A/res/2054A(XX), 1967.
42. International Convention on the Suppression and Punishment of the Crime of Apartheid, General Assembly resolution 3068(XXVIII), 1976. The Commission also passed a resolution on 1st March, 1976 that 'strongly condemned the attitude of any country which, by its political, military, economic and other forms of assistance, became an accomplice in apartheid and racial discrimination'.
43. Howard Tolley, *The United Nations Commission on Human Rights*, (Westview Press, London, 1987), p. 69.
44. Alexander Johnston, 'Weak states and national security: The case of South Africa in the era of total strategy', *Review of International Studies*, 17:2, 1991, pp. 149-66.
45. Tolley, op. cit., p. 69.
46. Martin Wight, *System of States*, (Leicester University Press, Leicester, 1977), p. 170.
47. Carey, op. cit., p. 295.
48. Jack Donnelly, 'International human rights: a regime approach', *International Organisation*, 40:3, 1986. p. 633.
49. For example, George F Kennan, 'Morality and foreign policy', *Foreign Affairs*, vol. 64:2, 1985, pp. 205-18.
50. R J Vincent, *Human Rights and International Relations*, (Cambridge University Press, Cambridge, 1986), p. 130.
51. For arguments concerning the importance of the Vietnam War and Watergate to the rise of human rights as a central issue for American foreign policy see Mark L Schneider, 'A new administration's new policy: the rise of power of human rights', in P G Brown and D Maclean (eds), *Human Rights and US Foreign Policy*, (Lexington Books, Lexington, 1979), pp. 3-13 and James Mayall, 'The United States', in R J Vincent (ed), *Foreign Policy and Human Rights*, (CUP, Cambridge, 1986), pp. 165-87.
52. For a recent discussion of the nature of democracy in an increasingly 'globalised' world see David Held (ed), *Prospects for Democracy*, (Polity Press, Oxford, 1992), particularly the introductory chapter by Held.
53. Jimmy Carter, speech at Notre Dame University, South Bend, Indiana, 22nd May, 1977.
54. Schneider, op. cit., p. 4.
55. David P Forsythe, *Human Rights and World Politics*, (University of Nebraska Press, Lincoln, 1989), p. 110.
56. Ali Mazrui, 'Human rights and the three worlds of power', *Round Table*, July, 1978, pp. 207-21.

57. Max L Stackhouse, *Creeds, Society and Human Rights*, (William B Eerdman, Grand Rapids, 1984). Stackhouse argues that the call for human rights reflected a breakdown of family life and society, together with concern for increasing government interference in almost all aspects of life.
58. Quoted in Stephen B Cohen, 'Conditioning the US security assistance on human rights practices', *American Journal of International Law*, vol.76, 1982, pp.264-79.
59. James Mayall, 'The United States', in Vincent, *Foreign Policy* op. cit., p. 184.
60. Lawyers Committee for Human Rights, *Linking Security Assistance and Human Rights*, (Project Series, New York, 1988).
61. For a discussion of the impact of domestic policy issues on foreign policy see B C Cohen, *The Public Impact on Foreign Policy*, (Lenham, University Press of America, 1983) and B B Hughes, *The Domestic Context of American Foreign Policy*, (San Francisco, W H Freeman, 1978).
62. Moynihan, op. cit., p. 19.
63. ibid. p. 22.
64. Vincent, *Human Rights* op. cit., pp. 132-37.
65. John Muravchik, The Uncertain Crusade: Jimmy carter and the Dilemma of Human Rights Policy, (Hamilton Press, London, 1986), ch. 7.
66. Warren Christopher, speech to the American Bar Association, 4th August, 1980.
67. Jimmy Carter, *Department of State Bulletin*, 30th June, 1977.
68. Lawyers Committee, op. cit., p. 17.
69. ibid., p. 24.
70. David Forsythe, *Human Rights and US Foreign Policy*, (University of Nebraska Press, London, 1987), p. 56.
71. Muravchik, op. cit.
72. Cohen, op. cit., p. 265.
73. Lawyers Committee, op. cit.
74. One explicit example of this is the introduction to the Department of State 'Reports on Human Rights Practices for 1981', Washington, 1981. This reads: 'Internationally recognised human rights can be grouped into broad categories: first, the right to be free from governmental violations of the integrity of the person....second, the right to enjoy civil and political rights'. There is no mention of economic, social and cultural rights.
75. Foreign Assistance Act, Section 116(a), sometimes referred to as the Harkin Amendment. In 1977 Congress imposed a similar restriction to the Food for Peace Program.
76. Lawyers Committee, op. cit.
77. Forsythe, 'Socioeconomic human rights', op. cit.
78. Sidney Weinberg, 'Human rights and basic needs in United States foreign aid policy', in P R Newberg, *The Politics of Human Rights*, (New York University Press, London, 1980), pp. 217-48.
79. R K Ramazani, *The United States and Iran*, (London, Praeger, 1982). Ramazani argues that the strategic importance of Iran to the United States meant that a blind eye was turned to the excess of the Shah's secret police. See also, Noel O'Sullivan, *Revolutionary Theory and Political Reality*, (London, Harvester Press, 1983), ch. 11.

7 Conclusion and Speculation

Human rights are now the most prominent idea in the rhetoric of international relations, except perhaps for democracy. This book has investigated the progress made during the last fifty years in turning this idea into something more than a slogan. Human rights lend themselves to regime analysis because international regimes are themselves understood to be normative structures. For most authors the existence of the Commission on Human Rights, the Universal Declaration of Human Rights, the major Covenants and the machinery for dealing with violations of human rights are sufficient to demonstrate the existence of a regime. According to the optimists, a regime already exists. However, for all this activity, and contrary to the optimists' claims, torture, political arrests, disappearances, wilful starvation and other gross violations of human rights remain common in many parts of the world. On the one hand the idea of human rights has become one of the most powerful political images of modern times, while on the other, and for all the activities of the United Nations and other international fora, little has been achieved in response to that image.

It was acknowledged that the regime concept lent itself to several interpretations from the outset. At one extreme found in the literature — referred to here as the statist discourse — international regimes reflect traditional thinking on international relations. That is to say, international regimes exist within the realm of a world of unitary state actors each engaged in the exercise of power maximisation. According to this model, to the extent that they exist at all, regimes are little more than formally constituted structures in which dominant state actors promote and maintain the rules and procedures that best suit their interests. International regimes are understood merely as arenas for acting out power relationships. Conceptualised in this way the idea of regimes has little to offer over what can be discovered through traditional, state-centric and interest-based means of analysis. Regimes are neither autonomous nor intervening variables: they do not have a life of their own nor do they affect international outcomes in any significant way.

A more subtle version of the statist discourse argues that regimes are an attempt to articulate the general obligations that guide state actions and should be understood as 'something more than temporary arrangements that change with every shift of power'.[1] In this approach states remain self-interested utility maximisers engaged in a continuous process of sifting possible alternative actions for maximising their own welfare. However, in an international environment characterised by both anarchy and interdependence, the single-minded pursuit of self-interest often leads to sub-optimal outcomes. Entering a regime therefore becomes a rational choice in areas of international life where complexity and uncertainty represent a challenge to expectations. Regimes are the outcome of bargaining and negotiating processes in which utility maximisers, cognisant that the environment in which they operate denies any possibility of achieving preferred options through self-help, adopt instead a strategy of 'satisficing'. Although this approach to regimes often displays some ambivalence towards the identity of the central actors in international regimes — acknowledging, for example, that regime rules are commonly directed at regulating the behaviour of non-state actors — the approach remains predominantly state-centric and concerned with formalised arrangements between states.

Opposed to this version of regimes is a cosmopolitan discourse. Those who employ this approach maintain that regimes are an unavoidable feature of international life. Indeed, they argue that '[w]e live in a world of international regimes'[2] and that 'regimes exist in all areas of international relations, even those such as major power rivalry, that are traditionally looked upon as clear-cut examples of anarchy'.[3] Cosmopolitans stress the social context of international regimes. They argue that actors are necessarily constrained by rules and norms when engaged in any social practice. These rules and norms should not be understood as empirical facts. Rather, they are the beliefs, values, expectations, mores and convictions about what is moral or legitimate in the context of the social situation in which actors are participating. Thus, in this approach it is possible to argue that a purely formal understanding of regimes — one that concentrates solely on formal bargaining and negotiating processes, legal rules and concrete international organisation — does not take proper account of the prevailing social environment as a determining factor of outcomes.[4] Indeed, cosmopolitans would argue that formalism deflects attention away from the part played by a variety of nongovernmental, domestic and transnational actors who collectively contribute to the social environment in which international relations is practised. Although states remain significant actors in regimes, cosmopolitans argue that regimes cannot be understood without taking proper account of domestic and transnational actors, since both influence the bargaining positions of state negotiators engaged in forming and maintaining regimes.

The diversity of interpretations placed on regime theory makes it open to the criticism of being all things to all theorists. However, in the case of human rights diversity can be a positive asset for it allows an insight into a central paradox of human rights. This is that countless millions of people throughout the world cannot secure their rights, though the idea of human rights has achieved near ubiquitous acclaim. Those who follow the statist approach to a human rights regime are inevitably optimists and point to a wealth of international law, legal argument, constitutions, and the activities of the United Nations and its agencies as evidence that the regime is operating successfully. Opposed to this are the pessimists who point to the continued violations of political and economic rights in Burundi, Indonesia, the Sudan and the former Yugoslavia. Pessimists argue that the statist approach to a human rights regime provides states with powerful political symbols that 'allow[s] everybody to declare themselves in favour of truth, beauty, goodness and world community'[5] but does not necessarily offer an insight into the way states and their peoples will actually respond in particular circumstances. The argument presented here is that regime theory allows a reconciliation of the optimists and pessimists by giving us an insight into the politics of human rights, as diplomats, governments and domestic and international interest groups struggle to respond to the idea of human rights.

Through an examination of the principles, norms, rules and decision-making procedures that constitute the human rights regime, the complex relationship between the idea of human rights emphasised by the optimists, and the failure to take any significant action to protect human rights emphasised by the pessimists, is brought into perspective. Although the tension between the principles of 'universalism' and 'internationalism' still haunts efforts to secure human rights, there is little doubt that 'internationalism' remains the dominant idea in international political thought and action. President Roosevelt and others raised the expectations of the world's peoples by using human rights imagery in speeches written to justify United States' involvement in the Second World War. These expectations were further reinforced as both the United States and the USSR sought to use their divergent approaches to human rights as a powerful weapon in Cold War politics. As the less developed states became the majority group in the Assembly, the call for universal human rights reinforced their demand for self-determination and the creation of a more egalitarian international economic system. However, the necessity to revise the principles of international society in order to secure human rights was resisted consistently. The response of most states to the growing demand for human rights remained at the level of rhetoric. This position remains unaltered today. Although there is much talk of a new post-Cold War order, this order remains an order of sovereign states.

Although there is little doubt that the Universal Declaration of Human Rights represents the most widely accepted expression of international human rights norms, and is therefore the strongest element of the regime, its status obscures continuing disagreements on what legitimately belongs in any list of rights. As discussed in chapter 3, the moral shock of Naziism, together with the image of protecting human rights as the rationale for engaging in the war, encouraged governments to seek a swift response to reassure the peoples of the world that such atrocities would not happen in future. This had several important effects on the future development of the regime. First, no time was given to questions that presented a challenge to the existing international system, for example, questions concerned with nonintervention, domestic jurisdiction and the state or individual as subjects of international law. Second, time constraints also meant that important philosophical questions to do with the nature of rights remained unresolved. In the context of the Cold War this was of particular significance. Third, as those engaged in developing the Declaration soon discovered, governments became increasingly uncertain about how human rights would impact on both their international and domestic politics. Although no state voted against the Declaration in the General Assembly this did not mean that full agreement on fundamental questions had been achieved. Consequently, although the Declaration assumes a central place in the debate on human rights, it does not represent the universal agreement on the norms of human rights that is often claimed.

The fundamental differences that began to emerge during the Declaration debate became more central once the Commission began work on developing the rules of the regime in the form of legally binding international law. With the emergence of the Cold War, and the gradual increase in the number of less developed states at the United Nations, human rights became increasingly politicised. Old disagreements that had surfaced during the Declaration debate were joined with new disputes that reflected the demands of less developed states. Included here were disagreements over self-determination, the right to economic development and the rights of peoples. Increasingly western states found themselves unable to retain control over lists of rights or over the definitions of particular rights.

This leads to a further conclusion concerning the role of hegemony in regime building. The presence of a hegemon is a necessary, if not sufficient, requirement for regime creation, as most regime theorists assert. It follows from this that the hegemon is in a position to obstruct the creation of any regime that does not serve its own purposes by failing to provide the resources necessary for regime creation. The United States of America found that it could not resist the challenge of the coalition of less developed and socialist states in the Assembly on human rights issues. As the regime emerged it took a form, content and character far removed from the limited liberal agenda set by the United States following the Second World War. Fearful of the challenge to racist, social and economic policies in many of the states, domestic interests embarked on a campaign to ensure that the United States would not ratify any legally binding agreement on human rights at all. The success of this campaign meant that hegemonic leadership was withdrawn, leaving the regime without an authoritative actor who could reconcile differences. Furthermore, doubts began to emerge concerning the limitations a human rights regime would impose upon the United States' ability to fulfil its new role as the dominant postwar power. The growing uncertainty over the international implications of entering a human rights regime, coupled with increasing domestic unrest over human rights, led the United States to withhold its support and thus deny the possibility of creating a strong human rights regime.[6]

Finally, methods of implementation have never received serious consideration. Even before the tensions between universal rights and the traditional principles of international relations emerged in the Declaration debate, few states seriously considered the possibility of setting up an institution like a High Commissioner for Human Rights or an International Court of Human Rights with potentially higher authority than the state. Such machinery that does exist often proves ineffectual, often deals with the least serious of violations and covers only a small percentage of complaints drawn to the attention of the United Nations.

This examination of the human rights regime suggests that none of the four components that define a regime exhibits evidence of widespread agreement among the members of international society. Changes to the principles of the international system to accommodate human rights are resisted by all states. Furthermore, the norms and rules of the regime are considered by many states to be incomplete. While statespeople and academics are prone to asserting that the two major Covenants on human rights are indivisible, and both now have an impressive number of ratifications, many western states pay little attention to economic and social rights, and resist any suggestion that this set of rights places a duty on them to assist less developed states. Finally, the only progress made in constructing machinery to ensure the implementation of universal human rights acts at the margins and is incapable of responding to gross violations that are widely reported.

The only conclusion that can be drawn from this perspective is that if a human rights regime can be said to exist at all then it is in the weakest of forms. However, the idea of human rights continues to attract the attention of peoples throughout the world. Evidence for this is seen in the growing number of organisations that devote all or part of their time to ensuring a dignified life for people everywhere. While states have often failed to make a satisfactory response to the demand for the promotion and protection of human rights, the activities of the United Nations continue to stimulate and strengthen further public interest. Furthermore, interest in the idea of human rights has been nourished by changes in social relations globally. Stimulated by technological improvements in communications, people are beginning to question first their own role in relation to their own immediate political community, and secondly their political community's role in relation to other political communities. This leads people to question established values that in previous periods helped define their social and political actions. In questioning these values people make a demand for greater participation in social and political spheres, which in turn is subversive of established institutionalised politics. The outcome of this is that ideas like human rights figure high on political agendas but fail to be realised.[7]

One way of addressing the tension between the demand for human rights and the inability of existing international political institutions to deliver satisfactory solutions to pressing human rights problems has been suggested by John Vincent. Vincent acknowledges that we are all now touched by the existence of a global economic system, and a global ecosystem, where our very survival is dependent upon our ability in the first instance to change our beliefs, expectations and values. This has increased our perceptions of the worth of the individual who, in order to claim economic, social and environmental rights, must accept responsibility for their own actions and for the actions of those officials who represent them beyond their borders. In this way international society, if not transformed, has at least yielded to modifications:

> It is not now enough for a state to be, and to be recognised as, sovereign. Nor is it enough for it to be a nation-state in accordance with the principles of self-determination. It must also act domestically so as not to offend against the basic rights of individuals and groups within its territory.[8]

Thus, Vincent claims that the rules of international society, which previously allowed each state to treat its own people in any way it saw fit, no longer apply. Intervention becomes legitimate, if only in a limited form. This is usually taken to mean support for popular movements opposed to a government that has lost all legitimacy, when suppression, genocide or enslavement is widely reported, or when counter intervention is justified to redress the balance after some other power has intervened without cause.[9] But even in these limited cases, intervention has often taken the form of ineffectual economic sanctions, or remained confined to the rhetoric of condemnation, often tinged with an air moral superiority. Mindful of this Vincent argues that 'any scheme for moral improvement has to find its way in this world of states',[10] and is cautious about claims that the call for human rights bears witness to an emerging cosmopolitan society. He rejects the idea that human rights represent a challenge to the existing state system and prefers instead to see rights claims as an addition to existing principles of international society. It is therefore not a revolutionary attack on the principles of sovereignty, but an additional attribute that helps define sovereignty in the contemporary international system. However the evidence presented here suggests that even Vincent's cautious approach may be an over-optimistic assessment of the progress made in the field of international human rights. While the idea of human rights has been encouraged through the development of new social relationships as Vincent argues, his conclusion that sovereignty is now in part defined by the acceptance of internationally recognised human rights seems premature.

This leaves the question of whether we can expect the human rights regime to gain in strength in the future. At present it seems that the call for human rights remains essentially a claim by individuals on their own state and not a call for a radical overhaul of the international system as a whole. As such, the analysis offered here suggests that human rights are unlikely to make any further progress as an issue that conditions the actions of international actors in any significant way. Indeed, if previous patterns of state behaviour over the promotion and protection of human rights are repeated, contrary to the view of many commentators, the state and state sovereignty will remain a barrier to progress in the field of human rights. However, now that the Cold War is over, the future of human rights may be undergoing renewed interest. In the same way that the Roosevelt Administration proclaimed a new world order following the end of the Second World War, President Bush proclaimed a new post-Cold War order that reflected the demand for democracy and human rights. It is worth concluding by speculating on the post-Cold War progress in the field of human rights, although the features that distinguish this new era from previous periods remain unclear.

A SPECULATION

Contradictions and tensions in the four defining features of the human rights regime have remained unresolved since human rights were first placed on the international political agenda at the end of the Second World War. The prospects for resolving these contradictions and tensions in the post-Cold War world are uncertain. Indeed, euphoria over the end of the Cold War promises to distract attention further from the failure to reconcile differences. The inclination to see all UN human rights activity as positive also leads to complacency and further encourages the tendency to overlook fundamental, unresolved problems. Indeed, the post-Cold War era has brought many problems that will confuse the project of universal human rights even more. Some of these problems suggest that the new post-Cold War world order may not offer the political and economic environment in which human rights can be secured, as President Bush and many other world leaders have tried to assert. The political, economic and social obstacles to furthering the project of universal human rights, that have existed since the founding of the United Nations, may present greater barriers than in the past, particularly now that the United States can claim to be the only superpower.

The most visible of these is the rise of nationalism. Since the collapse of the USSR, independence movements have emerged throughout eastern Europe, including the Solidarity movement in Poland, the movement to reunify Germany, independence movements in the old satellite states of the USSR, secessionist movements in the Russian Republics and nationalist movements in the former Yugoslavia. These activities have stimulated immense interest in a wide range of political and social questions. Perhaps most important of all are questions to do with human rights, particularly self-determination and the rights of the citizen. However, the history of oppression in many old socialist states has meant that these questions have remained unasked for nearly five decades. For many of those engaged in independence movements, concepts like nationalism and self-determination stimulate expectations more appropriately associated with pre-Second World War, if not nineteenth century, perceptions of statehood and international politics. In contrast to the current west European debate on the nature of sovereignty, which is conducted in the language of integration, interdependence and globalisation, the east European countries are more concerned with difference, separation and their own exceptionalism. The new nationalism of east Europe is therefore emerging at the interface of social identity founded on past ideas of community and new ideas of the nation-state.[11]

Questions of nationalism and self-determination are crucially important because they define the community in which rights can be claimed. They are also significant in the sphere of international politics because of questions to do with domestic jurisdiction and intervention. The practice of 'ethnic cleansing', a repugnant euphemism for genocide that has recently entered the language, is a striking example of the way some nationalists have attempted to define their community by branding certain groups as subhuman and therefore not qualified to make legitimate rights claims.[12] While Bosnia remains the most obvious example of this nationalist rationale for violating human rights, it is hardly the only one. The attempt by Chechenia to secede from Russia has seen both sides violate rights, and the rise of neo-fascist nationalism in both Germany and Austria has brought many attacks against foreign workers.

Although all this suggests that greater attention should be given to group rights in the post-Cold War order, it seems unlikely that this will be done.[13] The triumphalism that is common among western leaders suggests that winning the Cold War also means a return to the universal acceptance of individual rights claimed against the sovereign state. This may offer some relief to those governments less concerned with human rights, because the principle of sovereignty is central to their dream of achieving political and economic independence. This includes those who have freed themselves from colonial rule during recent decades, as much as the new states of eastern Europe. For newly independent, less developed countries the legitimation of intervention on grounds of human rights is treated with suspicion and understood as an attempt to retain some colonial control. The declarations of the three regional conferences that preceded the 1993 Vienna Conference on Human Rights give some indication of this. The Bangkok Declaration, for example, stressed the importance of national sovereignty and non-interference in the domestic affairs of the state. It also rejected the use of human rights as an instrument of political or economic conditionality.[14] Furthermore, while the Bangkok Declaration recognised the universality of human rights, it emphasised the importance of national, regional and religious particularities. Thus, although the worst cases of violation of human rights continue to concern minority and group rights, individual rights based on the central ordering principle of sovereignty will remain paramount in the post-Cold War order.

Secondly, the rhetoric of democracy favoured by the victorious West increasingly replaces human rights as a central feature of global politics. While establishing the formal institutions of democracy may be a necessary condition for claiming human rights, it is not a substitute for them. Many new democratic states, and even some with a longer history, are democratic in formal-institutional terms only. These states do not provide for the reform of social and legal systems that are essential to maintaining the conditions for protecting human rights, including a reduction in inequality, a free press and access to public office.

Until the end of the Cold War, the USA defended its record of sustaining relationships with authoritarian regimes simply because they were avowedly anticommunist. In the post-Cold War era this rationale is no longer available. The USA's support for the introduction of democratic institutions legitimates continuing economic relationships, strengthens calls to extend aid programmes and opens up the possibility of developing new trade. The USA's recent emphasis on democracy may also have more to do with preempting social unrest in previously authoritarian states prepared to embrace an economic system that supports American interests. This 'low level democracy'[15] is indifferent to rights claims and may encourage further violations. To sustain relations with powerful US economic interests, many new democratic governments legislate to create favourable conditions for foreign investment. This means that trade unions remain weak, wages remain below a level to sustain a dignified life, legislation on environmental, health and safety questions never reaches the statute books and all movements aimed at social reform are quashed.[16]

Furthermore, for many less developed states the institutions of national democracy have less significance for social, economic and political conditions than the activities of transnational corporations, the multilateral banks and trading organisations like the World Trade Organisation (WTO) and the North American Free Trade Association (NAFTA). The activities of these actors are often incompatible with the struggle for greater equality, justice and the strengthening of democracy. Indeed, sometimes these actors appear to legitimise undemocratic practices that lead to further violations of human rights.[17] The Narmada dam project in India, structural adjustment programmes and the policy of many multinational corporations to export dangerous industries to less developed states are all examples of this.

Thirdly, the new post-Cold War order is clearly a liberal-capitalist order based on free market principles that cannot accept economic claims as human rights. Accordingly, the old distinction between political rights and economic goals has been revived and the claim that 'the best hope for political freedom in some countries lies in opening them up through trade' is restated.[18] While economic rights have formal parity with political rights under international law, the West has been successful in maintaining a definition of human rights that emphasises the primacy of civil and political rights over economic claims. Less developed states will find it more difficult to sustain their claim for economic assistance and the right to development in a period when it is widely believed that the old ideological battles of the Cold War have been settled.[19] Even before the end of the Cold War the United States reemphasised its ideological objections to embracing economic rights by voting against the 1986 Declaration on the Right to Development. Japan, Germany and the United Kingdom abstained on the same resolution.

More recently the Uruguay Round of the General Agreement on Tariffs and Trade (GATT) has sought to open up markets in ways that show a disregard for the economic rights of many poor countries and peoples. It is predicted that the outcome of the Uruguay Round will boost world trade by over $200 billion a year from the beginning of the next century onwards. Two-thirds of this expected increased income will accrue to northern industrialised countries who support only one-third of the world's population. Against this the incomes of many Asian and African countries are expected to decline.

It is in the area of agricultural trade that the greatest indifference to human rights is found. New rules agreed under the Uruguay Round encourage the production of luxury foods for export to the North and open the markets of many less developed countries to the large food corporations based in the North. Consequently, local farmers will be less inclined to grow staple foods for less profitable domestic markets. Furthermore, intensive farming methods and the adoption of price support mechanisms in wealthy northern states puts further pressure on countries of the South not to grow their own food. This leaves a food deficit that many less developed countries must fill with imports paid for by exports of luxury foods to the North. In this way a system of deprivation is set in train that leads to poor nutrition, hunger, starvation and famine. If the industrialised capitalist countries of the North have any intention of increasing their support for internationally recognised economic rights, the Uruguay Round does not inspire confidence.[20]

Fourthly, the UN has recently engaged in several enterprises, ostensibly in the name of humanitarian intervention. Following these interventions it has become fashionable to talk of the new post-Cold War order as though a norm of humanitarian intervention has already been established. However, the decision to intervene is rarely inspired by a desire to protect individuals and communities against even the worst violations of rights as recognized under international law. The mandate given to UN troops in Rwanda, for example, gives testimony to the low priority given to human rights. During April 1995 that mandate obliged UN troops to stand by as the Rwandan army slaughtered over two thousand people in the Kibeho refugee camp. Furthermore, UN intervention in the name of human rights is unlikely to occur unless an issue embarrasses a permanent member of the Security Council. While Iraq is a regular target for condemnation, there is silence in the face of widely reported massacres by Indonesian troops in East Timor. The economic justification for this inconsistency is well known.[21]

Even when interventions are undertaken they are frequently retroactive and intended to tackle the consequences of violations that the international community has chosen to ignore, often for decades. There is also the problem of providing the necessary resources to ensure that peacekeepers can achieve the objectives set for them. These objectives include organising elections, bringing relief to the victims of war and the breakdown of government, and creating the minimum conditions for leading a dignified life in refugee camps. In 1994 the General Assembly created the position of High Commissioner for Human Rights with the task of coordinating UN human rights activities from the Centre for Human Rights in Geneva. This followed decades of resistance to creating such a post. However, early evidence suggests that the new post will make little difference unless the Commissioner is given the necessary material and political support. For example, the promise of the High Commissioner to send 22 human rights monitors to Rwanda by mid-1994 was not honoured. Furthermore, representatives of the UN Centre for Human Rights in Rwanda had to hire cars from neighbouring countries to conduct their investigations because no UN vehicles were made available.[22] If the UN is to fulfil its role to promote and protect human rights, then governments must stop using it as a way of appearing to be doing something without doing anything.[23] Threats by the United States and others to withdraw funding from certain humanitarian programmes do nothing to offer reassurance that human rights are taken as seriously as many hope.

Fifthly, what can be said of the future for UN human rights activity in the post-Cold War world? Much has been made of the International Criminal Tribunal for the Former Yugoslavia.[24] This Tribunal was brought into existence in 1993 through Security Council resolutions 808 and 827, under Article VII of the UN Charter. The use of tribunals for bringing to trial those accused of crimes against humanity was first tested at Nuremberg, although some have doubted the legality of such methods. Moreover, the decision to set up a tribunal is politically motivated and is part of a process of legitimation.[25] For example, why is a Tribunal on the former Yugoslavia considered legitimate, while no such action is taken following the bombing of innocent people in Libya or the killing of countless numbers of retreating Iraqi troops at the conclusion of Operation Desert Storm. The potential for taking positive action for the protection of human rights remains limited, but trials give the illusion of 'doing something' rather than achieving any lasting protection. The Tribunal for the former Yugoslavia, for example, has so far issued indictments charging twenty-one Serbians with 275 counts of crimes against humanity, genocide and breaches of the Geneva Conventions.

However, only one of the accused is in custody and the possibility of persuading the Serbian authorities to hand the others over seems slim.

Furthermore, many of the worst cases of violations result from negative outcomes inherent in existing economic and political structures rather than the intrinsic evil intentions of individual agents. This does not absolve the perpetrators of violations, but it does cast doubt on the importance given to tribunals and courts if economic and political structures are not reformed. In addition, while the authority of a court or tribunal may be a necessary feature of any programme for the protection of human rights, the retroactive nature of such procedures is of little value to those whose rights have already been abused. Furthermore, if structural arguments for violations are accepted, the argument that tribunals act as a deterrent cannot be sustained. The 1995 meeting of the Commission on Human Rights held at Geneva has begun to recognise this. During that meeting the discussion turned to developing preventive measures such as 'early warning systems' for potential violations of political and economic rights. Given the limited resources that the United Nations dedicates to human rights, this seems a more prudent approach. An exploration of preventive methods should therefore include a close examination of political and economic structures as causes of violations.[26]

While tribunal and other UN activity remain important in providing a focus for human rights activity in the post-Cold War period, this focus serves to highlight past failures as much as successes. The 1993 Vienna conference brought to the surface many disagreements over the way forward, particularly over universality, the role of nongovernmental organisations, the legitimacy of humanitarian intervention and the right to development. While western leaders asserted that the old ideological barriers to the protection of human rights had been removed, opening the way for implementing existing international law, many less developed countries feared they would become further ensnared by the North's political, economic and cultural hegemony. These concerns are not allayed by the United States and the West who continue to revel in their Cold War victory, promote the virtues of the free market and ignore the genuine claims of the less developed states. Unless the United Nations can act as a forum for creating greater understanding between all peoples, the idea of human rights that took root over fifty years ago will remain unfulfilled.

Finally, with the collapse of the USSR the United States is left as the unmatched superpower, suggesting that a single view of human rights will predominate for the foreseeable future. This is in contrast to the previous period when the United States failed to gain wide acceptance for a view of human rights that reflected its own ideology. After years of procrastination the United States has finally ratified the Covenant on Civil and Political

Rights. This may suggest that the USA has lifted its long-held objections to certain aspects of the human rights regime and is now prepared to become a full participant. However, while the ratification of the Covenant may be seen in this light, the reservations, declarations and understandings made by the USA suggest little has changed. Indeed, the influential Lawyers Committee on Human Rights has argued that ratifying the Covenant subject to important reservations, declarations and understandings suggests that 'one set of rules applies to the United States and another set to the rest of the world' and goes on to accuse the Administration of hypocrisy.[27] The reservations taken out by the USA underscore two features of the ratification that support the use of such strong language. Both will be familiar to the reader.

The first is that the United States does not undertake to make any alterations to existing arrangements for human rights. Since the purpose of the Covenant is to ensure that parties to it harmonise their human rights procedures with internationally agreed standards, the fact that existing standards do not conform cannot be accepted as a reason for reservations. For example, the USA reserves the right to impose capital punishment on persons below the age of 18 and to limit the scope of Article 7, which refers to the prohibition of cruel, inhuman and degrading treatment or punishment. By making these and similar reservations the USA appears to many as a boastful exemplar of human rights that needs no improvement.

The second feature is to declare that Articles 1–27 are not self-executing. Consequently, the force of the Covenant does not come into effect until Congress adopts the necessary legislation. This avoids old arguments about the treaty making powers of the Executive and the imposition of social norms on the states. Consequently, Articles that have proved politically contentious in the past are likely to remain unfulfilled. This declaration, which could be construed as a derogation from the central obligations undertaken in the treaty, is further reinforced by an understanding that the Federal Government accepts responsibility for the Covenant to the extent that a federal system allows. All other legislative changes are left to state and local governments.[28]

The argument offered here is not that the United Nations has no role to play in the protection of human rights. However, it has been argued that this role cannot develop unless the UN takes seriously the shortcomings of the principles upon which the current human rights regime is based. Furthermore, if the United States is taking international human rights seriously then it is important to recognise that other members of the international community also have important contributions to make. This book has attempted to highlight some fundamental shortcomings of the human rights regime. The post-Cold War era, like the post-Second World War era, will fail to produce an effective response to the idea of human rights unless there is a reexamination of the features on which existing UN machinery is built. To continue ignoring the difficulties presented by ideas of universalism in international society, disagreements over norms, or the problems of human rights talk in international law, will lead to further inadequate actions that cannot come close to protecting human rights. Social and political scientists, lawyers and commentators on human rights must also accept some responsibility for maintaining the myth that human rights are increasingly well protected because of UN activity. Unless these groups begin to recognize the fundamental problems of attempting to create a regime that can protect the rights of people everywhere, and cease to write as though all United Nations activity is *prima facie* for the good, then the project of universal human rights will continue to disappoint.

NOTES

1. Robert Keohane, *After Hegemony: Co-operation and Discord in the World Political Economy*, (Princeton University Press, Princeton, 1984), p. 26.
2. Oran Young, 'International regimes: Problems of concept formation', *World Politics*, 32:3, 1988, p. 331.
3. Raymond F Hopkins and Donald J Puchala, 'International regimes: Lessons from inductive analysis', *International Organization*, 36:2, 1982, p. 270.
4. ibid., p. 246.
5. Susan Strange, 'Cave! Hic dragones: A critique of regime analysis', *International Organization*, 36:2, 1982, p. 479-96
6. Recent research has demonstrated that the positions held by Senate staff on human rights have not altered in any significant way since 1953. The top ten arguments against the United States ratifying any human rights treaties whatsoever still include; i) a perceived threat to the basic rights of the citizen, ii) the potential threat to state rights, iii) the threat to the Constitution, iv) the promotion of world government, v) infringement of domestic sovereignty, and vi) the danger of increasing United States international entanglements. See Natalie Hevener Kaufman and David Whitman, 'Opposition to human rights treaties in the United States Senate: The legacy of the Bricker Amendment', *Human Rights Quarterly*, 10:3, 1988, p. 390-37.
7. This follows a similar argument concerning the idea of democracy put forward by Anthony Giddens, *The Nation State and Violence*, (Polity Press, London, 1985)
8. John Vincent, *Human Rights and International Relations*, (Cambridge University Press, Cambridge, 1986), p. 130.
9. J Slater and T Nardin, 'Non-intervention and human rights', *Journal of Politics*, vol. 48, 1986, pp. 86-95.
10. Vincent, op. cit., p. 124.
11. Demitris A Ziginis, 'Nationalism and the reality of the Nation State: The case of Greece and Turkey in relation to the European Orientation in the two countries', (unpublished PhD thesis, Essex University, 1993)
12. Jack Donnelly, 'Human rights and the New World Order', *World Policy Review*, 9:2, 1994, pp. 249-77.

13. Richard Falk, 'Human rights, humanitarian assistance and the sovereign state' in Kevin M Cahill (ed), *A Framework for Survival*, (Basic Books, 1993), and John Quinn, 'The General Assembly in the 1990s', in Philip Alston (ed), *The United Nations and Human Rights: A Critical Appraisal*, (Clarendon Press, Oxford, 1992), pp. 55-106.

14. For the Vienna Declaration and the declarations of the three regional conferences see *Human Rights Law Journal*, vol. 14, No. 9-10, 1993.

15. Barry Gill, Joel Rocamora and Richard Wilson, *Low Intensity Democracy: Political Power in the New World Order*, (Pluto Press, London, 1993).

16. Roger Burbach, 'The tragedy of American democracy', in ibid., pp. 100-123.

17. Smitu Kothari, 'Global economic institutions and democracy: A view from India', in J Gavanagh, D Wysham and M Arrunda (eds), *Beyond Breton Woods*, (Pluto Press, London, 1994), pp. 39-54.

18. 'The red and the blue', *The Economist*, 8 May 1993, p. 22.

19. Samir Amin, 'The Issue of Democracy in the Contemporary Third World', in Gill, Rocamora and Wilson, op. cit., pp. 59-78.

20. Kevin Watkins, *Fixing the Rules*, (CIIR, London, 1992). See also 'Cakes and Caviar', *The Ecologist*, 23:6, 1993, pp. 219-22. See also Annie Taylor, 'World trade and its environmental impacts', in Phil Sarre (ed), *Environment, Population and Development*, (Hodder and Stowghton, London, 1995)

21. 'UK in secret £2bn arms bid' and 'Making a killing with British aid', both in *The Observer*, 13th November 1994, p. 1 and 14 respectively.

22. 'Rwanda genocide probe chief quits over UN blunders', *The Observer*, 11th September 1994, p. 8.

23. 'Heart of gold, limbs of clay', *The Economist*, 12th June 1993, pp. 25-28.

24. Morten Bergsmo, 'The establishment of the International Tribunal on War Crimes', *Human Rights Law Journal*, vol. 14, No. 9-10, pp. 371-2.

25. C Douglas Lummis, 'Globocop? Time to watch the watchers', *Third World Resurgence*, No. 52, December 1994, pp. 39-42.

26. Johan Galtung, *Human Rights in Another Key*, (Polity Press, Cambridge, 1994)

27. Letter from the Lawyers Committee for Human Rights to Senator Claiborne Pell, 2 March 1992, published in *Human Rights Law Journal*, vol. 14, No. 3-4, p. 129.

28. For a full analysis of the reservations, declarations and understanding see *Human Rights Law Journal*, vol. 14, No. 3-4, pp. 125-8. For a defence of the reservations see 'U.S. ratification of the Covenant on Civil and Poltical Rights: The significance of the reservations, understandings and declarations', in *Human Rights Law Journal*, vol. 14, No. 3-4, pp. 77-83.

Appendix I: Universal Declaration of Human Rights

PREAMBLE

Whereas recognition of the inherent dignity and of the equal and inalienable rights of all members of the human family is the foundation of freedom, justice and peace in the world,

Whereas disregard and contempt for human rights have resulted in barbarous acts which have outraged the conscience of mankind, and the advent of a world in which human beings shall enjoy freedom of speech and belief and freedom from fear and want has been proclaimed as the highest aspiration of the common people,

Whereas it is essential, if man is not to be compelled to have recourse, as a last resort, to rebellion against tyranny and oppression, that human rights should be protected by the rule of law,

Whereas it is essential to promote the development of friendly relations between nations,

Whereas the peoples of the United Nations have in the Charter reaffirmed their faith in fundamental human rights, in the dignity and worth of the human person and in the equal rights of men and women and have determined to promote social progress and better standards of life in larger freedom,

Whereas Member States have pledged themselves to achieve, in cooperation with the United Nations, the promotion of universal respect for and observance of human rights and fundamental freedoms,

Whereas a common understanding of these rights and freedoms is of the greatest importance for the full realization of this pledge.

Now, Therefore,

THE GENERAL ASSEMBLY

proclaims

This universal declaration of human rights as a common standard of achievement for all peoples and all nations, to the end that every individual and every organ of society, keeping this Declaration constantly in mind, shall strive by teaching and education to promote respect for these rights and freedoms and by progressive measures, national and international, to secure their universal and effective recognition and observance, both among the peoples of Member States themselves and among the peoples of territories under their jurisdiction.

Article 1

All human beings are born free and equal in dignity and rights. They are endowed with reason and conscience and should act towards one another in a spirit of brotherhood.

Article 2

Everyone is entitled to all the rights and freedoms set forth in this Declaration, without distinction of any kind, such as race, colour, sex, language, religion, political or other opinion, national or social origin, property, birth or other status.

Furthermore, no distinction shall be made on the basis of the political, jurisdictional or international status of the country or territory to which a person belongs, whether it be independent, trust, non-self-governing or under any other limitation of sovereignty.

Article 3

Everyone has the right to life, liberty and security of person.

Article 4

No one shall be held in slavery or servitude; slavery and the slave trade shall be prohibited in all their forms.

Article 5

No one shall be subjected to torture or to cruel, inhuman or degrading treatment or punishment.

Article 6

Everyone has the right to recognition everywhere as a person before the law.

Article 7

All are equal before the law and are entitled without any discrimination to equal protection of the law. All are entitled to equal protection against any discrimination in violation of this Declaration and against any incitement to such discrimination.

Article 8

Everyone has the right to an effective remedy by the competent national tribunals for acts violating the fundamental rights granted him by the constitution or by law.

Article 9

No one shall be subjected to arbitrary arrest, detention or exile.

Article 10

Everyone is entitled in full equality to a fair and public hearing by an independent and impartial tribunal, in the determination of his rights and obligations and of any criminal charge against him.

Article 11

1. Everyone charged with a penal offence has the right to be presumed innocent until proved guilty according to law in a public trial at which he has had all the guarantees necessary for his defence.
2. No one shall be held guilty of any penal offence on account of any act or omission which did not constitute a penal offence, under national or international law, at the time when it was committed. Nor shall a heavier penalty be imposed than the one that was applicable at the time the penal offence was committed.

Article 12

No one shall be subjected to arbitrary interference with his privacy, family, home or correspondence, nor to attacks upon his honour and reputation. Everyone has the right to protection of the law against such interference or attacks.

Article 13

1. Everyone has the right to freedom of movement and residence within the borders of each state.
2. Everyone has the right to leave any country, including his own, and to return to his country.

Article 14

1. Everyone has the right to seek and to enjoy in other countries asylum from prosecution.
2. This right may not be invoked in the case of prosecutions genuinely arising from non-political crimes or from acts contrary to the purposes and principles of the United Nations.

Article 15

1. Everyone has the right to a nationality.
2. No one shall be arbitrarily deprived of his nationality nor denied the right to change his nationality.

Article 16

1. Men and women of full age, without any limitation due to race, nationality or religion, have the right to marry and to found a family. They are entitled to equal rights as to marriage, during marriage and at its dissolution.
2. Marriage shall be entered into only with the free and full consent of the intending spouses.
3. The family is the natural and fundamental group unit of society and is entitled to protection by society and the state.

Article 17

1. Everyone has the right to own a property alone as well as in association with others.
2. No one shall be arbitrarily deprived of his property.

Article 18

Everyone has the right to freedom of thought, conscience and religion; this right includes freedom to change his religion or belief, and freedom, either alone or in community with others and in public or private, to manifest his religion or belief in teaching, practice, worship and observance.

Article 19

Everyone has the right to freedom of opinion and expression; this right includes freedom to hold opinions without interference and to seek, receive and impart information and ideas through any media and regardless of frontiers.

Article 20

1. Everyone has the right to freedom of peaceful assembly and association.
2. No one may be compelled to belong to an association.   .

Article 21

1. Everyone has the right to take part in the government of his country, directly or through freely chosen representatives.
2. Everyone has the right of equal access to public service in his country.
3. The will of the people shall be the basis of the authority of government; this will shall be expressed in periodic and genuine elections which shall be by universal and equal suffrage and shall be held by secret vote or by equivalent free voting procedures.

Article 22

Everyone, as a member of society, has the right to social security and is entitled to realization, through national effort and international co-operation and in accordance with the organization and resources of each State, of the economic, social and cultural rights indispensable for his dignity and the free development of his personality.

Article 23

1. Everyone has the right to work, to free choice of employment, to just and favourable conditions of work and to protection against unemployment.
2. Everyone, without any discrimination, has the right to equal pay for equal work.

3. Everyone who works has the right to just and favourable remuneration ensuring for himself and his family an existence worthy of human dignity, and supplemented, if necessary, by other means of social protection.
4. Everyone has the right to form and to join trade unions for the protection of his interests.

Article 24

Everyone has the right to rest and leisure, including reasonable limitation of working hours and periodic holidays with pay.

Article 25

1. Everyone has the right to a standard of living adequate for the health and well-being of himself and of his family, including food, clothing, housing and medical care and necessary social services, and the right to security in the event of unemployment, sickness, disability, widowhood, old age or lack of livelihood in circumstances beyond his control.
2. Motherhood and childhood are entitled to special care and assistance. All children, whether born in or out of wedlock, shall enjoy the same social protection.

Article 26

1. Everyone has the right to education. Education shall be free, at least in the elementary and fundamental stages. Elementary education shall be compulsory. Technical and professional education shall be made generally available and higher education shall be equally accessible to all on the basis of merit.
2. Education shall be directed to the full development of the human personality and to the strengthening of respect for human rights and fundamental freedoms. It shall promote understanding, tolerance and friendship among all nations, racial or religious groups, and shall further the activities of the United Nations for the maintenance of peace.
3. Parents have a prior right to choose the kind of education that shall be given to their children.

Article 27

1. Everyone has the right to freely participate in the cultural life of the community, to enjoy the arts and to share in scientific advancement and its benefits.
2. Everyone has the right to the protection of the moral and material interests resulting from any scientific, literary or artistic production of which he is the author.

Article 28

Everyone is entitled to a social and international order in which the rights and freedoms set forth in this Declaration can be fully realized.

Article 29

1. Everyone has duties to the community in which alone the free and full development of his personality is possible.
2. In the exercise of his rights and freedoms, everyone shall be subject only to such limitations as are determined by law solely for the purpose of securing due recognition and respect for the rights and freedoms of others and of meeting the just requirements of morality, public order and the general welfare in a democratic society.
3. These rights and freedoms may in no case be exercised contrary to the purposes and principles of the United Nations.

Article 30

Nothing in this Declaration may be interpreted as implying for any State, group or person any right to engage in any activity or to perform any act aimed at the destruction of any of the rights and freedoms set forth herein.

Appendix II: International Covenant on Economic, Social, and Cultural Rights

PREAMBLE

The States Parties to the present Covenant,

Considering that, in accordance with the principles proclaimed in the Charter of the United Nations, recognition of the inherent dignity and of the equal and inalienable rights of all members of the human family is the foundation of freedom, justice and peace in the world,

Recognizing that, in accordance with the Universal Declaration of Human Rights, the ideal of free human beings enjoying freedom from fear and want can only be achieved if conditions are created whereby everyone may enjoy his economic, social and cultural rights, as well as his civil and political rights,

Considering the obligation of States under the Charter of the United Nations to promote universal respect for, and observance of, human rights and freedoms,

Realizing that the individual, having duties to other individuals and to the community to which he belongs, is under a responsibility to strive for the promotion and observance of the rights recognized in the present Covenant,

Agree upon the following articles:

PART I

Article 1

1. All peoples have the right of self-determination. By virtue of that right they freely determine their political status and freely pursue their economic, social and cultural development.
2. All peoples may, for their own ends, freely dispose of their natural wealth and resources without prejudice to any obligations arising out of international economic co-operation, based upon the principle of mutual

benefit, and international law. In no case may a people be deprived of its own means of subsistence.

3. The States Parties to the present Covenant, including those having responsibility for the administration of Non-Self-Governing and Trust Territories, shall promote the realization of the right of self-determination, and shall respect that right, in conformity with the provisions of the Charter of the United Nations.

PART II

Article 2

1. Each State Party to the present Covenant undertakes to take steps, individually and through international assistance and co-operation, especially economic and technical, to the maximum of its available resources, with a view to achieving progressively the full realization of the rights recognized in the present Covenant by all appropriate means, including particularly the adoption of legislative measures.
2. The States Parties to the present Covenant undertake to guarantee that the rights enunciated in the present Covenant will be exercised without discrimination of any kind as to race, colour, sex, language, religion, political or other opinion, national or social origin, property, birth or other status.
3. Developing countries, with due regard to human rights and their national economy, may determine to what extent they would guarantee the economic rights recognized in the present Covenant to non-nationals.

Article 3

The States Parties to the present Covenant undertake to ensure the equal right of men and women to the enjoyment of all economic, social and cultural rights set forth in the present Covenant.

Article 4

The States Parties to the present Covenant recognize that, in the enjoyment of those rights provided by the State in conformity with the present Covenant, the State may subject such rights only to such limitations as are determined by law only in so far as this may be compatible with the nature of these rights and solely for the purpose of promoting the general welfare in a democratic society.

Article 5

1. Nothing in the present Covenant may be interpreted as implying for any State, group or person any right to engage in any activity or to perform any act aimed at the destruction of any of the rights or freedoms recognized herein, or at their limitation to a greater extent than is provided for in the present Covenant.
2. No restriction upon or derogation from any of the fundamental human rights recognized or existing in any country in virtue of law, conventions, regulations or custom shall be admitted on the pretext that the present Covenant does not recognize such rights or that it recognizes them to a lesser extent.

PART III

Article 6

1. The States Parties to the present Covenant recognize the right to work, which includes the right of everyone to the opportunity to gain his living by work which he freely chooses or accepts, and will take appropriate steps to safeguard this right.
2. The steps to be taken by a State Party to the present Covenant to achieve the full realization of this right shall include technical and vocational guidance and training programmes, policies and techniques to achieve steady economic, social and cultural development and full and productive employment under conditions safeguarding fundamental political and economic freedoms to the individual.

Article 7

The States Parties to the present Covenant recognize the right of everyone to the enjoyment of just and favourable conditions of work, which ensure, in particular:
(a) Remuneration which provides all workers, as a minimum with:
    (i) Fair wages and equal remuneration for work of equal value without distinction of any kind, in particular women being guaranteed conditions of work not inferior to those enjoyed by men, with equal pay for equal work;
    (ii) A decent living for themselves and their families in accordance with the provisions of the present Covenant;
(b) Safe and healthy working conditions;

(c) Equal opportunity for everyone to be promoted in his employment to an appropriate higher level, subject to no considerations other than those of seniority and competence;

(d) Rest, leisure and reasonable limitation of working hours and periodic holidays with pay, as well as remuneration for public holidays.

Article 8

1. The States Parties to the present Covenant undertake to ensure:
   (a) The right of everyone to form trade unions and to join the trade union of his choice, subject only to the rules of the organization concerned, for the promotion and protection of his economic and social interests. No restrictions may be placed on the exercise of this right other than those prescribed by law and which are necessary in a democratic society in the interests of national security or public order or for the protection of the rights and freedoms of others;
   (b) The right of trade unions to establish national federations or con-federations and the right of the latter to form or join international trade union organizations;
   (c) The right of trade unions to function freely subject to no limitations other than those prescribed by law and which are necessary in a democratic society in the interests of national security or public order or for the protection of the rights and freedoms of others;
   (d) The right to strike, provided that it is exercised in conformity with the laws of that particular country.
2. This article shall not prevent the imposition of lawful restrictions on the exercise of these rights by members of the armed forces or of the police or of the administration of the State.
3. Nothing in this article shall authorize States Parties to the International Labour Organization Convention of 1948 concerning Freedom of Association and Protection of the Right to Organize to take legislative measures which would prejudice, or apply the law in such a manner as would prejudice, the guarantees provided for in that Convention.

Article 9

The States Parties to the present Covenant recognize the right of everyone to social security, including social insurance.

Article 10

The States Parties to the present Covenant recognize that:
1. The widest possible protection and assistance should be accorded to the family, which is the natural and fundamental group unit of society, particularly for its establishment and while it is responsible for the care and education of dependent children. Marriage must be entered into with the free consent of the intending spouses.
2. Special protection should be accorded to mothers during a reasonable period during and after childbirth. During such period working mothers should be accorded paid leave with adequate social security benefits.
3. Special measures of protection and assistance should be taken of all children and young persons without any discrimination for reasons of parentage or other conditions. Children and young persons should be protected from economic and social exploitation. Their employment in work harmful to their morals or health or dangerous to life or likely to hamper their normal development should be punishable by law. States should also get limits below which the paid employment of child labour should be prohibited and punishable by law.

Article 11

1. The States Parties to the present Covenant recognize the right of everyone to an adequate standard of living for himself and his family, including adequate food, clothing and housing, and to the continuous improvement of living conditions. The States Parties will take appropriate steps to ensure the realization of this right, recognizing to this effect the essential importance of international co-operation based on free consent.
2. The States Parties to the present Covenant, recognizing the fundamental right of everyone to be free from hunger, shall take, individually and through international co-operation, the measures, including specific programmes, which are needed:
   (a) To improve methods of production, conservation and distribution of food by making full use of technical and scientific knowledge, by disseminating knowledge of the principles of nutrition and by developing or reforming agrarian systems in such a way as to achieve the most efficient development and utilization of natural resources;
   (b) Taking into account the problems of both food-importing and food-exporting countries, to ensure an equitable distribution of world food supplies in relation to need.

Article 12

1. The States Parties to the present Covenant recognize the right of everyone to the enjoyment of the highest attainable standard of physical and mental health.
2. The steps to be taken by the States Parties to the present Covenant to achieve the full realization of this right shall include those necessary for:
   (a) The provision for the reduction of the stillbirth rate and of infant morality and for the healthy development of the child;
   (b) The improvement of all aspects of environmental and industrial hygiene;
   (c) The prevention, treatment and control of epidemic, endemic, occupational and other diseases;
   (d) The creation of conditions which would assure to all medical service and medical attention in the event of sickness.

Article 13

1. The States Parties to the present Covenant recognize the right of everyone to education. They agree that education shall be directed to the full development of the human personality and the sense of its dignity, and shall strengthen the respect for human rights and fundamental freedoms. They further agree that education shall enable all persons to participate effectively in a free society, promote understanding, tolerance and friendship among all nations and all racial, ethnic or religious groups, and further the activities of the United Nations for the maintenance of peace.
2. The States Parties to the present Covenant recognize that, with a view to achieving the full realization of this right:
   (a) Primary education shall be compulsory and available free to all;
   (b) Secondary education in its different forms, including technical and vocational secondary education, shall be made generally available and accessible to all by every appropriate means, and in particular by the progressive introduction of free education;
   (c) Higher education shall be made equally accessible to all, on the basis of capacity, by every appropriate means, and in particular by the progressive introduction of free education;
   (d) Fundamental education shall be encouraged or intensified as far as possible for those persons who have not received or completed the whole period of their primary education;

(e) The development of a system of schools at all levels shall be actively pursued, an adequate fellowship system shall be established, and the material conditions of teaching staff shall be continuously improved.

3. The States Parties to the present Covenant undertake to have respect for the liberty of parents and, when applicable, legal guardians, to choose for their children schools, other than those established by the public authorities, which conform to minimum educational standards as may be laid down or approved by the State and to ensure the religious and moral education of their children in conformity with their own convictions.

4. No part of this article shall be construed so as to interfere with the institutions, subject always to the observance of the principles set forth in paragraph 1 of this Article and to the requirement that the education given in such institutions shall conform to such minimum standards as may be laid down by the State.

Article 14

Each State Part to the present Covenant which, at the time of becoming a Party, has not been able to secure in its metropolitan territory or other territories under its jurisdiction compulsory primary education, free of charge, undertakes, within two years, to work out and adopt a detailed plan of action for the progressive implementation, within a reasonable number of years, to be fixed in the plan, of the principle of compulsory education free of charge for all.

Article 15

1. The States Parties to the present Covenant recognize the right of everyone:
   (a) To take part in cultural life;
   (b) To enjoy the benefits of scientific progress and its applications;
   (c) To benefit from the protection of the moral and material interests resulting from any scientific, literary or artistic production of which he is the author.

2. The steps to be taken by the States Parties to the present Covenant to achieve the full realization of this right shall include those necessary for the conservation, the development and the diffusion of science and culture.

3. The States Parties to the present Covenant undertake to respect the freedom indispensable for scientific research and creative activity.

4. The States Parties to the present Covenant recognize the benefits to be derived from the encouragement and development of international contacts and co-operation in the scientific and cultural fields.

PART IV

Article 16

1. The States Parties to the present Covenant undertake to submit in conformity with this part of the Covenant reports on the measures which they have adopted and the progress made in achieving the observance of the rights recognized herein.
2. (a) All reports shall be submitted to the Secretary-General of the United Nations, who shall transmit copies to the Economic and Social Council for consideration in accordance with the provisions of the present Covenant.
   (b) The Secretary-General of the United Nations shall also transmit to the specialized agencies copies of the reports, or any relevant parts therefrom, from States Parties to the present Covenant which are also members of these specialized agencies in so far as these reports, or parts therefrom, relate to any matters which fall within the responsibilities of the said agencies in accordance with their constitutional instruments.

Article 17

1. The Sates Parties to the present Covenant shall furnish their reports in stages, in accordance with a programme to be established by the Economic and Social Council within one year of entry into force of the present Covenant after consultation with the States Parties and the specialized agencies concerned.
2. Reports may indicate factors and difficulties affecting the degree of fulfilment of obligations under the present Covenant.
3. Where relevant information previously has been furnished to the United Nations or to any specialized agency by any State Party to the present Covenant, it will not be necessary to reproduce that information, but a precise reference to the information so furnished will suffice.

Article 18

Pursuant to its responsibilities under the Charter of the United Nations in the field of human rights and fundamental freedoms, the Economic and Social Council may make arrangements with the specialized agencies in respect of their reporting to it on the progress made in achieving the observance of the provisions of the present Covenant falling within the scope of their activities. These reports may include particulars of decisions and recommendations on such implementation adopted by their competent organs.

Article 19

The Economic and Social Council may transmit to the Commission on Human Rights for study and general recommendation or as appropriate for information the reports concerning human rights submitted by States in accordance with Articles 16 and 17, and those concerning human rights submitted by the specialized agencies in accordance with Article 18.

Article 20

The States Parties to the present Covenant and the specialized agencies concerned may submit comments to the Economic and Social council on any general recommendation under Article 19 or reference to such general recommendation in any report of the Commission on Human Rights or any documentation referred to herein.

Article 21

The Economic and Social Council may submit from time to time to the General Assembly reports with recommendations of a general nature and a summary of the information received from the States Parties to the present Covenant and the specialized agencies on the measures taken and the progress made in achieving general observance of the rights recognized in the present covenant.

Article 22

The Economic and Social Council may bring to the attention of other organs of the United Nations, their subsidiary organs and specialized agencies concerned with furnishing technical assistance any matters arising out of the reports referred to in this part of the present Covenant which may assist such bodies in deciding, each within its field of competence, on the advisability of international measures likely to contribute to the effective progressive implementation of the present Covenant.

Article 23

The States Parties to the present Covenant agree that international action for the achievement of the rights recognized in the present Covenant includes such methods as the conclusions of conventions, the adoption of recommendations, the furnishing of technical assistance and the holding of regional meetings for the purpose of consultation and study organized in conjunction with the Governments concerned.

Article 24

Nothing in the present Covenant shall be interpreted as impairing the provisions of the Charter of the United Nations and of the constitutions of the specialized agencies which define the respective responsibilities of the various organs of the United Nations and of the specialized agencies in regard to the matters dealt with in the present Covenant.

Article 25

Nothing in the present Covenant shall be interpreted as impairing the inherent right of all peoples to enjoy and utilize fully and freely their natural wealth and resources.

PART V

Article 26

1. The present Covenant is open for signature by any State Member of the United nations or member of any of its specialized agencies, by any State Party to the Statute of the international Court of Justice, and by any other State which has been invited by the General Assembly of the United Nations to become a party to present Covenant.
2. The present Covenant is subject to ratification. Instruments of ratification shall be deposited with the Secretary-General of the United Nations.
3. The present Covenant shall be open to accession by any State referred to in paragraph 1 of this Article.

4. Accession shall be effected by the deposit of an instrument of accession with the Secretary-General of the United Nations.
5. The Secretary-General of the United Nations shall inform all States which have signed the present Covenant or acceded to it of the deposit of each instrument of ratification or accession.

Article 27

1. The present Covenant shall enter into force three months after the date of the deposit with the Secretary-General of the United Nations of the thirty-fifth instrument of ratification or instrument of accession.
2. For each State ratifying the present Covenant or acceding to it after the deposit of the thirty-fifth instrument of ratification or instrument of accession, the present Covenant shall enter into force three months after the date of the deposit of its own instrument of ratification or instrument of accession.

Article 28

The provisions of the present Covenant shall extend to all parts of federal States without any limitations or exceptions.

Article 29

1. Any State Party to the present Covenant may propose amendment and file it with the Secretary-General of the United Nations. The Secretary-General shall thereupon communicate any proposed amendments to the States Parties to the present Covenant with a request that they notify him whether they favour a conference of States Parties for the purpose of considering and voting upon the proposals. In the event that at least one third of the States Parties favours such a conference, the Secretary-General shall convene the conference under the auspices of the United Nations. Any amendment adopted by a majority of the States Parties present and voting at the conference shall be submitted to the General Assembly of the United Nations for approval.
2. Amendments shall come into force when they have been approved by the General Assembly of the United Nations and accepted by a two-thirds majority of the States Parties to the present Covenant in accordance with their respective constitutional processes.
3. When amendments shall come into force they shall be binding on those States Parties which have accepted them, other States Parties still being

bound by the provisions of the present Covenant and any earlier amendments which they have accepted.

Article 30

Irrespective of the notifications made under Article 26, paragraph 5, the Secretary-General of the United Nations shall inform all States referred to in paragraph 1 of the same article of the following particulars:
(a) Signatures, ratifications and accessions under Article 26;
(b) The date of the entry into force of the present Covenant under Article 27 and the date of the entry into force of any amendments under Article 29.

Article 31

1. The present Covenant, of which the Chinese, English, French, Russian and Spanish texts are equally authentic, shall be deposited in the archives of the United Nations.
2. The Secretary-General of the United Nations shall transmit certified copies of the present Covenant to all States referred to in Article 26.

Appendix III: International Covenant on Civil and Political Rights

PREAMBLE

The States Parties to the present Covenant,

Considering that, in accordance with the principles proclaimed in the Charter of the United Nations, recognition of the inherent dignity and of the equal and inalienable rights of all members of the human family is the foundation of freedom, justice and peace in the world,

Recognizing that, these rights derive from the inherent dignity of the human person,

Recognizing that, in accordance with the Universal Declaration of Human Rights, the ideal of free human beings enjoying civil and political freedom and freedom from fear and want can only be achieved if conditions are created whereby everyone may enjoy his civil and political rights, as well as his economic, social and cultural rights,

Considering the obligation of States under the Charter of the United Nations to promote universal respect for, and observance of, human rights and freedoms,

Realizing that the individual, having duties to other individuals and to the community to which he belongs, is under responsibility to strive for the promotion and observance of the rights recognized in the present Covenant,

Agree upon the following articles:

PART I

Article 1

1. All peoples have the right of self-determination. By virtue of that right they freely determine their political status and freely pursue their economic, social and cultural development.
2. All peoples may, for their own ends, freely dispose of their natural wealth and resources without prejudice to any obligations arising out of

international economic co-operation, based upon the principle of mutual benefit, and international law. In no case may a people be deprived of its own means of subsistence.

3. The States Parties to the present covenant, including those having responsibility for the administration of Non-Self-Governing and Trust Territories, shall promote the realization of self-determination, and shall respect that right, in conformity with the provisions of the Charter of the United Nations.

PART II

Article 2

1. Each State Party to the present Covenant undertakes to respect and to ensure to all individuals within its territory and subject to its jurisdiction the rights recognized in the present Covenant, without distinction of any kind, such as race, colour, sex, language, religion, political or other opinion, national or social origin, property, birth or other status.

2. Where not already provided for by existing legislative or other measures, each State Party to the present Covenant undertakes to take the necessary steps, in accordance with its constitutional processes and with the provisions of the present Covenant, to adopt such legislative or other measures as may be necessary to give effect to the rights recognized in the present Covenant.

3. Each State Party to the present Covenant undertakes:
   (a) To ensure that any person whose rights or freedoms as herein recognized are violated shall have an effective remedy, notwithstanding that the violation has been committed by persons acting in an official capacity;
   (b) To ensure that any person claiming such remedy shall have his right thereto determined by competent judicial, administrative legislative authorities, or by any other competent authority provided for by the legal system of the State, and to develop the possibilities of judicial remedy;
   (c) To ensure that the competent authorities shall enforce such remedies when granted.

Article 3

The States Parties to the present Covenant undertake to ensure the equal right of men and women to the enjoyment of all civil and political rights set forth in the present Covenant.

Article 4

1. In time of public emergency which threatens the life of the nation and the existence of which is officially proclaimed, the States Parties to the present Covenant may take measures whereat from their obligations under the present Covenant to the extent strictly required by the exigencies of the situation, provided that such measures are not inconsistent with their other obligations under international law and do not involve discrimination solely on the ground of race, colour, sex, language, religion or social origin.
2. No derogation from Articles 6, 7, 8 (paragraphs 1 and 2), 11, 15, 16 and 18 may be made under this provision.
3. Any State Party to the present Covenant availing itself of the right of derogation shall immediately inform the other States Parties to the present Covenant, through the intermediary of the Secretary-General of the United Nations of the provisions from which it has derogated and of the reasons by which it was actuated. A further communication shall be made, through the same intermediary on the date on which it terminates such derogation.

Article 5

1. Nothing in the present Covenant may be interpreted as implying for any State, group or person any right to engage in any activity or perform any act aimed at the destruction of any of the rights and freedoms recognized herein or at their limitation to a greater extent that is provided for in the present Covenant.
2. There shall be no restriction upon or derogation from any of the fundamental human rights recognized or existing in any State Party to the present Covenant pursuant to law, regulations or custom on the pretext that the present Covenant does not recognize such rights or that it recognizes them to a lesser extent.

PART III

Article 6

1. Every human being has the inherent right to life. This right shall be protected by law. No one shall be arbitrarily deprived of his life.
2. In countries which have not abolished the death penalty, sentence of death may be imposed only for the most serious crimes in accordance with the law in force at the time of the commission of the crime and not contrary to the provisions of the present Covenant and to the Convention on the Prevention and Punishment of the Crime Genocide. This penalty can only be carried out pursuant to a final judgement rendered by a competent court.
3. When deprivation of life constitutes the crime of genocide, it is understood that nothing in this article shall authorize any State Party to the present Covenant to derogate in any way from any obligation assumed under the provisions of the Convention on the Prevention and Punishment of the Crime Genocide.
4. Anyone sentenced to death shall have the right to seek pardon or commutation of the sentence. Amnesty, pardon or commutation of the sentence of death may be granted in all cases.
5. Sentence of death shall not be imposed for crimes committed by persons below eighteen years of age and shall not be carried out on pregnant women.
6. Nothing in this article shall be invoked to delay or prevent the abolition of capital punishment by any State Party to the present Covenant.

Article 7

No one shall be subjected to torture or to cruel, inhuman or degrading treatment or punishment. In particular, no one shall be subjected without his free consent to medical or scientific experimentation.

Article 8

1. No one shall be held in slavery; slavery and the slave-trade in all their forms shall be prohibited.
2. No one shall be held in servitude.
3. (a) No one shall be required to perform forced or compulsory labour;
   (b) Paragraph 3 (a) shall not be held to preclude, in countries where imprisonment with hard labour may be imposed as a punishment for a

crime, the performance of hard labour in pursuance of a sentence to such punishment by a competent court;

(c) For the purpose of this paragraph the term 'forced or compulsory labour' shall not include:

  (i) Any work or service, not referred to in sub-paragraph (b), normally required of a person who is under detention in consequence of a lawful order of a court, or of a person during conditional release from such detention;

  (ii) Any service of a military character and, in countries where conscientious objection is recognized, any national service required by law of conscientious objectors;

  (iii) Any service exacted in cases of emergency or calamity threatening the life or well-being of the community;

  (iv) Any work or service which forms part of normal civil obligations.

Article 9

1. Everyone has the right to liberty and security of person. No one shall be subjected to arbitrary arrest or detention. No one shall be deprived of his liberty except on such grounds and in accordance with such procedures as are established by law.

2. Anyone who is arrested shall be informed, at the time of arrest, of the reasons for his arrest and shall be promptly informed of any charges against him.

3. Anyone arrested or detained on a criminal charge shall be brought promptly before a judge or other officer authorized by law to exercise judicial power and shall be entitled to trial within a reasonable time or to release. It shall not be the general rule that persons awaiting trial shall be detained in custody, but release may be subject to guarantees to appear for trial, at any other stage of the judicial proceedings, and, should occasion arise, for execution of the judgement.

4. Anyone who is deprived of his liberty by arrest or detention shall be entitled to take proceedings before a court, in order that the court may decide without delay on the lawfulness of his detention and order his release if the detention is not lawful.

5. Anyone who has been the victim of unlawful arrest or detention shall have an enforceable right to compensation.

Article 10

1. All persons deprived of their liberty shall be treated with humanity and with respect for the inherent dignity of the human person.
2. (a) Accused persons shall, save in exceptional circumstances, be segregated from convicted persons and shall be subject to separate treatment appropriate to their status as unconvicted persons;
   (b) Accused juvenile persons shall be separated from adults and brought as speedily as possible for adjudication.
3. The penitentiary system shall comprise treatment of prisoners the essential aim of which shall be their reformation and social rehabilitation. Juvenile offenders shall be segregated from adults and be accorded treatment appropriate to their age and legal status.

Article 11

No one shall be imprisoned merely on the ground of inability to fulfil a contractual obligation.

Article 12

1. Everyone lawfully within the territory of a State shall, within that territory, have the right to liberty of movement and freedom to choose his residence.
2. Everyone shall be free to leave any country, including his own.
3. The above-mentioned rights shall not be subject to any restrictions except those which are provided by law, are necessary to protect national security, public order (*ordre public*), public health or morals or the rights and freedoms of others, and are consistent with the other rights recognized in the present Covenant.
4. No one shall be arbitrarily deprived of the right to enter his own country.

Article 13

An alien lawfully in the territory of a State Party to the present Covenant may be expelled therefrom only in pursuance of a decision reached in accordance with law and shall, except where compelling reasons of national security otherwise require, be allowed to submit the reasons against his expulsion and to have his case reviewed by, and be represented for the purpose before, the competent authority or a person or persons especially designated by the competent authority.

Article 14

1. All persons shall be equal before the courts and tribunals. In the determination of any criminal charge against him, or of his rights and obligations in a suit law, everyone shall be entitled to a fair and public hearing by a competent, independent and impartial tribunal established by law. The Press and the public may be excluded from all or part of a trial for reasons of morals, public order (*ordre public*) or national security in a democratic society, or when the interest of the private lives of the parties so requires, or to the extent strictly necessary in the opinion of the court in special circumstances where publicity would prejudice the interests of justice; but any judgement rendered in a criminal case or in a suit at law shall be made public except where the interest of juvenile persons otherwise requires or the proceedings concern matrimonial disputes or the guardianship of children.
2. Everyone charged with a criminal offence shall have the right to be presumed innocent until proved guilty according to law.
3. In the determination of any criminal charge against him, everyone shall be entitled to the following minimum guarantees, in full equality:
   (a) To be informed promptly and in detail in a language which he understands of the nature and cause of the charge against him;
   (b) To have adequate time and facilities for the preparation of his defence and to communicate with counsel of his own choosing;
   (c) To be tried without undue delay;
   (d) To be tried in his presence, and to defend himself in person or through legal assistance of his own choosing; to be informed, if he does not have legal assistance, of this right; and to have legal assistance assigned to him, in any case where the interests of justice so require, and without payment by him in any such case if he does not have sufficient means to pay for it;
   (e) To examine, or have examined, the witnesses against him and to obtain the attendance and examination of witnesses on his behalf under the same conditions as witnesses against him;
   (f) To have the free assistance of an interpreter if he cannot understand or speak the language used in court;
   (g) Not to be compelled to testify against himself or to confess to guilt.
4. In any case of juvenile persons, the procedure shall be such as will take account of their age and the desirability of promoting their rehabilitation.
5. Everyone convicted of a crime shall have the right to his conviction and sentence being reviewed by a higher tribunal according to law.

6. When a person has by a final decision been convicted of a criminal offence and when subsequently his conviction has been reversed or he has been pardoned on the ground that a new or newly discovered fact shows conclusively that there has been a miscarriage of justice, the person who has suffered punishment as a result of such conviction shall be compensated according to law, unless it is proved that the non-disclosure of the unknown fact in time is wholly or partly attributable to him.

7. No one shall be liable to be tried or punished again for an offence for which he has already been finally convicted or acquitted in accordance with the law and penal procedure of each country.

Article 15

1. No one shall be held guilty of any criminal offence on account of any act or omission which he did not constitute a criminal offence, under national or international law, at the time when it was committed. Nor shall a heavier penalty be imposed than the one that was applicable at the time when the criminal offence was committed. If, subsequent to the commission of the offence, provision is made by law for the imposition of a lighter penalty, the offender shall benefit thereby.

2. Nothing in this article shall prejudice the trial and punishment of any person for any act or omission which, at the time when it was committed, was criminal according to the general principles of law recognized by the community of nations.

Article 16

Everyone shall have the right to recognition everywhere as a person before the law.

Article 17

1. No one shall be subjected to arbitrary or unlawful interference with his privacy, family, home or correspondence, nor to unlawful attacks on his honour and reputation.

2. Everyone has the right to the protection of the law against such interference or attacks.

Article 18

1. Everyone shall have the right to freedom of thought, conscience and religion. This right shall include freedom to have or to adopt a religion or belief of his choice, and freedom, either individually or in community with others and in public or private, to manifest his religion or belief in worship, observance, practice and teaching.
2. No one shall be subject to coercion which would impair his freedom to have or to adopt a religion or belief of his choice.
3. Freedom to manifest one's religion or beliefs may be subject only to such limitations as are prescribed by law and are necessary to protect public safety, order, health, or morals or the fundamental rights and freedoms of others.
4. The States Parties to the present Covenant undertake to have respect for the liberty of parents and, when applicable, legal guardians to ensure the religious and moral education of their children in conformity with their own convictions.

Article 19

1. Everyone shall have the right to hold opinions without interference.
2. Everyone shall have the right to freedom of expression; this right shall include freedom to seek, receive and impart information and ideas of all kinds, regardless of frontiers, either orally, in writing or in print, in the form of art, or through any other media of his choice.
3. The exercise of the rights provided for in paragraph 2 of this Article carries with it special duties and responsibilities. It may therefore be subject to certain restrictions, but these shall only be such as are provided by law and are necessary:
   (a) For respect of the rights or reputation of others;
   (b) For the protection of national security or of public order (*ordre public*), or of public health or morals.

Article 20

1. Any propaganda for war shall be prohibited by law.
2. Any advocacy of national, racial or religious hatred that constitutes incitement to discrimination, hostility or violence shall be prohibited by law.

Article 21

The right of peaceful assembly shall be recognized. No restrictions may be placed on the exercise of this right other than those imposed in conformity with the law and which are necessary in a democratic society in the interests of national security or public safety, public order (*ordre public*), the protection of public health or morals or the protection of the rights and freedoms of others.

Article 22

1. Everyone shall have the right to freedom of association with others, including the right to form and join trade unions for the protection of his interests.
2. No restriction may be placed on the exercise of this right other than those which are prescribed by law and which are necessary in a democratic society in the interests of national security or public safety, public order (*ordre public*), the protection of public health or morals or the protection of the rights and freedoms of others. This Article shall not prevent the imposition of lawful restrictions on members of the armed forces and of the police in their exercise of this right.
3. Nothing in this article shall authorize States Parties to the International Labour Organization Convention of 1948 concerning Freedom of Association and Protection of the Right to Organize to take legislative measures which would prejudice, or to apply the law in such a manner as to prejudice, the guarantees provided for in that Convention.

Article 23

1. The family is the natural and fundamental group unit of society and is entitled to protection by society and the State.
2. The right of men and women of marriageable age to marry and to found a family shall be recognized.
3. No marriage shall be entered into without the free and full consent of the intending spouses.
4. States Parties to the present Covenant shall take the appropriate steps to ensure equality of rights and responsibilities of spouses as to marriage, during marriage and at its dissolution. In the case of dissolution, provision shall be made for the necessary protection of any children.

Article 24

1. Every child shall have, without any discrimination as to race, colour, sex, language, national or social origin, property or birth, the right to such measures of protection as are required by his status as a minor, on the part of his family, society and the State.
2. Every child shall be registered immediately after birth and shall have a name.
3. Every child has the right to acquire a nationality.

Article 25

Every citizen shall have the right and the opportunity, without any of the distinctions mentioned in Article 2 and without unreasonable restrictions:
(a) To take part in the conduct of public affairs, directly or through freely chosen representatives;
(b) To vote and to be elected at genuine periodic elections which shall be by universal and equal suffrage and shall be held by secret ballot, guaranteeing the free expression of the will of the electors;
(c) To have access, on general terms of equality, to public service in his country.

Article 26

All persons are equal before the law and are entitled without any discrimination to the equal protection of the law. In this respect, the law shall prohibit any discrimination and guarantee to all persons equal and effective protection against discrimination on any ground such as race, colour, sex, language, religion, political or other opinion, national or social origin, property, birth or other status.

Article 27

In those States in which ethnic, religious or linguistic minorities exist, persons belonging to such minorities shall not be denied the right, in community with the other members of their group, to enjoy their own culture, to profess and practise their own religion, or to use their own language.

PART IV

Article 28

1. There shall be established a Human Rights Committee (hereafter referred to in the present Covenant as the Committee). It shall consist of eighteen members and shall carry out the functions hereinafter provided.
2. The Committee shall be composed of nationals of the States Parties to the present Covenant who shall be persons of high moral character and recognized competence in the field of human rights, consideration being given to the usefulness of the participation of some persons having legal experience.
3. The members of the Committee shall be elected and shall serve in their personal capacity.

Article 29

1. The members of the Committee shall be elected by secret ballot from a list of persons processing the qualifications prescribed in Article 28 and nominated for the purpose by the States Parties to the present Covenant.
2. Each State Party to the present Covenant may nominate not more than two persons. These persons shall be nationals of the nominating State.
3. A person shall be eligible for renomination.

Article 30

1. The initial election shall be held no later than six months after the date of the entry into force of the present Covenant.
2. At least four months before the date of each election to the Committee, other than an election to fill a vacancy declared in accordance with Article 34, the Secretary-General of the United Nations shall address a written invitation to the States Parties to the present Covenant to submit their nominations for membership of the Committee within three months.
3. The Secretary-General of the United Nations shall prepare a list in alphabetical order of all the persons thus nominated, with an indication of the States Parties which have nominated them, and shall submit it to the States Parties to the present Covenant no later than one month before the date of each election.
4. Elections of the members of the Committee shall be held at a meeting of the States Parties to the present Covenant convened by the Secretary-General of the United Nations at the Headquarters of the United

Nations. At that meeting, for which two thirds of the States Parties to the present Covenant shall constitute a quorum, the persons elected to the Committee shall be those nominees who obtain the largest number of votes and an absolute majority of the votes of the representatives of States Parties present and voting.

Article 31

1. The Committee may not include more than one national of the same State.
2. In the election of the Committee, consideration shall be given to equitable geographical distribution of membership and to the representation of the different forms of civilization and of the principal legal systems.

Article 32

1. The members of the Committee shall be elected for a term of four years. They shall be eligible for re-election if re-nominated. However, the terms of nine of the members elected at the first election shall expire at the end of two years; immediately after the first election, the names of those nine shall be chosen by lot by the Chairman of the meeting referred to in Article 30, paragraph 4.
2. Elections at the expiry of office shall be held in accordance with the proceeding articles of this part of the present Covenant.

Article 33

1. If, in the unanimous opinion of the other members, a member of the Committee has ceased to carry out his functions for any cause other than absence of a temporary character, the Chairman of the Committee shall notify the Secretary-General of the United Nations, who shall then declare the seat of that member to be vacant.
2. In the event of the death or the resignation of a member of the Committee, the Chairman shall immediately notify the Secretary-General of the United Nations, who shall declare the seat vacant from the date of death or the date on which the resignation takes effect.

Article 34

1. When a vacancy is declared in accordance with Article 33 and if the term of office of the member to be replaced does not expire within six months of the declaration of the vacancy, the Secretary-General of the United

Nations shall notify each of the States Parties to the present Covenant, which may within two months submit nominations in accordance with Article 29 for the purpose of filling the vacancy.

2. The Secretary-General of the United Nations shall prepare a list in alphabetical order of the persons thus nominated and shall submit it to the States Parties to the present Covenant. The election to fill the vacancy shall then take place in accordance with the relevant provisions of this part of the present Covenant.

3. A member of the Committee elected to fill a vacancy declared in accordance with Article 33 shall hold office for the remainder of the term of the member who vacated the seat on the Committee under the provisions of that Article.

Article 35

The members of the Committee shall, with the approval of the General Assembly of the United Nations, receive emoluments from United Nations resources on such terms and conditions as the General Assembly may decide, having regard to the importance of the Committee's responsibilities.

Article 36

The Secretary-General of the United Nations shall provide the necessary staff and facilities for the effective performance of the functions of the Committee under the present Covenant.

Article 37

1. The Secretary-General of the United Nations shall convene the initial meeting of the Committee at the Headquarters of the United Nations.

2. After its initial meeting, the Committee shall meet at such times as shall be provided in its rules of procedure.

Article 38

Every member of the Committee shall, before taking up its duties, make a solemn declaration in open committee that he will perform his functions impartially and conscientiously.

Article 39

1. The Committee shall elect its officers for a term of two years. They may be re-elected.
2. The Committee shall establish its own rules of procedure, but these rules shall provide, *inter alia,* that;
   (a) Twelve members shall constitute a quorum;
   (b) Decisions of the Committee shall be made by a majority vote of the members present.

Article 40

1. The States Parties to the present Covenant undertake to submit reports on the measures they have adopted which give effect to the rights recognized herein and on the progress made in the enjoyment of those rights;
   (a) Within one year of the entry into force of the present Covenant for the States Parties concerned;
   (b) Thereafter whenever the Committee so requests.
2. All reports shall be submitted to the Secretary-General of the United Nations, who shall transmit them to the Committee for consideration. Reports shall indicate the factors and difficulties, if any, affecting the implementation of the present Covenant.
3. The Secretary-General of the United Nations may, after consultation with the Committee, transmit to the specialized agencies concerned copies of such parts of the reports as may fall within their field of competence.
4. The Committee shall study reports submitted by the States Parties to the present Covenant. It shall transmit its reports, and such general comments as it may consider appropriate, to the States Parties. The Committee may also transmit to the Economic and Social Council these comments along with the copies of the reports it has received from States Parties to the present Covenant.
5. The States Parties to the present Covenant may submit to the Committee observations on any comments that may be made in accordance with paragraph 4 of this Article.

Article 41

1. A State Party to the present Covenant may at any time declare under this article that it recognizes the competence of the Committee to receive and consider communications to the effect that a State Party claims that another State Party is not fulfilling its obligations under the present

Covenant. Communications under this Article may be received and considered only if submitted by a State Party which has made a declaration recognizing in regard to itself the competence of the Committee. No communication shall be received by the Committee if it concerns a State Party which has not made such a declaration. Communications received under this article shall be dealt with in accordance with the following procedure:

(a) If a State Party to the present Covenant considers that another State Party is not giving effect to the provisions of the present Covenant, it may, by written communication, bring the matter to the attention of that State Party. Within three months after the receipt of the communication, the receiving State shall afford the State which sent the communication an explanation or any other statement in writing clarifying the matter, which should include, to the extent possible and pertinent, reference to domestic procedures and remedies taken, pending, or available in the matter.

(b) If the matter is not adjusted to the satisfaction of both States Parties concerned within six months after the receipt by the receiving State of the initial communication, either State shall have the right to refer the matter to the Committee, by notice given to the Committee and to the other State.

(c) The Committee shall deal with a matter referred to it only after it has ascertained that all domestic remedies have been invoked and exhausted in the matter, in conformity with the generally recognized principles of international law. This shall not be the rule where the application of the remedies is unreasonably prolonged.

(d) The Committee shall hold closed meetings when examining communications under this Article.

(e) Subject to the provisions of sub-paragraph (c), the Committee shall make available its good offices to the States Parties concerned with a view to a friendly solution of the matter on the basis of respect for human rights and fundamental freedoms as recognized in the present Covenant.

(f) In any matter referred to it, the Committee may call upon the States Parties concerned, referred to in sub-paragraph (b), to supply any relevant information.

(g) The States Parties concerned, referred to in sub-paragraph (b), shall have the right to be represented when the matter is being considered in the Committee and to make submissions orally and/or in writing.

(h) The Committee shall, within twelve months after the date of receipt of notice under sub-paragraph (b), submit a report:

(i) If a solution within the terms of sub-paragraph (e) is reached, the Committee shall confine its report to a brief statement of the facts; the written submissions and record of the oral submissions made by the States Parties concerned shall be attached to the report.

In every matter, the report shall be communicated to the States Parties concerned.

2. The provisions of this article shall come into force when ten States Parties to the present Covenant have made declarations under paragraph 1 of this article. Such declarations shall be deposited by the States Parties with the Secretary-General of the United Nations, who shall transmit copies thereof to the other States Parties. A declaration may be withdrawn at any time by notification to the Secretary-General. Such a withdrawal shall not prejudice the consideration of any matter which is the subject of a communication already transmitted under this Article; no further communication by any State Party shall be received after the notification of withdrawal of the declaration has been received by the Secretary-General, unless the State Party concerned has made a new declaration.

Article 42

1. (a) If a matter referred to the Committee in accordance with Article 41 is not resolved to the satisfaction of the States Parties concerned, the Committee may, with the prior consent of the States Parties concerned, appoint an *ad hoc* Conciliation Commission (herein after referred to as the Commission). The good offices of the Commission shall be made available to the States Parties concerned with a view to an amicable solution of the matter on the basis of respect for the present Covenant;

(b) The Commission shall consist of five persons acceptable to the States Parties concerned. If the States Parties concerned fail to reach agreement within three months on all or part of the composition of the Commission the members of the Commission concerning whom no agreement has been reached shall be elected by secret ballot by a two-thirds majority vote of the Committee from among its members.

2. The members of the Commission shall serve in their personal capacity. They shall not be nationals of the States Parties concerned, or of a State not party to the present Covenant, or of a State Party which has not made a declaration under Article 41.

3. The commission shall elect its own Chairman and adopt its own rules of procedure.

4. The meetings of the commission shall normally be held at the Headquarters of the United Nations or at the United Nations Office at Geneva. However, they may be held at such other convenient places as the Commission may determine in consultation with the Secretary-General of the United Nations and the States Parties concerned.

5. The Secretariat provided in accordance with Article 36 shall also service the commissions appointed under this article.

6. The information received and collated by the Committee shall be made available to the Commission and the Commission may call upon the States Parties concerned to supply any other relevant information.

7. When the Commission has fully considered the matter, but in any event not later than twelve months after having been seized of the matter, it shall submit to the Chairman of the Committee a report for communication to the States Parties concerned.

   (a) If the Commission is unable to complete its consideration of the matter within twelve months, it shall confine its report to a brief statement of the status of its consideration of the matter.

   (b) If an amicable solution to the matter on the basis of respect for human rights as recognized in the present Covenant is reached, the Commission shall confine its report to a brief statement of the facts and of the solution reached.

   (c) If a solution within the terms of sub-paragraph (b) is not reached, the Commission's report shall embody its findings on all questions of fact relevant to the issues between the States Parties concerned, and its views on the possibilities of an amicable solution of the matter. This report shall also contain the written submissions and a record of the oral submissions made by the States Parties concerned.

   (d) If the Commission's report is submitted under sub-paragraph (c), the States Parties concerned shall, within three months of the receipt of the report, notify the Chairman of the Committee whether or not they accept the contents of the report of the Commission.

8. The provisions of this Article are without prejudice to the responsibilities of the Committee under Article 41.

9. The States Parties concerned shall share equally all the expenses of the members of the Commission in accordance with estimates to be provided by the Secretary-General of the United Nations.

10. The Secretary-General of the United Nations shall be empowered to pay the expenses of the members of the Commission, if necessary, before reimbursement by the States Parties concerned, in accordance with paragraph 9 of this Article.

Article 43

The members of the Committee, and of the *ad hoc* conciliation commissions which may be appointed under Article 42, shall be entitled to the facilities, privileges and immunities of experts on mission for the United Nations as laid down in the relevant sections of the Convention on the Privileges and Immunities of the United Nations.

Article 44

The provisions for the implementation of the present Covenant shall apply without prejudice to the procedures prescribed in the field of human rights by or under the constituent instruments and the conventions of the United Nations and of the specialized agencies and shall not prevent the States Parties to the present Covenant from having recourse to other procedures for settling a dispute in accordance with general or special international agreements in force between them.

Article 45

The Committee shall submit to the General Assembly of the United Nations through Economic and Social Council, an annual report on its activities.

PART V

Article 46

Nothing in the present Covenant shall be interpreted as impairing the provisions of the Charter of the United Nations and of the constitutions of the specialized agencies which define the respective responsibilities of the various organs of the United Nations and of the specialized agencies in regard to the matters dealt with in the present Covenant.

Article 47

Nothing in the present Covenant shall be interpreted as impairing the inherent right of all peoples to enjoy and utilize fully and freely their natural wealth and resources.

PART VI

Article 48

1. The present Covenant is open for signature by any State Member of the United Nations or member of any of its specialized agencies, by any State Party to the Statute of the International Court of Justice, and by any other State which has been invited by the General Assembly of the United Nations to become a party to the present Covenant.
2. The present Covenant is subject to ratification. Instruments of ratification shall be deposited with the Secretary-General of the United Nations.
3. The present Covenant shall be open to accession by any State referred to in paragraph 1 of this Article.
4. Accession shall be effected by the deposit of an instrument of accession with the Secretary-General of the United Nations.
5. The Secretary-General of the United Nations shall inform all States which have signed this Covenant or acceded to it of the deposit of each instrument of ratification or accession.

Article 49

1. The present Covenant shall enter force three months after the date of the deposit with Secretary-General of the United Nations of the thirty-fifth instrument of ratification or instrument of accession.
2. For each State ratifying the present Covenant or acceding to it after the deposit of the thirty-fifth instrument of ratification or instrument of accession, the present Covenant shall enter into force three months after the date of deposit of its own instrument of ratification or instrument of accession.

Article 50

The provisions of the present Covenant shall extend to all parts of federal States without any limitations or exceptions.

Article 51

1. Any State Party to the present Covenant may propose an amendment and file it with the Secretary-General of the United Nations. The Secretary-General of the United Nations shall thereupon communicate any proposed amendments to the States Parties to the present Covenant

with a request that they notify him whether they favour a conference of States Parties for the purpose of considering and voting upon the proposals. In the event that at least one third of the States Parties favours such a conference, the Secretary-General shall convene the conference under the auspices of the United Nations. Any amendment adopted by a majority of the States Parties present and voting at the conference shall be submitted to the General Assembly of the United nations for approval.

2. Amendments shall come into force when they have been approved by the General Assembly of the United Nations and accepted by a two-thirds majority of the States Parties to the present Covenant in accordance with their respective constitutional processes.

3. When amendments come into force, they shall be binding on those States Parties which have accepted them, other States Parties still being bound by the provisions of the present Covenant and any earlier amendment which they have accepted.

Article 52

Irrespective of the notifications made under Article 48, paragraph 5, the Secretary-General of the Untied Nations shall inform all States referred to in paragraph 1 of the same article of the following particulars:

(a) Signatures, ratifications and accessions under Article 48;

(b) The date of the entry into force of the present Covenant under Article 49 and the date of the entry into force of any amendments under Article 51.

Article 53

1. The present Covenant, of which the Chinese, English, French, Russian and Spanish texts are equally authentic, shall be deposited in the archives of the United Nations.

2. The Secretary-General of the United Nations shall transmit certified copies of the present Covenant to all States referred to in Article 48.

Bibliography

Action, Philip, 'Regimes and hegemony', *Paradigms: The Kent Journal of International Relations*, 3:1, 1987, pp. 47-55

Akhurst, Michael, 'Humanitarian intervention', in Hedley Bull (ed), *Intervention in World Politics*, (Clarendon Press, Oxford, 1984), pp, 95-118.

An-Na'im, Abdullahi Ahmed, *Towards an Islamic Reformation: Civil Liberties, Human Rights, and International Law*, (Syracuse University Press, Syracuse, 1990).

Archer, Peter, 'Action by unofficial organizations on human rights', in Evan Luard (ed), *The International Protection of Human Rights*, (Thames and Hudson, London, 1967), 165-78.

Ashley, Richard K, 'Untying the sovereign state: a double reading of the anarchy problematique', *Millennium*, 17:2, 1988, pp. 227-62.

Augelli, Enrico, and Craig Murphy, *America's Quest and the Third World*, (Pinter Publishers, London, 1988).

Axelrod, Robert, *The Evolution of Co-operation*, (Princeton University Press, Princeton, 1984).

Barkun, Michael, *Law Without Sanctions*, (Yale University Press, London, 1968).

Barry, Brian, 'Can states be moral? International morality and the compliance problem', in Anthony Ellis (ed) *Ethics and International Relations*, (Manchester University Press, Manchester, 1986).

Beitz, Charles R, 'Bounded morality: justice and the state in world politics', *International Organization*, 33:3, 1979, pp. 405-24.

Beitz, Charles R, *Political Theory and International Relations*, (Princeton University Press, New Jersey, 1979).

Beitz, Charles R, 'Human rights and social justice', in PG Brown and D Maclean, *Human Rights and US Foreign Policy*, (Lexington Books, Lexington, 1979), pp. 45-63.

Bergesen, Helge Ole, 'The power to embarrass: the UN human rights regime between realism and utopia', (Paper presented to the International Studies Association, Rio de Janeiro, August, 1982).

Bozeman, Adda, *The Future of Law in a Multicultural World*, (Princeton University ess, New Jersey, 1971).

Brown, Peter G and Douglas Maclean (eds), *Human Rights and US Foreign Policy*, (Lexington Books, Lexington, 1979).

Brown, Chris, 'Ethics of coexistence: the international theory of Terry Nardin', *Review of International Studies*, 14:3, 1988, PP. 213-22.

Brown, Chris 'Not my department? Normative theory and international relations', *Paradigms: Kent Journal of International Relations*, 1:2, 1987, pp. 104-13.

Brownlie, Ian, *Basic Documents on Human Rights*, (Clarendon Press, Oxford, 1981).

Bull, Hedley, *The Anarchical Society*, (Macmillan, Basingstoke, 1988).

Bull, Hedley, 'Human rights and world order', in Ralf Pettman (ed), *Moral Claims in World Affairs*, (Croom Helm, London, 1979), pp. 79-91.

Buzan, Barry, and R J Barry Jones, *Change in the Study of International Relations*, (Pinter, London, 1981).

Capotorli, F, 'Human rights: The hard road towards universality', in R MacDonald & D M Johnson (eds), *The Structure and Process of International Law*, (Mijhoff, Dordrecht, 1983).

Carey, John, 'Procedures for the protection of human rights', *Iowa Law Review*, vol. 53, 1967, pp. 291-324.

Cassese, Antonio, 'Progressive transnational promotion of human rights', in B Ramcharan (ed), *Human Rights: Thirty Years After the Universal Declaration*, (Mijhoff, London, 1979).

Cassese, Antonio, 'The Helsinki Declaration and Self-determination', in T Buergenthal (ed), *Human Rights, International Law and the Helsinki Accord*, (Allenheld, Osmun, New York, 1977), pp. 83-110.

Cassese, Antonio, 'The self-determination of peoples', in Louis Henkin (ed) *The International Bill of Rights*, (Columbia University Press, NY, 1981), pp. 92-113.

Cassese, Antonio, *International Law in a Divided World*, (Clarendon Press, Oxford,1986).

Cassin, Rene, 'Looking back on the Universal Declaration of 1948', *Review of Contemporary Law*, No. 1, 1968, pp. 13-26.

Chiang-Pie Leng, *Non-governmental organizations at the United Nations*, (Praeger, NY,1981)

Chomsky, Noam, *Human Rights and American Foreign Policy*, (Spokesman Books, Nottingham, 1978).

Clark, Roger Stenson, *A United Nations Commissioner for Human Rights*, (Nijhoff, The Hague, 1972).

Cohen, Stephen B, 'Conditioning US security assistance on human rights practice', *American Journal of International Law*, vol. 76, 1982, pp. 246-79.

Cohn, Cindy A, 'The early harvest: Domestic legal changes related to the Human Rights Committee and the Covenant on Civil and Political Rights' *Human Rights Quarterly*, 3:3, 1991, pp. 295-321.

Cox, Robert, 'Social forces, states and world orders: Beyond international relations theory', *Millennium*, 10:2, 1981, pp. 126-55.

Cox, Robert, 'Production, the state and changes in world order', in Ernst-Otto Czempiel and James Rosenau (eds), *Global Changes and Theoretical Challenges*, (Lexington Books, Lexington, 1989), pp. 37-50.

Cox, Robert, 'Gramsci, hegemony and international relations: An essay in method', *Millennium*, 12:2, 1983, pp. 162-75.

Cranston, Maurice, 'Are there human rights?', *Daedalus*, 112:4, 1983, pp. 1-18.

Cranston, Maurice, 'Human rights, real and supposed', in D D Raphael (ed), *Political Theory and the Rights of Man*, (Macmillan, London, 1967), pp. 43-53.

Cranston, Maurice, *What Are Human Rights?*, (Bodley Head, London, 1973).

Crawford, James, 'The rights of peoples: Some conclusions' in J Crawford, (ed) *The Rights of Peoples*, (Clarendon Press, Oxford, 1988) pp. 159-75.

Dean, Richard N, 'Beyond Helsinki: The Soviet view of human rights in international law', *Virginia Journal of International Law*, 21:1, 1981, pp. 55-95.

Delbrueck, Jost, 'International protection of human rights and state sovereignty', *Indiana Law Journal*, 57:4, 1982, pp. 567-78.

Donnelly, Jack, 'Recent trends in UN human rights activity: Description and polemic', *International Organization*, 35:4, 1981, pp. 653-55.

Donnelly, Jack, *Universal Human Rights in Theory and Practice*, (Cornell University Press, Itica, 1989).

Donnelly, Jack, 'International human rights: A regime analysis', *International Organization*, 40:3, 1986, pp. 599-642.

Donnelly, Jack, *The Concept of Human Rights*, (Croom Helm, London, 1985).

Donnelly, Jack, and R Howard, 'Human dignity, human rights and political regimes' *American Political science Review*, 80:3, 1984, pp. 801-17.

Eagleton, Clyde, 'Self-determination in the United Nations', *American Journal of International Law*, vol. 47, 1953, pp. 88-93.

Evans, Tony, 'Human rights: A reply to Geoffrey Best', *Review of International Studies*, 17:1, 1991, pp. 87-94.

Evans, Tony and Peter Wilson, 'International regimes and the English school of international relations: A comparison', *Millennium*, 22:1, 1993, pp. 329-51.

Falk, Richard, *Human Rights and State Sovereignty*, (Holmes and Meier, London, 1981).

Falk, Richard, 'The reality of international law', *World Politics*, vol. 14, 1962, pp. 353-63.

Falk, Richard, 'Theoretical foundations of human rights', in RP Newburg (ed), *The Politics of Human Rights*, (New York University Press, NY, 1980), pp. 65-109.

Farer, Tom, 'The United Nations and human rights: More than a whimper, Less th⌐n a Roar', *Human Rights Quarterly*, vol. 9, 1987, pp. 550-86,

Femia, Joseph, *Gramsci's Political Thoughts: Hegemony, Consciousness and the Revolutionary Process*, (Clarendon Press, Oxford 1987).

Field, G Lowell, 'Law as an objective political concept', *The American Political Science Review*, 43:2, 1949, pp. 229-249.

Finlayson, J A and M Zacher, 'The GATT and the regulation of trade barriers: regime dynamics and function', *International Regimes*, (Cornell University Press, London, 1983), pp. 237-314.

Fisher, Dana, 'Reporting Under the Covenant on Civil and Political Rights: The First Five Years of the Human Rights Committee', *American Journal of International Law*, vol. 70, 1982, pp. 142-53.

Forsythe, David, *Human Rights and US Foreign Policy*, (University of Nebraska Press, London, 1987).

Forsythe, David P, *Human Rights and World Politics*, (University of Nebraska Press, Lincoln, 1989).

Forsythe, David, 'Socio-economic human rights: The United Nations, the United States, and Beyond', *Human Rights Quarterly*, 4:4, 1982, pp. 435-49.

Galtung J *Human Rights in Another Key*, (Polity Press, Cambridge, 1994)

Gourevitch, Peter A, 'The second image reversed: The international sources of international politics', *International Organization*, 32:4, 1978, pp. 881-911.

Gowa, Joanne, 'Anarchy, egoism and the third image: the evolution of co-operation in international relations', *International Organization*, 40:1, 1986, pp. 167-86.

Gross-Espiell, H, 'The evolving concept of human rights - Western, Socialist and Third World views', in B G Ramcharan, *Human Rights: Thirty Years After the Universal Declaration*, (Nijhoff, London, 1979), pp. 42-65.

Haas, Ernst, *When Knowledge is Power*, (University of California Press, Oxford, 1990).

Haas, Ernst, 'Human rights: to act or not to act?', in Kenneth A Oye, David Rothchild and R J Lieber (eds), *Eagle Entangled*, (Longman, London, 1979).

Haas, Ernst, 'Why collaborate? Issue linkage and international regimes', *World Politics*, 32:2, 1980, pp. 357-405.

Haas, Ernst, 'On systems and international regimes', *World Politics*, 27:2, 1975, pp. 147-74.

Haas, Ernst, 'Words can hurt you; or who said what to whom about regimes', *International Organization*, 36:2, 1982, pp. 207-43.

Haggard, Stephen, and Beth A Simmons, 'Theories of international regimes', *International Organization*, 41:3, 1987, pp. 419-517.

Hardin, Russell, 'The emergence of norms', *Ethics*, vol. 90, 1979, pp. 575-87.

Hart, HLA, 'Are there any natural rights', in A Quinton (ed), *Political Philosophy*, (Oxford University Press, Oxford, 1977), pp. 53-66.

Held, David, (ed), *Prospects for Democracy*, (Polity Press, Oxford, 1992).

Henkin, Louis, *The Rights of Man Today*, (Stevens and Sons, London, 1979).

Henkin, Louis, 'The United Nations and human rights', *International Organization*, 19:3, 1965, pp. 504-17.

Henkin, Louis, 'International human rights as rights', in J R Pennock and J W Chapman (eds), *Human Rights*, (New York University Press, NY, 1981), pp. 257-80.

Henkin, Louis, (ed), *The International Bill of Rights: The Covenant on Civil and Political Rights*, (University of Chicago Press, Chicago, 1967).

Hoffmann, Stanley, 'The hell of good intentions', *Foreign Policy*, vol. 29, winter 1977, pp. 3-26.

Hoffmann, Stanley, *Duties Beyond Borders*, (Syracuse University Press, New York, 1981).

Hughes, B B, *The Domestic Context of American Foreign Policy*, (San Francisco, W H Freeman, 1978).

Humphrey, John, 'The Universal Declaration of Human Rights: Its history, impact and judicial character', in B G Ramcharan (ed), *Human Rights: 30 Years After the Universal Declaration*, (Nijhoff, London, 1979), pp. 21-37.

Humphrey, John, *Human Rights and the United Nations: The Great Adventure*, (Transnational Publishers, Dobbs Ferry, 1984).

Humphrey, John P, 'The UN Charter and the Universal Declaration of Human Rights' in, Evan Luard (ed), *The International Protection of Human Rights*, (Thomas and Hudson, London, 1967), pp. 43-54.

Humphrey, John P, 'The international law of human rights in the middle twentieth century' in, M Bos (ed), *The Present State of International Law*, (Kluwer, Netherlands, 1973), pp. 75-105.

Humphrey, John, 'Human rights, the United Nations and 1968', *Journal of the International Committee of Jurists*, 8:2, 1968, pp. 1-13.

Humphrey, John, *No Distant Millennium: The International Law of Human Rights*, (UNESCO, Paris, 1989).

Humphrey, John, 'The International Bill of Rights', in *Philosophical Foundations of Human Rights*, (UNESCO, 1986), pp. 59-72.

Jackson, Robert, *Quasi-States: Sovereignty, International Relations and the Third World*, (Cambridge University Press, Cambridge, 1990).

Jacobson, Harold K, 'The global system and the realization of human dignity and justice', *International Studies Quarterly*, 26:2, 1982, pp. 315-32.

Johnson, M Glenn, 'Human rights in divergent conceptual settings: How do ideas influence policy choices?', in D L Cingranelli (ed), *Human Rights: Theory and Measurement*, (Macmillan, London, 1988). pp. 46-55.

Kaplan, M A and N B Katzenbach, *The Politics and Foundations of International Law*, (John Wiley, London, 1961).

Kaufman, Natalie Hevener and David Whiteman, 'Opposition to human rights treaties in the United States: The legacy of the Bricker Amendment', *Human Rights Quarterly*, 10:3, 1988, pp. 309-37.

Keeley, James, 'Towards a Foucauldian analysis of international regimes', *International Organization*, 44:1, 1990, pp. 83-105.

Kelman, Herbert C, 'The conditions, criteria and dialectics of human dignity', *International Studies Quarterly*, 21:3, 1977, pp. 529-52.

Kennan, George, 'Morality and foreign policy', *Foreign Affairs*, 64:2, 1985, pp. 205-18.

Keohane, Robert O, 'The theory of hegemonic stability and changes in international economic regimes, 1967-77', in Ole Holsti et al., *Change in the International System*, (Westview Press, Boulder, 1980), pp. 131-62.

Keohane, Robert O, *After Hegemony: Co-operation and Discord in the World Political Economy*, (Princeton University Press, Princeton, 1984).

Khan, Muhammad Zafrulla, *Islam and Human Rights*, (The London Mosque, London, 1976).

Kleinig, John, 'Human rights, legal rights and social change', in E Kamenka & A Erh-Soon Tay (eds), *Human Rights*, (Edward Arnold, London, 1978), pp. 36-47.

Korey, William, 'Human rights treaties: Why the US is stalling', *Foreign Affairs*, 45:3, 1967, pp. 414-24.

Krasner, Stephen (ed), *International Regimes*, (Cornell University Press, London, 1983).

Krasner, Stephen, 'Sovereignty: An institutional perspective', *Comparative Political Studies*, 21:1, 1988, pp. 66-94.

Krasner, Stephen, 'Structural causes and regime consequences: Regimes as intervening variables', *International Organization*, 36:2, 1982, pp. 1-21.

Kratochwil, Friedrich and John Ruggie, 'International organizations: a state of the art or the art of the state' *International Organization*, 40:4, 1986, pp. 753-75.

Kratochwil, Friedrich, *Rules, Norms and Decisions*, (Cambridge University Press, Cambridge, 1989).

Kratochwil, Friedrich, 'The force of prescription', *International Organization*, 38:4, 1984, pp. 685-708.

Kudryartov, VN, 'Human rights and the Soviet Constitution', in *Philosophical Foundations of Human Rights*, (UNESCO, New York, 1986).

Lauterpacht, Hersch, *International Law and Human Rights*, (Archon Books, 1968).

Lerche, Charles O, *The Cold War....and After*, (Prentice-Hall, Englewood Cliffs, NJ, 1965).

Loth, Wilfred, *The Division of the World - 1941-45*, (Routledge, London, 1988).

Luard, Evan, *Human Rights and Foreign Policy*, (Pergamon Press, London, 1981).

Luard, Evan, *A History of the United Nations: The Years of Western Domination, 1945-55*, vol. 1, (Macmillan Press, London, 1982).

Luard, Evan, *A History of the United Nations: The Age of Decolonization - 1955-1965*, (Macmillan, Basingstoke, 1989).

Luard, Evan, *The Globalization of Politics: The Changing Focus of Political Action in the Modern World*, (Macmillan, Basingstoke, 1990).

Luban, David, 'The romance of the nation-state', *Philosophy and Public Affairs*, 9:4, 1980, pp. 392-97.

Mayall, James, 'The United States', in R J Vincent (ed), *Foreign Policy and Human Rights*, (Cambridge, CUP, 1986), pp. 165-87.

Mayall, James, 'International society and intervention', in Michael Donelan (ed), *The Reason of States*, (Allen & Unwin, London, 1978), pp. 122-42.

McGoldrick, Dominic, *The Human Rights Committee*, (Clarendon Press, Oxford, 1991).

Miller, Lynn H, *Global Order: Values and Power in International Politics*, (Westview, London, 1985).

Minogue, Kenneth, 'Natural rights, ideology and the game of life', in E Kamenka & A Erh-Soon Tay (eds), *Human Rights*, (Edward Arnold, London, 1978), pp. 13-35.

Minogue, Kenneth 'The history of the idea of human rights', in, W Laqueur and B Rubin (eds), *The Human Rights Reader*, (Meridian Books, NY, 1977).

Mitchell, Neil J, and James M McCormick, 'Economic and political explanations of human rights violations', *World Politics*, 40:4, 1988, pp. 476-98.

Mower, A Glenn, *The United States, the United Nations, and Human Rights*, (Greenwood Press, Westport, 1979).

Mower, A Glenn, 'Implementing United Nations Covenants', in AA Said (ed), *Human Rights and World Politics*, (Praeger Publishers, New York, 1978), pp. 108-16.

Muravchik, Joshua, *The Uncertain Crusade: Jimmy Carter and the Dilemma of Human Rights Policy*, (Hamilton Press, London, 1986).

Nardin, Terry, *Law, Morality, and the Relations of States*, (Princeton University Press, Princeton, NJ, 1983).

O'Meara, Richard L, 'Regimes and their implications of international theory', *Millennium*, 13:3, 1984, pp. 245-64.

Onuf, N G, 'The principle of non-intervention, the United Nations, and the international system', *International Organization*, 25:2, 1971, pp. 209-27.

Onuf N G and V Spike Peterson, 'Human rights from an international regime perspective', *Journal of International Affairs*, 32:2, 1984, pp. 329-43.

Opsahl, Torkel, 'Instruments of implementation of human rights', *Human Rights Law Journal*, 10:1, 1989, pp. 13-33.

Pechota, V, 'The development of the Covenant on Civil and Political Rights', in Louis Henkin (ed), *The International Bill of Rights: Covenant on Civil and Political Rights*, (Columbia University Press, NY, 1981), pp. 31-71.

Pettman, Ralph, *State and Class: A Sociology of International Affairs*, (Croom Helm, London, 1979).

Puchala, Donald J and Raymond Hopkins, 'International regimes: Lessons from inductive analysis', *International Organization*, 36:2, 1982, pp. 245-75.

Rajan, M, *United Nations and Domestic Jurisdiction*, (Asia Publications, London, 1958).

Ramazani, R K, *The United States and Iran*, (London, Praeger, 1982).

Ramcharan, B G, 'Implementing the International Covenants on Human Rights', in B G Ramcharan, *Human Rights: Thirty Years After the Universal Declaration*, (Nijhoff, The Hague, 1979), pp. 159-95.

Ramcharan, R, *The Concept and Present Status of International Protection of Human Rights*, (Nijhoff, The Hague, 1989).

Ramcharan, B H (ed), *Human Rights: Thirty Years After the Universal Declaration*, (Nijhoff, London, 1979).

Raphael, D D, 'The liberal western tradition of human rights', *International Social Science Journal*, 18:1, 1966, pp. 22-30.

Raphael, D D, 'Human rights old and new', in D D Raphael (ed), *Political Theory and the Rights of Man*, (London, Macmillan, 1967), pp. 54-67.

Reisman, David, 'Prospects for human rights', in AA Said (ed), *Human Rights and World Politics*, (Praeger Publishers, NY, 1978), pp. 22-30.

Robertson, A H, 'The implementation system: international measures', in Louis Henkin (ed), *The International Bill of Rights: The Covenant on Civil and Political Rights*, (University of Chicago Press, Chicago, 1967), pp. 332-66.

Roosevelt, Eleanor, *The Autobiography of Eleanor Roosevelt*, (Hutchinson, London, 1962).

Roosevelt, Eleanor, *As He Saw It*, (Hutchinson, London, 1968).

Rostow, Dankwart A, 'Man or citizen? Global modernization and human rights', in P R Newberg (ed), *The Politics of Human Rights*, (New York University Press, NY, 1980), pp. 19-32.

Ruggie, John G, 'Human rights and the future of international community', *Daedalus*, 112:4, 1983, pp. 93-110.

Ruggie, John G, 'International responses to technology: Concepts and trends' *International Organization*, 29:3, 1975, pp.557-83.

Said, A A (ed), *Human Rights and World Politics*, (Praeger Publishers, NY, 1978).

Schachter, Oscar, 'Towards a theory of obligation', *Virginia Journal of International Law*, 8:2, 1968, pp. 300-22.

Schachter, Oscar, 'The obligation to implement the Covenant in domestic law', in Louis Henkin, *The International Bill of Rights: The Covenant on Civil and Political Rights*, (Columbia University Press, Columbia, 1970), pp. 313-31.

Schachter, Oscar, 'The twilight existence of non-binding international agreements', *American Journal of International Law*, 71:2, 1977, pp. 296-304.

Schneider, Mark L, 'A new administration's new policy: the rise of power of human rights', in P G Brown and D Maclean (eds), *Human Rights and US Foreign Policy*, (Lexington Books, Lexington, 1979), pp. 3-13.

Schwelb, Egon, *Human Rights and the International Community*, (Quadrangle Books, Chicago, 1964).

Shue, Henry, *Basic Rights: Subsistence, Affluence and US Foreign Policy*, (PUP, Princeton, 1980).

Shue, Henry, 'Rights in the light of duties', in P G Brown and D Maclean (eds), *Human Rights and US Foreign Policy*, (Lexington Books, Lexington, 1979), pp. 65-81.

Sieghart, P, *The International Law of Human Rights*, (Clarendon Press, Oxford, 1983).

Sieghart, P, *The Lawful Rights of Mankind: An Introduction to the Legal Code of Human Rights*, (Oxford University Press, Oxford, 1986).

Slater, J and T Nardin, 'Non-intervention and human rights', *Journal of Politics*, vol. 48, 1986, pp. 86-95.

Smith, Roger, 'Institutionalization as a measure of regime stability: Insights for international regime analysis from the study of domestic politics', *Millennium*, 18:2, 1989, pp. 227-44.

Sohn, Louis, 'The development of the Charter of the United Nations: The Present State', in M Bos (ed), *The Present State of International Law and Other Essays*, (Kluwer, The Netherlands, 1973), pp. 39-58,

Sohn, Louis and Thomas Buergenthal, *International Protection of Human Rights*, (Bobbs-Merrill Company, NY, 1973).

Stackhouse, Max L, *Creeds, Society and Human Rights*, (William B Eerdman, Grand Rapids, 1984).

Stark, J G, 'Human rights and international law', in E Kamenka and A Erh-Soon Tay (eds), *Human Rights*, (Edward Arnold, London, 1978), pp. 113-131.

Strange, Susan, 'Cave! hic dragones: A critique of regime analysis', in, Stephen Krasner (ed), *International Regimes*, (Cornell University Press, London, 1983), pp. 337-54.

Strong, Tracy B, 'Taking the rank with what is ours: American political thought, foreign policy, and the question of rights', in P R Newburg (ed), *The Politics of Human Rights*, (New York University Press, London, 1980), pp. 33-64.

Tananbaum, Duane, *The Bricker Amendment Controversy: A Test of Eisenhower's Political Leadership*, (Cornell University Press, Ithica, 1988).

Tardu, M E, 'United Nations Responses to Gross Violations of Human Rights: The 1503 Procedure' *Santa Clara Law Review*, vol. 20, 1980, pp. 553-601.

Teson, Ferdinando R, 'The Kantian theory of international law', *Columbia Law Review*, 92:1, 1992, pp. 53-102.

Tetreault, Mary Ann, 'Regimes and liberal world order' *Alternatives*, vol. 13, 1988, pp. 5-26.

Thaper, R, 'The Hindu and Buddhist tradition', *International Social Science Journal*, 18:1, 1966, pp. 31-40.

Tolley, Howard, *The United Nations Commission on Human Rights*, (Westview Press, London, 1987).

Vasak K (ed), *The International Dimensions of Human Rights*, (Greenwood Press, Westpoint, 1982).

Vincent, John, *Human Rights and International Relations*, (Cambridge University Press, Cambridge, 1986).

Vincent, John, *Nonintervention and International Order*, (Princeton University Press, NJ, 1974).

Vincent, John, 'Human rights and foreign policy', *Australian Outlook*, 22:3, 1982, pp. 1-5.

Vogelgesang, Sandra, 'What price principles? US policy on human rights', *Foreign Affairs*, 56:4, 1978, pp, 818-41.

Watson, J S, 'Legal theory, efficacy and validity in the development of human rights norms in international law' *University of Illinois Law Forum*, vol. 3, 1979, pp. 609-41.

Weisbrodt, David, 'The role of international non-governmental organizations in the implementation of human rights', *Texas International Law Journal*, vol. 12, spring, 1977, pp. 293-320.

Young, Oran, 'Regime dynamics: the rise and fall of international regimes', *International Organization*, 36:2, 1982. pp. 277-97.

Young, Oran, 'International regimes: Towards a new theory of institution', *World Politics*, 39:1, 1986, pp. 104-22.

Young, Oran, *International Co-operation: Building Regimes for Natural Resources and the Environment*, (Cornell University Press, London, 1989).

Young, Oran, 'International regimes: problems of concept formation', *World Politics*, 32:3, 1980, pp. 331-56.

Young, Oran, 'The politics of international regime formation: managing natural resources and the environment', *International Organization*, 43:3, 1989, pp. 349-75.

Zacher, Mark W, 'Towards a theory of international regimes', *Journal of International Affairs*, 44:1, 1990, pp. 139-57.

Index